# EVERY NATION
## IN OUR GENERATION

R I C E   B R O O C K S

EVERY NATION IN OUR GENERATION by Rice Broocks
Published by Creation House Press
A part of Strang Communications Company
600 Rinehart Road
Lake Mary, Florida 32746
www.creationhouse.com
        and
Every Nations Productions
783 Old Hickory Boulevard, Suite 210 E.
Brentwood, Tennessee 37027

Unless otherwise noted, Scripture quotations are from The Holy Bible, New International version, © 1973, 1978, 1984 by the International Bible Society. Used by permission.

Scripture quotations marked NASB are from the *New American Standard Bible*, © 1960, 1962, 1963, 1968, 1971, 1972, 1975, 1977 by the Lockman Foundation. Used by permission.

Scripture quotations marked NKJV are from the New King James Version of the Bible. Copyright © 1979, 1980, 1982 by Thomas Nelson, Inc., publishers. Used by permission.

Scripture quotations marked KJV are from the King James Version of the Bible.

Library of Congress Control Number: 2002107847

International Standard Book Number: 0–88419–934–7

Printed in the United States of America.

02 03 04 05 06   8 7 6 5 4 3 2 1

# DEDICATION

*To my five children:*
*Elizabeth, Louisa,*
*William, Wyatt and*
*Charles Spurgeon.*

# ACKNOWLEDGMENTS

I offer my deepest thanks and gratitude to:

Eric Holmberg, Lynn Nawata and Stephen Mansfield—for their tireless work in editing this manuscript and helping to make this book a reality.

Walter Walker, who initially encouraged me to write and helped me launch this project.

The Morning Star International pastors and leaders worldwide, who lay down their lives daily for the cause of Christ.

To Bethel World Outreach Center in Nashville, thank you for your prayers and for being a church that strives to model what this book teaches.

My wife, Jody, for enduring the time it took me to write this book. Thank you for making my life such a joy.

# TABLE OF CONTENTS

# "THE TIPPING POINT"

I t is curious how simple things can change the world. Malcolm Gladwell, in his best-seller *The Tipping Point*, chronicled this phenomenon: "We need to prepare ourselves for the possibility that sometimes big changes follow from small events, and that sometimes these changes can happen very quickly."[1]

Whether it's a fashion craze, a crime wave or a viral epidemic, the "tipping point" is the moment of critical mass, the threshold or boiling point where a minor trend suddenly surges to become a significant movement. And while the kingdom of heaven is like leaven that works its way incrementally throughout the earth,[2] there are moments—these tipping points—when either an individual or an entire culture can be suddenly transformed for the glory of God. The New Testament declares, "The Word of God grew mightily and prevailed."[3] The preaching of the Gospel in the first century eventually caused a tipping point in the Roman Empire. Over the next few hundred years, Christianity would grow from a small, persecuted minority to see even the emperor declare that Jesus was Lord.

In 1517, another seemingly minor event triggered a tipping point that radically changed Europe and eventually the entire world. On the last day of October, a monk by the name of Martin Luther nailed a series of theses—articles for discussion—to the door of a church in Wittenberg, Germany. The Protestant Reformation followed in the wake of that act.

In the fall of 1900, John R. Mott, a thirty-year-old man from Iowa, published the book, *The Evangelization of the World in this Generation*.

"Practically the whole world is open," he declared as he challenged the Church to abandon its malaise along with the failed strategies of the past. With a renewed vision and commitment, Mott asserted that it was "…entirely possible to fill the earth with the knowledge of Christ before the present generation passes away."[4] His book precipitated another tipping point, and the Student Volunteer Movement was born. Eventually, over twenty-five thousand young people were sent overseas as missionaries. Mott later received the Nobel Prize, and President Woodrow Wilson offered him the post of U. S. Ambassador to China. One Japanese leader would describe him as "…the father of the young people of the world."

Mott's central theme was simple: "The primary work of the Church is to make Jesus Christ known and obeyed and loved throughout the world."[5] A century later, the work remains. If anything, recent global events have created an even greater need—and hence a potential tipping point—for the kingdom of God.

## OUR WAKE-UP CALL

The great challenge is in keeping the Church's focus in the right direction—reaching the nations of the world. Deep down, Christians know this is important and, furthermore, that they are personally responsible to help make it happen. But the concerns and busyness of our modern lives have made this call far too easy to dismiss or ignore. "Besides, we have needs in our own families, churches and cities," many would say. "We really need to be focusing on them." Thinking this way, though, has blinded people to the world around them.

*September 11 was the wake-up call.* Suddenly, it was much easier to understand how people and events halfway around the world can dramatically impact our lives. As our eyes have been opened, we see that these nations have now moved into our own cities and neighborhoods. From language options at the ATM to the growth of restaurants and supermarkets catering to specific ethnicities, we are all more aware of the different nations now represented in our own backyard. Tragically, suspicion and prejudice have taken root in some hearts, taking what should be a wonderful ministry opportunity and twisting it into a liability.

But for those truly sensitive to the heart of God, our modern landscape has produced a growing compassion—and a sense of urgency—to help build a bridge of peace to others. It has been quite a shock to see the commitment of terrorists and suicide bombers; people who are literally willing to die on behalf of their causes. Their commitment, though twisted and misguided, should provoke the Church to evaluate its own level of dedication. Love is stronger than hate and death, faith more powerful than fear. But these great promises of God's Word are just that, promises, until they are claimed and then unleashed through the lives of God's people on the earth.

If life were a chess match, it would certainly be the Church's move.

## AN INCREDIBLE OPEN DOOR

An extraordinary "tipping point" moment is upon us. The rationalism of the Enlightenment has run out of gas and its postmodern replacement has come up empty-handed as well.[6] Pain, suffering and uncertainty about the future have produced an unprecedented openness, even among people who not too long ago would have been singularly resistant to the Gospel.

As I walked the streets of New York City two days after 9/11, I saw signs of this new openness all around me. People weren't just combing the streets looking for loved ones; thousands searched for answers to the hard questions bleeding from the wound that was the World Trade Center. Doors into hearts and lives were swinging open; doors that I also knew could just as suddenly swing shut.

Our ministry, Morning Star International, seized the opportunity and planted a church in Manhattan. Had we waited, I'm not sure our efforts would have been as effective. This same openness existed in Asia in the eighties, Eastern Europe in the nineties, and now seems to be everywhere you look. Nations are beckoning to someone—anyone—to come and help.

My book, *Finding Faith at Ground Zero*, recounted General Douglas MacArthur's request for ten thousand "missionary reinforcements"[7] to move to post-war Japan and evangelize that nation. Here was another door God had sovereignly swung open. Sadly and all too predictably, only a few hundred missionaries were sent. Today, the economic downturn is once again opening hearts and minds in Japan, presenting another strategic opportunity for ministry. What will be the response in our generation?

Much of Africa is experiencing a tremendous spiritual awakening, as are significant regions of Asia and Latin America. But these massive numbers of converts are in desperate need of teaching and training in the foundations of biblical knowledge and Christian character. This wide-open door could represent another tipping point if the Church responds properly in this hour. If this fails to happen, Scripture as well as history tells us the enemy stands ready to devour the young in faith if they are not properly grounded and discipled. In spite of all the religious fervor, the needs of these places are still enormous. Many nations in Africa are suffering from the pandemic of AIDS, poverty, warfare, hunger and unrelenting oppression. For example, it is projected that the nation of Malawi will cease to exist in eight years if AIDS continues to spread at its current rate.[8] The United Nations estimates there will be forty million orphans there by the year 2010. It's going to take radical commitment and mountain-moving faith to raise this continent out of the grip of death. Again the question presents itself: Are we willing to try?

## DIFFERENT TIMES, SAME ATMOSPHERE

Many of the same characteristics of the first century mark the landscape of the twenty-first, setting the stage perhaps for even greater results than those the early Church experienced. In his book, *Revolution in Leadership: Training Apostles for Tomorrow's Church*, Reggie McNeal points out several amazing parallels between then and now. Among them are:

◆ *Globalism*: Comparatively speaking, the world has been brought together to form at least the outline of a global village. In the first century this was accomplished through the dominance of Greco-Roman culture over most of the known world. Today it's the hegemony of Western culture (the arts, particularly Hollywood and pop music), telecommunications, democratization, international trade and modern transportation—over the entire planet. Contributing to this is the common language factor: in the first century it was Greek, today it's English.

◆ *Religious pluralism*: Just as today there is a wide assortment of religious expressions, there was a similar phenomenon in the first century. It was just this kind of atmosphere that Paul confronted in Athens when he called on its citizens to deal with the "unknown God" that made heaven and earth.

◆ *Heightened spiritual awareness:* Both eras can be character-
ized by a high degree of interest in spirituality. Although in
the West, church attendance today is down, the percentage
of people expressing belief in God and the importance of
spirituality has increased. As people lose faith in organized
religion, they can't escape their spiritual needs. This
hunger of the heart persists, regardless of the objections in
the mind.

Even as this fog of spiritual confusion covered the nations in the
first century, the Church pressed forward with the clear message of
the cross. Amid the (relative) peace Rome had won (the famous *Pax
Romana*), Christian missionaries traveled Roman roads, speaking the
Empire's language. Within a generation, people would say as the
Church advanced: "These who have turned the world upside down
have come here too."[9] As Andrew Murray said at the turn of the twentieth century,

To evangelize the world in this generation is entirely possible…in view of the achievements of the Christians of the
first generation. They did more to accomplish the work
than succeeding generations. In studying the secret of
what they accomplished, one is led to the conclusion that
they employed no vitally important method which cannot
be used today, and they availed themselves of no power
which we can not utilize.[10]

In this first century of a new millennium, there is a new opportunity for the Church to once again have the same kind of
determination and see the same kind of world-shaking results.

## LEFT BEHIND…OR LEFT OUT?

We must stress that there's more to our message to the world in this
hour than simply, "Don't get left behind." In the July 1, 2002, issue of
*Time* magazine, Nancy Gibbs noted, "The experience of last fall—the
terrorist attacks, the anthrax deaths—not only deepened the interest
among Christians fluent in the language of Armageddon and apocalypse. It broadened it as well." Instead of using this opportunity to
inspire greater passion for reaching and discipling the nations, the
events were simply interpreted by many Christians as just one more

set of clues as to when the end of the world will come. How ironic that it was left to a secular magazine to question the wisdom of this mindset. As Gibbs concludes, "If Christians are called to put their faith in Christ whatever trials they face, then it undermines that trust to try and read the signs, unlock the code, and focus on what can't be known, rather than what must be done: heal the sick, tend the poor and spread the Gospel."[11]

The grand and glorious fact is that this Gospel has answers that will heal hearts, homes and, yes, even homelands. The real challenge of the hour isn't "Don't get left behind" but rather "Don't get 'left out'…of God's purposes during such a crucial time in history." The Welsh Revival and the Great Awakenings in America are examples of tipping points when suddenly crime rates fell, families were strengthened and every social institution was affected. Anything is possible when God pours out His Spirit.

The apostle Paul declared, "His intent was that now, through the church, the manifold wisdom of God should be made known to the rulers and authorities in the heavenly realms."[12] Note the use of the qualifier "now" in this passage. As the Church, we have a present responsibility to make known the "manifold [multi-faceted or multi-colored] wisdom of God." Grace has been given to us now to present the unfathomable riches of our Lord before He returns.

This is to be the primary focus for the Church. As God promised through the prophet Isaiah: "See, darkness covers the earth and thick darkness is over the peoples, but the LORD rises upon you and his glory appears over you." Christ is returning for "a glorious bride without spot or wrinkle," a church that is "occupying until He comes." Isaiah continues, "Nations will come to your light, and kings to the brightness of your dawn."[13]

## THE GREAT RECOVERY

The Church is to be a "light to the nations" of the world. For this calling to become a reality, we must recover and embrace the lost mandate Jesus gave to His disciples. In Matthew 28, Mark 16 and Luke 24, the Lord commissioned them to "Go into all the world… preach the Gospel…and make disciples of all nations." These marching orders have come to be known as the "Great Commission" and should be the heart and soul of everything we do. As we will see in the next chapter, at certain times throughout the history of the

Church this mandate has been lost, distorted, or—most common of all—simply ignored. In one recent survey of American evangelicals, 75 percent of those polled weren't even familiar with the term "Great Commission." It should be obvious that there is no way to obey orders one doesn't even know exist!

To help reintroduce and redefine this awesome task—as well as to impress a sense of the urgency of the Lord's calling on this present generation—we have coined the phrase "Apostolic Mandate" as a synonym for the Great Commission. It is "apostolic" in that it focuses on the challenge of reaching and discipling the world by sending "ambassadors of the Gospel" to plant churches in every nation in the world.[14] It is a "mandate" because it is a strategic command from a higher (the highest, of course) authority to His appointed representatives. As with any true mandate, it carries within it the power and the delegated authority to ensure the mission's success.[15] Furthermore, it is a "mandate" because it is not optional or reserved for members of some spiritual elite; these orders must be communicated to every person who responds to the Gospel message. From the very beginning, a convert should know that, by coming to Christ, they are not only forgiven and placed in God's family through Jesus' death and resurrection, but they also have been commissioned by Him to take His Gospel to the nations.

Church leaders must obey these orders and not allow them to be pushed down the priority ladder of the church. Doing this will amount to a revolution in how every Christian lives his or her life. No longer is the Apostolic Mandate the responsibility of a committed few; it is the mandate of every believer.

## RECOVERING THE MESSAGE

In order to recover this mandate, we must also regain the apostolic message the early Church took to the world: the belief that Jesus Christ is *Lord*. His substitutionary death and resurrection validated His claim to being "...the way and the truth and the life"[16]—the only way for man to be redeemed from the power of sin and come back to God. This conviction compelled the early Church to go into the entire world.

Today, many who call themselves Christians question this foundational truth. A *U.S. News & World Report* survey revealed that 77 percent of Christians felt that all religions have elements of truth, and therefore they couldn't claim any sense of exclusivity for their faith.[17]

No wonder there has been a lack of motivation to reach out to other cultures and religions. If in the end people can make it to heaven without the shedding of Christ's blood upon the cross, what's the point in evangelizing?[18] All of this demonstrates a tragic lack of understanding concerning the nature of man, sin, Christ, the Trinity, the Gospel—really the entire fabric of the Christian faith. If Jesus didn't have to give His life on the cross for the sins of the world, then not only was He either confused or lying,[19] but His sacrifice was also the greatest waste of a life in history.

Our message remains unchanged from the one Paul preached in Jerusalem, Samaria and to the outmost parts of the world: "Jesus Christ and Him crucified."[20] His death uniquely satisfied the claims of God's justice, and His resurrection opened the way for all mankind to be forgiven and transformed. It is imperative that we preach a message that produces an authentic commitment and the life change that the Scripture promises.

The Lordship of Christ has enormous implications for every area of life. He isn't just the Lord of church services and religious affairs. He is King of kings, Lord of lords, the Ruler of the kings of the earth.[21] This means that there is no area of life that is not subject to Him. The vestiges of platonic dualism that have plagued the Church for centuries—separating what people believe from what they do as well as creating a false dichotomy between the material and spiritual world—must be "cast down" and replaced with a biblical worldview: one that honors God and strives to extend His kingdom rights over the earth.

## RECOVERING THE METHOD

This points to the heart and soul of the Apostolic Mandate, *making disciples*, which has been referred to by some as the "Great Omission of the Great Commission."[22] We have tried every method imaginable, without producing lasting results. As has been said, "The problem is not that Christianity has been tried and found wanting, but that it has never been tried at all." While other religions and ideologies thoroughly train their adherents, Christianity continues to act as if great character and great leaders will "just happen." Although Jesus spoke to the masses, His primary strategy was to pour His life into twelve men. He then commanded them to go and do the same.

In order to do this, the vital ministries of Ephesians 4 and 1 Corinthians 12 must be recovered as well. It is the responsibility of these ministries to "prepare God's people for works of service."[23] The result will be the mightiest force for the Gospel the world has ever seen, as people from every walk of life are trained to reach *their* world for Christ.

## RECOVERING THE MANDATE

Much of this introduction was written while I was visiting two of the world's great capital cities, London and Paris. While walking their streets, I was deeply moved by the realization that their grandeur and glory were now mostly remnants of a bygone era. Spiritual decay was now all around me—and not just in these two centers of civilization; most of Europe is reeling from the latter stages of a great apostasy. The spiritual need is immense... and yet comparatively little attention and effort are being invested by the Church to meet it. Like a child dying of hunger in a world filled with food, if these cities perish, it will be from utter neglect. I couldn't help but recall Jesus' warnings to the religious establishment of Israel:

> It will be more bearable on that day for Sodom than for that town...For if the miracles that were performed in you had been performed in Tyre and Sidon, they would have repented long ago.
>
> —LUKE 10:12–13

If the meetings, conferences and church plantings that have taken place throughout America had happened in London or Paris, I am convinced these cities would have responded. We can't assume that they aren't open and then make our prophecy self-fulfilling by not reaching out to them. We can't look at the advance of darkness as an excuse for not obeying the Lord's command to make disciples of *all nations,* especially when Jesus has said *all authority in heaven and earth belongs* to Him.

In the meantime, while a significant portion of the Church is preoccupied with endtime scenarios, another dramatic "tipping point" is upon us. If we do nothing, the circumstances will, no doubt, "tip" in the wrong direction. Rather than viewing the challenges around us negatively and thus lowering our expectations, we should echo the words of the apostle Paul when he was thrown into prison: "What has happened to me has really served to advance the Gospel."[24] This is the spirit of faith so desperately needed in this epochal moment in history.

# PART I

# VISION

## CHAPTER 1

# EVERY NATION IN OUR GENERATION

*Things cannot go on as they are if the world is really to be evangelized in this generation.*

—ANDREW MURRAY
NEW YORK MISSIONS CONFERENCE, 1900

*I*t's one of my favorite scenes in movie history. *Chariots of Fire* tells the true story of Scottish runner and missionary, Eric Liddell. The film focuses on the events surrounding his gold medal win at the 1924 Olympics. But it also powerfully depicts another great moment in his athletic career—an event that took place in a far less impressive setting.

During a local race in Scotland, Liddell was tripped and fell to the ground. The crowd gasped as the front-runner, the man everyone expected to win, appeared out of the race. Pulling himself to his feet, Liddell found the other runners well ahead on the short 400-meter course. Refusing to quit, the "Flying Scotsman" began to run with an abandon that brought the stunned crowd to its feet. Incredibly, he caught the field and won the race, virtually collapsing across the finish line. His recovery and victory were truly remarkable.

In many ways, the Church today finds itself in the same position as Liddell: knocked down, counted out of the race for the destiny of the planet.

Increasingly we are ignored as a political voice, scoffed at as a moral authority, and discounted as a credible force in influencing society. The vibrant Christian worldview that at one time ruled America and much of Western culture[1] is now muffled and trivialized.

In *The State of the Church 2002*, cultural analyst George Barna noted that there are far more churches than schools, post offices and McDonald's restaurants. And yet "the church has less impact on our culture than any of those less-prolific entities, despite missions that are far less significant or compelling."[2]

As the light of truth dims over the western world, the threat of a new dark age of spiritual confusion and bondage becomes increasingly real. The forces of false religion have stepped into the void with a counterfeit vision of reality that is sweeping up millions of people.

In 1950, two-thirds of the world's missionaries came from the United States.[3] Now, a generation later, the majority of the mission force emanates from what has been called the "two-thirds world"—in particular, Africa, Asia and Latin America. While we celebrate the increase of Christianity in these other nations, the sad fact is that America is sending fewer and fewer missionaries abroad. This spectacular growth is certainly being challenged in these areas by the forces of Islam and Hinduism. The nation of Nigeria, which now boasts the world's largest churches, could also be called the world's greatest battleground over the soul of a nation—and possibly the continent. Despite great gains in certain areas, the Church has no room for a false sense of security. As Philip Jenkins comments in *New Christendom: The Coming of Global Christianity,*

> No church or religion has a guaranteed market share in any country. It is quite possible to imagine a scenario in which the proportion of Nigerian Christians could fall as low as 10% (presently it's 40%), in the event of persecutions or successful jihad by the nation's Muslim majority. The figure could rise far higher if a sweeping Christian revival should occur.[4]

In nation after nation, the advance of the kingdom of God is contested. Countries like Sierra Leone are being bought piece-by-piece by terrorist states and then rebuilt around mosques.

Meanwhile, back in the West, once a bastion of Christianity, the darkness advances virtually unchallenged. The false messiah of secularism has swept through Europe. In nations like Belgium and Greece—where the Christian faith once thrived—it is now virtually illegal to preach the Gospel.

At the same time, the stronghold of ritualism and superstition twists the vision of the real Christ into a pale substitute, ever hanging upon the cross, offering forgiveness but almost powerless to set men free from sin. The scandal of those who have violated their trust as ministers has been heralded by the popular media as a failure of "the Church." In fact, the Gallup Poll showed people who had confidence in religion fell from 60 percent in 2001 to 45 percent in 2002. "This is religion's lowest ranking in the history of the Gallup surveys."[5] At a time in history when courageous moral leadership is so desperately needed, the last place many would look is within the Christian faith.

## THE GATES OF HELL WILL NOT PREVAIL

But the true Church isn't like this. Jesus declared, "You will know them by their fruits."[6] In the end, God will have a people who obey His commands and are empowered by His Spirit, modeling on Earth the righteousness and integrity of His kingdom in heaven.

And this is what the forces of darkness fear. Satan knows that the Church founded upon the rock of Christ's Lordship will plunder his dark kingdom and foil every evil scheme for the cities and nations of the world. Jesus boldly promised, "I will build My church, and the gates of Hades shall not prevail against it."[7] Keep in mind that gates are stationary objects; they can't attack or pursue. Jesus' choice of words can mean only one thing: we are to be advancing against, not retreating from, hell's gates. In the end, they will not be able to withstand the Lord of hosts' attack.[8]

With the many promises of victory that God has granted us, it is puzzling why we have consistently failed to advance the Gospel from one generation to the next. Why have we so often gained ground only to find ourselves knocked down, looking at the backs of the competing worldviews that have raced past us?

This is not God's plan. Nor is He pleased with this cycle of defeat. That which He births carries within it the seed of victory, a destiny to overcome the world.[9] Eric Liddell liked to say that the Lord made him fast. No doubt that was true, but it took courage and steadfastness on his part to become a champion. God made the Church to inherit the nations, but how will our generation respond to this calling? We may be troubled on every side, but we need not be distressed. We may be "persecuted, but not abandoned; struck down, but not destroyed."[10] Will we, like Liddell, get up and run the race with renewed passion? The destiny of lives and nations hangs in the balance, waiting for the answer.

## THE STRUGGLES AND SUCCESSES OF THE EARLY CHURCH

Look back at the first disciples. They met the Son of God face-to-face. They listened to His teachings and saw His miracles—even participating in them at times.[11] They were His friends—they hung out with Him, ate food He had created out of nothing or had prepared with His own hands.[12] Yet, in spite of this, they had difficulty grasping His essential mission.

From the very beginning of His public ministry, Jesus' "fame spread throughout all the region around Galilee."[13] In the hometown of Peter and Andrew, the entire city showed up at their house to see Him. Finding Jesus praying in a secluded place, the disciples told Him about the waiting crowds. No doubt they were a bit stunned when He replied, "Let us go somewhere else—to the nearby villages—so I can preach there also. That is why I have come."[14] It wasn't really until well after Pentecost that they finally understood: He had come to save the entire world—not just one city or nation.

Jesus had what many Jews considered an unfortunate habit of ministering to people from different cultures—minorities who were considered off-limits or unimportant. Time and again, He would reach out to Gentiles and even honor them as examples of true faith. In talking about His approaching struggle with the Prince of Darkness, Jesus confidently declared that He would also draw *all* men to Himself when He was "lifted up from the earth."[15] When that cataclysmic moment came and He was crucified, His followers at first despaired, frightened that their cause had failed and their mission was lost. Three days later, their fear turned to faith. The Lord of life conquered death, and His bodily resurrection became a heavenly declaration that not only was He indeed the Son of God, but that He had become the world's new Ruler. He now possessed "all authority in heaven and on earth." Calling His disciples together, He instructed them to "go and make disciples of all nations."[16]

In sending them to the nations as His ambassadors and granting them the power and authority of His name, the "disciples" were transformed into "apostles." The original twelve not only thoroughly preached the Gospel,[17] but they also set a precedent upon which future generations could build. The era of the apostles remains the "benchmark of missional effectiveness."[18]

> Apostolic-age believers adopted the spread of the Gospel as their marching orders. In the face of skepticism, unbelief, and hostility, they courageously shared their faith—with stunning results. Their fervor launched a movement that gained momentum in its early centuries. Between A.D. 250 and 350, the number of Christians increased dramatically from 1.7 million to 33.8 million.[19]

This success, however, did not come without a struggle for the focus and heart of the Church.

## STUCK IN JERUSALEM

Old habits and paradigms die hard. Despite Jesus' clear command to reach all nations and not just stay in Jerusalem, the leaders of the new Church had a hard time "thinking outside the box" of their Jewish traditions. The holy city had been the center of the universe for God's covenant people; surely it would remain the Lord's focus. And not only that, so much was going on in the city of David! People were beginning to complain that the apostles couldn't keep up with the needs in their own backyard.[20] It also seemed as though the world might be coming to them. The Holy Spirit instructed Philip to head just south of town and, sure enough, he was able to help lead an African—a powerful government official, no less—to Christ. Build it in Jerusalem, they might have thought, and the rest of the world will come.[21]

In the meantime, the Lord was preparing to shake up both the apostles and the world. The mighty hand of His grace fell on the most unlikely of vessels. Saul of Tarsus was a Jew of Jews. Educated at the Harvard of his day, he possessed the type of résumé that made him a natural to hit the lecture circuit in the Jewish world.[22] And not only was he uniquely qualified to minister to his own brethren, the pharisaical culture in which he had been raised would have only aggravated his innate Jewish prejudice against the Gentile world. And yet, when he finally met the Lord and received his call as an apostle, Jesus told Paul right up front that he was being sent "to carry my name before the Gentiles and their kings and before the people of Israel."[23] It was no accident that the Gentiles were mentioned first. Paul was to focus on an area that the other apostles were, for the most part, neglecting.

## PETER'S SECOND SET OF DENIALS

Few people in history have had more reason to be grateful for a second chance than Simon Peter. Three times he denied knowing his master and friend at the very time when Jesus needed Peter's support the most. After the apparent finality of the Lord's death on the cross, the weight of the whole world must have fallen on the disciple's shoulders. He might well have feared that he would never be able to say he was sorry or in some way make it up to Him.

Three days later, Peter—and with him each one of us—got a second chance. What a relief it was to see his Lord alive; to not only be able to tell Him three times that he loved Him, but also to hear Jesus entrust him with the care of His flock. Later, Peter stood atop a mountain with the other ten disciples and heard Jesus officially commission him with the greatest and most glorious task in human history. He was to be a "witness [for Christ] in Jerusalem, Judea and Samaria and to the ends of the earth."[24]

Perhaps Peter, like most of us when we hear the word of the Lord, focused on the part he liked the most. Despite the broader command, despite the Lord's clear example in ministering to non-Jews, Peter focused his attention on his own people and their capital city, Jerusalem. The rest of the world seemed to drop off his radar screen.

Ever faithful to complete the work He has begun in us,[25] God then sends a vision to His reluctant disciple; one so powerful that it knocks him into a trance.[26] Peter sees a four-cornered sheet—a reference to the entire "four-cornered" earth[27]—filled with animals that were ritually unclean under the ceremonial law of the Old Testament. "Rise [get up and get going!] Peter, kill and eat," the Lord commands. "No, Lord," Peter responds. "What God has cleansed you must not call unclean," Jesus counters, driving the point home. Three times this happens. Three times Peter tells the Lord "No."

Having awakened from his trance, the three-fold nature of his refusal must have brought back a flood of memories for the chastened apostle. *Have I done it again?* he might have wondered.

While absorbed with what the vision means, he is suddenly met by emissaries from a Gentile leader who wants to know more about God. Peter goes and meets Cornelius. The Holy Spirit falls and Cornelius, his family and friends are wonderfully converted. Upon their baptism, the apostolic outreach to the Gentile world officially begins. And the mystery of Peter's vision is solved: There is no part of the world, no corner of culture or human endeavor, where Jesus does not extend His claims.

Over the next few generations, people from all nationalities and ethnicities flooded into the kingdom of God. The Gospel was preached to "all the world" and "brought forth fruit," swelling the ranks of the Church and slowly transforming the culture.[28]

## THE PROGRESS OF THE MANDATE

Sadly, the momentum gained by these early victories did not always continue unabated. God's people—as they did throughout the Bible—cycled between seasons of great fervor for God and periods of lukewarm-ness and apostasy. During these latter phases, the attempts of the mainstream Church to fulfill the Apostolic Mandate tended to look more like the "city of man" than the "city of God." The unconverted were too often "compelled to come in" not by the power of the Spirit, but by intimidation, social pressure and even brute force. Such was the case with the Christianization of the Roman Empire under Constantine and subsequent "Christian" emperors. Years later the Crusades, which began in A.D. 1095, became an even more egregious example of this perversion of the missionary impulse. And even as recently as the eighteenth century, many missions efforts had more to do with colonization and the expansion of an empire than with genuine spiritual transformation.

But just when it would seem that the Apostolic Mandate was in danger of being lost, God would always open someone's ears to His call for the nations. The testimonies of each of these people, and the movements they birthed, stand as a beacon to our generation. As *Time* magazine observed in an article written after the tragedy of September 11: "In times of crisis great leaders reach back in time to receive counsel from leaders of another generation, waiting to guide them."[29]

Among these leaders were two simple men—one a former slave, the other a cobbler—who by faith virtually changed the world.

## PATRICK OF IRELAND

Born in Scotland in 387 of noble parents, Patricus was kidnapped in his sixteenth year, taken to Ireland and sold into slavery. For the next six years, he prayed day and night as he labored in solitude as a shepherd. Years later, Patrick, as he would come to be called, would describe this period of God-ordained preparation:

> The love of God and His fear increased in me more and more, and the faith grew in me, and the spirit was roused, so that, in a single day, I have said as many as a hundred prayers, and in the night nearly the same, so that whilst in the woods and on the mountain, even before the dawn, I was roused to prayer and felt no hurt from it, whether there was snow or ice or rain; nor was there any slothfulness, such as I see now, because the spirit was then fervent within me.[30]

Patrick wouldn't understand until later just how fervently the Spirit of God was watching over and preparing him for the Lord's service. During these six years of captivity, he became fluent in the Celtic tongue and the intricacies of the Druid religion that ruled the island with a satanic fist. When his season of training drew to a close, an angel appeared to him and told him he was free to leave. His journey home was a remarkable one, arduous but attended by much grace and supernatural intervention; a pattern that would come to characterize his entire life and ministry.

Once back with his family and friends, it wasn't long before Patrick felt the call to return to Ireland and preach freedom in Christ to the very people who once held him in slavery. More than once he was visited by a vision of children from his adopted homeland saying, "O holy youth, come back to Ireland 'and walk once more among us.'"[31]

In the summer of 433, Patrick landed again on the Emerald Isle, attended by a small band of missionary companions. Over the next sixty years, the "apostle to Ireland" would experience more challenges, struggles and supernatural victories than perhaps any man in history other than Paul the Apostle. Twelve times he was taken captive; on a number of other occasions people tried to kill him. But in all these, Patrick was more than a conqueror through Christ who strengthened him. Village by village, pagan chieftain by pagan chieftain, the Gospel of peace made its way over the island as a refiner's fire. The druidic cult was virtually extinguished. The Christian faith was embraced with a fervency that would later spawn a missionary movement that reintroduced the Gospel to Europe and rekindled the Apostolic Mandate's march toward the other nations of the world. As Thomas Cahill noted in his bestseller, *How the Irish Saved Civilization*, Patrick's apostolic legacy was far more than just an entire nation won for Christ. By preserving Christian scholarship, training disciples (he would personally ordain some three hundred and fifty bishops) and bequeathing to them a passion for the nations, it is not an exaggeration to say that God used Patrick not only to save a nation, but also to preserve much of the Christian faith for the world as a whole.

It is interesting and perhaps more than a little significant to our generation today that, before he died, Patrick had a vision of Ireland bathed in the light of God's glory. In this vision, the glory continued unabated for many centuries and then began to wane. Disturbed, the great apostle cried out to the Lord, beseeching Him that the light would return. As he prayed, the glimmering gradually grew in intensity until the entire island was once again lit up in pristine splendor.

In a time when Ireland, like most of Europe, has all but succumbed to the darkness of humanism, an obvious challenge presents itself.[32] Will we be the instruments that God uses to see this prophetic vision of restoration fulfilled?

## WILLIAM CAREY

Of all the champions of the Apostolic Mandate since the time of Patrick, there are few more remarkable than William Carey. The birth of what we now know as the Modern Missions Movement occurred in a humble shop where the young Carey repaired and sold second-hand shoes.

The simple cobbler had been struck by Jesus' straightforward command to go into the world and preach the Gospel to every nation. Carey became so absorbed with the thought of fulfilling this forgotten mandate that he pieced together a leather globe of the world, praying over it as he worked. And then one day the call from the Lord came: "If it be the duty of all men to believe the Gospel, then it be the duty of those who are entrusted with the Gospel to endeavor to make it known among all nations."[33] Carey responded with the cry, "Here am I; send me!"[34]

To surrender to the Lord's call was one thing; actually going was an entirely different matter. At the time, there were no missionary societies and little real missionary interest. When Carey approached some church leaders for aid in reaching the lost in other nations, he was stunned at their indifferent reply. "When God pleases to convert the heathen, he will do it without your aid or mine," he was told.[35]

Undaunted, he set out to publish a pamphlet that would present his burden—or more properly, the Lord's—to reach the nations with the Gospel. In 1791, an English merchant gave the young shoemaker £10 to print *Enquiry into the Obligation of Christians to Use Means for the Conversion of Heathens.* The small book had one primary aim: to recover the commission Jesus bestowed upon His disciples before His ascension into heaven as the primary purpose for both the Christian and the Church. He argued that nothing had changed, that both the Apostolic Mandate and the power to fulfill it were just as pressing in his day as they were in ages past. The book brimmed with passion and confidence that the Lord was more than able to accomplish through the Church the very thing He had commanded.

Carey wrote:

> Yet God repeatedly made known His intention to prevail finally over all the power of the devil, and to destroy all his works, and to set up His own kingdom and interests among men, and extend it as universally as Satan had extended his. It was for this purpose that the Messiah came and died, that God may be just, and the justifier of all that should believe in Him. When He had laid down His life, and taken it up again, He sent forth His disciples to preach the good tidings to every creature, and to endeavor by all possible methods to bring over a lost world to God. They went forth according to their divine commission, and wonderful success attended their labors; the civilized Greeks, and uncivilized barbarians, each yielded to the cross of Christ, and embraced it as the only way of salvation.[36]

The book's publication and Carey's subsequent forty-one year ministry in India launched the Modern Missions Movement. Since he penned these words over two hundred years ago, the Gospel has spread and prospered. Many nations that were all but unreached in his day have seen strong and growing churches established. Carey's motto still stands as a bold challenge: "Expect great things from God; attempt great things for God."[37]

## THE HALL OF CHAMPIONS

Patrick and Carey are but two of the many faithful witnesses who served the purpose of God in their generation, passing the baton of the Apostolic Mandate to the ones who followed. Among the other giants of the faith stands the Irish missionary Aidan (c. 600–651), who continued Patrick's legacy and, with the help of King Oswald, spread Christianity throughout much of Britain. The English nobleman, Boniface (c. 680–754), in turn spent almost forty years laboring among the Old Saxons, earning the title "the Apostle to Germany." John Amos Comenius (1592–1670), the "Father of Modern Education," was also a devoted missionary to the people of Poland and Europe. His "Via Lucis"—or "way of light"—set the stage for the great Moravian missionary movement. At the age of seventeen, Count Nicholas von Zinzendorf (1700–1760) helped found The Order of the Grain of Mustard Seed, a secret society made up of influential people who wanted to use their positions to help spread the Gospel. Joining later with the Moravians, von Zinzendorf was able to help birth a missions movement that powerfully touched Africa, the Americas and Russia. Out of the Moravian renewal sprang John and Charles Wesley and the Methodists, men and a movement that would literally transform the moral landscape of England and America. Speaking of the Apostolic Mandate, it was John Wesley who declared:

> Give me a hundred men who hate nothing but sin and love God with all their hearts, and I will shake the world for Christ.[38]

Echoing the words of Hebrews 11, what more shall I say? Time would fail me to tell of the many other champions of the faith: David Brainerd, Robert Moffat, David Livingstone, John Geddie, John Paton, Hudson Taylor, Mary Slessor, Jonathan Goforth, Solomon Ginsburg, James Chalmers, Amy Carmichael, James Gilmour—people "who through faith conquered kingdoms, administered justice, and gained what was promised;…whose weakness was turned to strength; and who became powerful in battle and routed foreign armies."[39] Together they made the nineteenth century one of the most potent eras in the history of the Church as regards the Apostolic Mandate.

However, by the twentieth century, modernism, higher criticism and a host of other spiritual ills had eaten into the foundations of much of the mainstream Church. While the Baptists and the Assemblies of God, most notably, were able to avoid many of the snares of liberal theology and remain a vital force on the field of apostolic missions, they were the exception and not the rule. As was true so many times in the past, it was often left to young pioneers and parachurch organizations, rather than the Church, to keep the mandate for the nations alive.

Most notable among them were Robert Wilder, John R. Mott and the "Student Volunteer Movement" (SVM). Birthed out of a campaign of prayer that stretched all the way back to 1810 in what was then called the "Haystack Movement," the SVM was officially launched in 1886. During that summer, Wilder attended a missions conference for college students hosted by the great evangelist, D. L. Moody. One hundred students responded to the call to support missionaries through prayer and financial giving as well as to sincerely seek the Lord about volunteering for the mission field themselves. By 1925, the SVM was considered to be the source for one-half to two-thirds of all the missionaries sent from North America. Ultimately, some twenty-five thousand workers rose up to meet the challenge articulated by Wilder and his co-worker Mott: "Evangelize the world in this generation."

As the first half of the century progressed, however, the movement began to decline. World War I sent a wave of pessimism throughout the culture. Hard on its heels came the twin shocks of the Roaring Twenties and the Great Depression. The movement's watchword, "The Evangelization of the World in this Generation" was increasingly attacked as being too presumptuous. By the 1932 SVM conference, the phrase, which had been the movement's crowning glory, was conspicuous by its absence. Quoting a critical synopsis of the meeting that took place four years later:

> The mass of delegates had little or no knowledge of the Bible and spiritual things. They had evidently not studied the Bible in their homes, in churches or in colleges and universities. They lacked the background and foundations for the appreciation of missionary themes.... The audience was the mission field rather than the missionary force.[40]

Overall, the cynicism whipped up by two world wars produced "a marked decline in missionary interest and activity on the part of the mainline denominations in the United States. With few exceptions, they have retreated all along the line."[41] The result was that, as the twentieth century drew to a close, books were being written on missions with subtitles such as, "Where Have We Gone Wrong?"[42]

It was time to recover again the mandate passed down from Jesus. It was time to start getting it right.

## TO 2000 AND BEYOND

Approaching the year 2000, there was a mixture of fear and anticipation by the Church at large. The threat of Y2K, and the myriad speculations that surrounded it, presented another opportunity to become distracted from our mission. At the same time, there were eschatological predictions of the work of evangelizing the nations being finished by the year 2000, and thus the "end will come." There were numerous programs and strategies that put the "finish line" for the Church at the end of the second millennium. Well, that time has come and gone, and *we are still here.* The year 1988—forty years after Israel became a nation—came and went, and *we are still here.* Y2K came, and *we are still here.* Because we are, it falls upon every ministry, movement, denomination and family to reexamine its efforts and find a way to get back in the race and regain our place as the "salt of the earth." Finishing the task means more than giving every person a basic Gospel presentation. Again, somehow, we have heard only part of the Lord's instructions.

## EVERY NATION IN OUR GENERATION

In 1999, while standing on the precipice of this new millennium, I was impressed by the Lord to articulate this 2000-year-old Apostolic Mandate in a fresh way to our ministry, Morning Star International (MSI). I will never forget the sense of awe and surprise I experienced when a simple, memorable phrase came to my heart and mind. As I shared it with other leaders, it seemed to produce the same kind of enthusiastic response. This phrase—almost a slogan really—was to become the rallying cry for our ministry, one that would sum up the mission for us but hopefully mobilize people everywhere to the greatness and urgency of our call:

*Every nation in our generation.*

At the time, I had never heard anything like it. As I later researched the history of missions, I was intrigued to find echoes of it in the slogans of other movements.

It was stunning to find out that, almost one hundred years ago, Mott released *The Evangelization of the World in this Generation.* Clearly, a theme that was very much on the heart of God was being rebirthed. Let me say here that I don't believe this is just a word given to Morning Star International; this phrase is simply a restating of the

Apostolic Mandate given to all the Church by Jesus before He ascended into heaven. "Every nation" is the scope of the mandate— and has been ever since God made the covenant with Abraham that He would bless all the nations through him. "Our generation" is the timing, one that has become progressively more achievable over the last two hundred years. "Write the vision and make it plain on tablets, that he may run who reads it."[43] So the Lord commanded the prophet Habakkuk over twenty-five hundred years ago. In a fundamental sense, this is the primary purpose of this book—to record the vision and make it plain, to challenge everyone who calls on the name of the Lord to read it and run to find their role in fulfilling the Apostolic Mandate.

*Every nation in our generation.* A grand and glorious goal...but how to get there? As I sought the Lord for specific direction, a few preeminent truths stood out in my mind. First, it is the Church that is the "pillar and foundation of the truth."[44] The missionaries we sent were to function apostolically, planting churches in every nation of the world. Second, their purpose wasn't to just pluck "brands from the fire" as the surrounding culture succumbed to the flames of sin. The goal was to obey the command of Christ: to disciple the nations, teaching them to observe all the things (He) has commanded. Again, the Church was the key. We were to establish true "outposts of the kingdom of heaven" where people could be set free from the bondage of sin, trained and then sent to salt their culture and the world. Multiply, divide and spread! So Jesus fed the multitudes. So works the leaven of God's kingdom in the "loaf of this world."[45]

## THE 2010 INITIATIVE

With the vision and these guiding principles in mind, a plan began to unfold...a plan that came to be called the *2010 Initiative,* the first ten-year installment of a generational blueprint. In a nutshell, the goal is for every one of our local churches to help plant at least one new church every two years.[46] This would result in exponential church planting in the years to come.

In the end, only God can bring this type of increase. Without His presence and power, the 2010 Initiative is mere wishful thinking. But to sit around and wait for the Apostolic Mandate to be fulfilled without plans and goals is presumption and disobedience.

The Bible declares that the Lord "is able to do exceedingly abundantly beyond all that we ask or think."[47] God does it…but we still have to ask and think! We plan according to the will of God and can then stand back in awe when He blesses our efforts and accomplishes more than we ever anticipated. Plans neither limit God nor force His hand—they are His appointed means by which His grace is manifested in the earth.

And these plans also provide us with a useful ruler by which we can measure the success of our grand adventures in the kingdom of God. Hopefully, from the vantage point of the momentum achieved by doing this and arriving at the year 2010, there will be a second initiative—the 2020 Initiative—that could potentially result in our having planted a church in every nation of the world by the end of that decade. Whether we reach every nation by 2020 or 2030 isn't as important as pressing on to accomplish this mandate, believing that by the power of God it can be done.

As the Lord declared to another generation who desired to see the fulfillment of His purposes: "Not by might, not by power, but by My Spirit says the Lord."[48]

The first step is getting to the nations. The next step is to spread out and infiltrate the culture. Who knows what a 2030 Initiative might include, as we plant churches in every nation and have these strategic bases in place from which to advance God's kingdom in the earth.

## THE MOTIVATION OF THE MANDATE

Many would say that our ultimate motivation in embracing the Apostolic Mandate should be our love for God and our fellow man. On one level this is absolutely true. As the most well known verse in the Bible makes very clear, it was because of the Father's love for the whole world—not just one nation or people—that the Son was delivered to the cross.[49] As a people who are to follow in His footsteps, who are to model the "greater love" that is willing to "lay down his life for his friends," our call to the nations should be rooted and grounded in love and service.[50]

But there is another motivating factor that is just as important as love (I would argue that it is just another dimension of divine love), though it doesn't play as well in our self-centered, "feel-good-at-all-costs" age. The Bible declares in several places that the fear of the Lord is the beginning of wisdom. Numerous times the Book of Acts records how the fear of God fell on everyone present as the Church experienced the presence and power of the Holy Spirit.

Our present generation desperately needs a baptism in this same fear of the Lord. It isn't an option or some higher call for a spiritual elite. It is the antidote—the "red pill," to use a metaphor from the popular movie, *The Matrix*—for a culture infected with the virus of humanism.

This virus leads many to think that the Gospel creates nothing but a cozy familiarity with God. Because Christians "aren't perfect, just forgiven" (with the emphasis on the word *just*) we can blithely ignore the call to obedience. Yet it is from a very different perspective—a place of trembling before a Holy God—that Paul wrote, "knowing the terror [or fear] of the Lord we persuade men."[51] While avoiding speculative scenarios about the "end times," there is a vital truth that cannot be ignored: The Lord will return and there will be a "day of judgment." Just as fear of an IRS audit keeps many Americans honest about their taxes, there is a dimension of this fear that keeps us focused even when our inclinations would be otherwise.

"Historically, the telling of the final judgment has transformed entire epochs."[52] From the preaching of the early Church that Christ would return to judge the living and the dead, to the vivid picture of Dante's *Divine Comedy*, this is a very real motivator to a culture evaluating its actions. "In the 19th century, abolitionists like William Lloyd Garrison preached the judgment of God with such fire that President Lincoln admitted that he shuddered at what God would do if slavery continued."[53] There is a chilling reference to the source of this fear in the Gospel records—this great and terrible day of the Lord.[54] Jesus referred to the men of Nineveh standing up against this generation at the judgment:

> The men of Nineveh shall stand up with this generation at the judgment, and shall condemn it because they repented at the preaching of Jonah; and behold, something greater than Jonah is here. The Queen of the South shall rise up with this generation at the judgment and shall condemn it, because she came from the ends of the earth to hear the wisdom of Solomon; and behold, something greater than Solomon is here.
>
> —Matthew 12:41–42, NASB

I had always thought of judgment day as a fairly private affair. But what the Lord is describing here sounds more like a public courtroom. In fact, it even has echoes of the television talk shows that have become so popular around the world. You know the type of program I'm talking about—our modern equivalent of the gladiatorial games, except that people use words (and the occasional fist) to attack their opponents. Besides the combatants, there is always a host to moderate the proceedings (and to stir the pot when things become tame) and a studio audience to throw gas on the fire. After the pathetic exchange between the people on the stage, members of the audience rise up, condemning the person they think is wrong and pointing out the fallacies in their presentation.

Then it hit me. In a way, these talk shows reflect something of the judgment described in the twelfth chapter of Matthew. On Judgment Day, all the generations that have ever lived will in some sense be in the audience. One by one, each of them will take the stage to give an account of their actions, their stewardship of the grace of God. Focusing now on our own generation, it is going to be very difficult explaining to John the Baptist or the believers who suffered under Nero or the pilgrims who settled New England, how "tough" it was for us to fulfill Christ's command to reach the world. (I have a hard enough time now keeping my head up when I'm around members of the underground church in China.)

From our bookshelves to our computers, we're awash in Bibles and biblical teaching. Two thousand years of Church history and sacrifice have given us an incredible head start. Any young believer can, in a matter of a few years, have a better understanding of orthodoxy than all but the greatest scholars of 500 years ago, if they are diligent. We have more freedom to worship and serve God than almost any generation in history. Telecommunications, jets that can circle the globe, modern medicine, education, wealth, abundance, on and on it goes—there has never been a generation with so many advantages.

Referring to the parable Jesus told in Matthew 25, our generation is the one that has been given the most "talents." And with them comes the greatest expectation of return from our Master.

The parable raises another interesting point. After bestowing upon his subjects a certain number of talents, the master in Luke's parallel account tells them to "do business till I come."[55] There is no mention of specific orders concerning what to do with the money. This is because there is a broad understanding that the talents and gifts must be used to prosper the kingdom of God.

The Bible assures us that the Holy Spirit, by the Word of God, will guide anyone who is listening to Him, so that they can fulfill their specific calling in regard to the talents they have been given. The key to unlock the door of divine destiny is simply believing—knowing—that the Spirit of God will lead and empower His people as they stand ready to obey Him.

The Lord has given us the command to reach the world. He has also granted us the gifts necessary to accomplish this command. The question is, can we open our eyes and utilize all that He has set before us?

## WE CAN CATCH UP

What will be the response of our generation? Every era of believers has its chance to rise up and make its mark while preparing to successfully hand off the baton in this trans-generational race. If we can learn from the mistakes of the past while giving our whole heart to this eternal cause, we can make a quantum leap from the back of the pack to the front like Eric Liddell. The choice is before us: to stay on the ground and concede the race, or to do as the Scripture says: "For though a righteous man falls seven times, he rises again."[56] We have faced this same choice and were able to join together and commit our lives to God's purposes. Therefore, before we explore the vital principles that are involved in recovering the Apostolic Mandate, it's necessary to give you a glimpse of our journey and the obstacles we overcame to regain this focus. May our story inspire you to do the same and to get back in the race for the destiny of this planet.

## CHAPTER 2

# THE MIRACLE
# IN MANILA

*We mutually pledge to each other our lives, our for-
tunes and our sacred honor.*

—THE DECLARATION OF INDEPENDENCE

*I*t seemed like the right thing to say; one of those nice-sounding
prayers you pray when you think you already know the answer. At
the time, I was feeling really good about the way things were going
in my life. In three months, my wife, Jody, and I were expecting the
birth of our first child. After having traveled for years, we had just
moved into a beautiful new home in Scottsdale, Arizona. To top it off, I
could walk out my back door, drop a golf ball and aim for the twelfth
green. Everything seemed right with God and my place in the world.

And so when I leaned back in my office chair one beautiful, sunny
day in January of 1984, casually looked at a map of the world and said,
"Lord, is there anything You want me to do?" I expected my sense of
contentment to continue. "No, no," the Lord would say, "you're doing
just great!" But there was no mistaking the still, small voice that broke
through my reverie. The Holy Spirit impressed upon my heart a command that was to explode my comfortable, sanctified American
dream: "I want you to get up and go plant a church in the Philippines."

The Philippines at that time was a nation on the verge of chaos.
Almost daily, large numbers of students were marching through the
streets, protesting against the government of President Ferdinand

Marcos. Often these demonstrations turned into full-scale riots. The economy was teetering, and the communist threat was mounting in anticipation of a move to seize power. You couldn't pick up the paper or turn on the news without something telling you that the Philippines was among the last places any intelligent Westerner would want to visit—much less stay and plant a church.

Later, as plans for the new church began to move ahead, it was difficult telling Jody that only three months after the baby was born we would be leaving for this dangerous area of the world. Talking to our families was even harder. We love and honor them a great deal and have often been helped by their sage advice. But now we had to listen as they pled with us not to go. Humanly speaking, of course, their counsel made perfect sense; but we knew that God was leading us. Even so, it was a painful and awkward moment.

After receiving the word to plant a church in the Philippines, the first thing I did was call my friend, Phil Bonasso. Phil and I had worked together pioneering a campus church at the University of Southern California. The ministry began in an old fraternity house where we held meetings in the evening while our ministry team witnessed to students during the day. One night, a young student by the name of Al Manamtam rode up to our house on a bicycle. Al had been born in Hawaii, but both his parents were Filipino. Well, not only did Jesus save him that evening, He commissioned him as well. Al knew from the moment he met the Lord that someday he was going back to his parents' homeland to preach the Gospel. Now, two years later, Al was the leading candidate on my very short list of people who could help plant the new church. I ran the idea by Phil, and he said he thought Al was ready.

There was a profound sense of destiny in the air when we sat down with Al. All of us remembered the evening when a boy on a bicycle was turned into a man with a calling. Not surprisingly, Al had become increasingly burdened for the Philippines as he had watched the news pouring out of that troubled country. When I asked if he was prepared and sensed the call to go and help lead this church plant, he said yes. One major part of our team was now in place.

Next I called another close friend, Steve Murrell. Steve and his wife, Deborah, were leading a church in Starkville, Mississippi. Steve is a great leader and organizer and also someone you can count on to keep a cool head in the midst of a storm—the perfect man to help hold together the team we were planning to drop into the center of the student unrest in Manila. The Murrells sensed the call to go, as well, though at the time they thought it was only going to be for a short time.

And so in June of 1984, less than six months after the initial word from God—after a flurry of organizing, recruiting and fund-raising—Al, Steve, Deborah, Jody, our new baby and I were on a plane headed for the Philippines with sixty college students.

## THE PRICE OF VISION

There's a common idea that once you enter into the center of God's will, it's all smooth sailing. Obviously, all the heroes of the faith would tell you otherwise.

The apostle Paul learned this lesson after receiving a vision to go to Macedonia.[1] As he discussed this divine calling with his partner, Silas, there must have been a tremendous sense of excitement and anticipation. And yet, not long after they arrived in the Macedonian city of Philippi, they found themselves beaten and in jail! Nursing his wounds while in chains, it would have been easy for Silas to look over at Paul and say, "Some vision! Paul, you really missed this one." Instead, he joined with his friend in praying and singing hymns to God. An earthquake came…and a powerful Church was born. But there was a price to be paid to fulfill the true vision.

While our tribulations were not nearly as intense, we had our storms—both figurative and literal. First, we arrived in Manila to find ourselves in the middle of typhoon season. Now a typhoon is not just a bad storm; here in the West we call them hurricanes. We would go out to minister and find ourselves slogging through knee-deep water. Sometimes even our meeting place was flooded. Then there was the hotel our advance person had secured for us. We got a great deal on the rooms, but then found out why. Let's just say that the establishment catered to a less than "family-friendly" clientele.

We started our nightly meetings at the Girl Scout Auditorium, but soon secured a permanent location for our new church—the basement of a movie theater. It was all we could find. Like many basements, it was filled with years of accumulated dirt and clutter. All the pipes and duct-work for the theater—including the sewer pipes—ran across the ceiling, and most had been leaking for a long time. The smell that hit you as you went down the stairs was awful; you thought you were entering a stable. It was just the type of place where miracles are born.

Every day, tens of thousands of students and young protesters would pass right by our doorstep. It would have been hard to imagine a more opportune time to preach the Gospel or a more strategic place to plant a church. We started having meetings every night, and many began coming. Before long we were trying to figure out how to cram hundreds of people into our little basement. A new wave of student protests began, and we found ourselves in the very epicenter of the riots.

After every service, we would challenge those who responded to the altar call to stay afterwards for some one-on-one discipleship training. Each of the sixty American students had made it their goal to train a Filipino counterpart before going back home. And so every night there were dozens of little groups of American and Filipino young people huddled over their Bibles and talking about Jesus until the early hours of the morning. Each new convert was also encouraged to come an hour before the next night's meeting and attend a class with Bob Perry, now the leader of our church plant in Latvia. Bob taught them the foundations of the faith, as well as how to share the Gospel with their friends.

## A DRAMATIC SIGN

During the day we were either sharing the Gospel on the streets or cleaning that awful basement and patching leaky sewer pipes. The evenings found us in meetings, helping lead kids to Christ and then training them as disciples. This had been going on every day for several weeks. It was an exciting time and God was doing great things, but the pace was taking its toll. The whole team was becoming physically and emotionally drained.

Almost a month had gone by when one night, while still in the Girl Scout Auditorium, the most astounding thing occurred. I was about to close the meeting when I saw what appeared to be a cloud up in the balcony at the back of the room. At first I thought it was smoke from a fire or fog coming out of an air conditioning duct. As I watched, the cloud moved from the balcony and down to the floor. I looked over at Al and asked, "Do you see what I see?" Staring at the cloud, he nodded. It was like nothing we had ever seen before.

We watched as the cloud moved over the crowd and toward the stage. As it passed through the congregation, the people instantly sensed the presence of God. Spontaneous worship broke out and continued for over an hour. Afterwards, each person felt completely restored, as fresh as when the outreach had just begun. The Holy Spirit had literally and dramatically renewed our strength by His manifest presence. It was one of the most supernatural moments of my life.

A few weeks later, the summer outreach drew to a close. Many hundreds of people had come to Christ and there were almost two hundred, most of them young people, who were committed to being a part of the new Church. The team had worked so hard, and I couldn't stand the thought of losing even one inch of the ground that we had gained. As I have done so many times in the past, I turned to my old college roommate for help.

"Steve, would you and Deborah pray about staying for another six months to help Al and work with these new disciples?" Pastors and servants that they are, the Murrells quickly agreed to extend their stay.

Their decision ended up being a great blessing to both the Philippines and eventually for Morning Star International. Steve is a very methodical kind of guy. He is singularly focused about his mission: Win the world for Christ. And his strategy never changes: *Make disciples, train leaders and plant churches.* To any Christian who wonders what God is saying today to the Church, Steve would reply, "The same thing He has been saying for 2000 years: Make disciples, train leaders and plant churches!"

Almost two decades—and three earthquakes, twenty typhoons and a dozen brownouts later—Steve, Deborah and the three boys are still in Manila. Steve jokingly explains it this way: "I heard an audible voice calling me to stay in Manila—Rice's! Later, God Himself called me to stay." The result of their obedience has been nothing short of supernatural.

As I write this, there are scores of churches that have sprung from that initial outreach. Many thousands of lives have been radically changed by the power of the Holy Spirit, including very influential people in government, business and the entertainment industry. Many of the young people who came to Christ in 1984 are now planting and pastoring churches. The vision of touching the nations is very real to the hearts of these Filipinos. In their minds, if no one else obeys the Apostolic Mandate, they will. Day in and day out, their focus remains on making disciples, training leaders and planting churches.

In essence, this is a clear model of what God has commissioned us to do: Each believer is to be equipped and empowered to change his or her world. Each church must believe to not only reach their city, but also to transform their nation. Every person counts—no one is *left behind*. Whenever I go to Manila and see the fire and excitement in the peoples' hearts, my priorities are brought back into focus. The miracle in Manila was not only God using us to affect a nation, but also God changing us as a result of our ministry there. What happened there is an example of what we should see happen in every nation of the world.

## BIG VISIONS, SMALL BEGINNINGS

Steve and I had met years before while students at Mississippi State University. Meeting him was a critical step in my own journey toward discovering my destiny in Christ. As a college junior, I had been in hot pursuit of answers for my life. Everyone has some measure of fear and insecurity; mine had grown to the point where they had begun to dominate my life. I watched as my natural self-confidence began to erode. Having a Christian background that was at best nominal, the essential principles of the Lordship of Jesus, repentance and faith for salvation were foreign to me. Needless to say, I had no real answers for the guilt and condemnation that had begun to weigh heavily on my heart. Desperate to escape their burden, the Lord had placed within me a desire for a genuine relationship with Him.

I would routinely watch Christian television, pray and read motivational books, but nothing seemed to work. The truth was, I was trying to overcome fear and depression instead of facing the real problem: *I was lost.* Because I had been brought up going to church, I presumed I was a Christian. It never occurred to me that my real problem was the need for salvation.

Finally, I approached a pastor from my denominational background and asked for help. I supposed that people who were hungry to find God went to see him all the time. I was certain he would have answers for my questions, so I unloaded it all, right there in his office. He seemed taken aback by the candor and passion with which I poured out my problems. As I was finishing, he lit up a cigarette and said rather nervously, "Rice, maybe you need to get professional counseling." That was really the last thing I wanted or needed to hear. My girlfriend was suffering from an eating disorder that was eroding her faith. She was convinced that God couldn't or wouldn't do anything about her problem or mine. My talk with the minister only confirmed the pessimism she had shared with me.

Like many guys, I didn't like talking to my parents about issues that were emotional and deeply personal. On top of that, my father was an oil company executive who traveled the world, with little time for long, emotional talks. I went home looking for advice anyway. I was soon referred to my older brother.

Ben, my older brother, was in law school and had already received degrees in psychology and counseling. He rendered his verdict in a tone of expert finality: "The biggest part of your problem, Rice, is that you're thinking too much about God. Religion just messes people up! Remember the Crusades? Remember the Inquisition?" On and on he went. In the end, I more or less gave up. "I'm going back to school," I told my parents, "and just try to act like I'm normal."

## COMING TO CHRIST

True to my word, once I got back to Mississippi State I made up my mind to forget about God and just try to regain my confidence through dating, partying and all the other "normal" pursuits. That lasted about a week. As God would have it, one night I wandered into a Christian meeting on campus where they were having a spaghetti supper. The atmosphere was a fairly typical one as far as church services go. On top of that, the guy up front was a little annoying. He kept repeating the phrase, "We just want everything to be free tonight." Then from across the room someone shouted, "Hey, if it's supposed to be free, why did it cost me $2.50?" The sudden burst of humor was indeed a refreshing bit of reality that got my attention. I made my way across the room and introduced myself to the student who was brave enough to have interjected life into a rather dull setting. His name was Greg Anthony. Though he was younger than I, I was ready to listen to anything he had to say.

Later that night, I followed him back to his apartment. The funny thing was, he didn't really want to hear my story. He just wanted to share with me about God and how powerful His Word was. I had never before met anyone so bold and confident about his relationship with God and his own identity in Christ. What a contrast it was to my fear, doubt and insecurity. Greg had what I wanted, and I determined right then and there to get it. I had prayed before, but this was different. For the first time in my life I had actually met young people who were committed to Christ. Something changed in my heart. I can truly identify with John Wesley's testimony of his heart being "strangely warmed."[2] Though I still felt that I had issues to deal with, something had definitely changed in my heart. Christ had come to rescue me and give me a new life.

Weeks went by, and every day I returned to Greg Anthony's apartment where he would pour faith and encouragement into my hungry soul. Dramatic changes began to take place. Faith in God's Word took the place of my fears and doubts about God and myself. I had taken the first step on the road to freedom.

Naturally, I began to hang around other people who also loved Jesus in this way. Among the most significant new friends I made were two freshmen from Jackson, Mississippi: Steve Murrell and another Greg, Greg Ball. Both had become Christians in high school and had come to campus already intent on serving the Lord there. We didn't realize it then, but our friendship was to blossom into a ministry relationship that would last a lifetime. It was Steve who introduced me to a new Christian group that was meeting on campus. The most intriguing thing about this fellowship was that they believed in the gifts of the Spirit. That really piqued my curiosity.

As someone who had grown up in church, I had heard about the experience people referred to as the "baptism in the Holy Spirit." One of my old friends had warned me that it was something sought by people who were "trying to get closer to God"—as if that were a bad thing to do. While I had been confused before about what it meant to know and serve God, I needed to know whether there was anything to this alleged supernatural experience.

The meeting place for the group's church was actually a small house. I didn't realize until later that they were trying to have a church service; I thought it was some sort of a prayer meeting. After speaking for a few minutes, the pastor, Walter Walker, paused to look at his notes. I figured he was waiting for someone else to say something, so I raised my hand and asked, "Excuse me, do you folks believe in the experience known as the 'Baptism in the Holy Spirit'?" Walter hesitated, trying to decide whether to go on with his message or answer my question. Mercifully, he responded, "Yes, we do."

Realizing now that I had interrupted the pastor's sermon, I glanced around the room. Instead of the looks of disgust or embarrassment I expected, I found young, excited faces that seemed to encourage me on in my hunger for God. I looked back at the pastor and said, "I've got to have that."

The meeting adjourned, and Walter, Steve and I made our way to a more private room. I was told later that there was some high-powered intercession going on outside. As they laid hands on me and asked God to fill me with the Spirit, I felt the presence of God in an unusual way and knew that something significant had happened in my life. Jesus promised, "You shall receive power when the Holy Spirit has come upon you; and you shall be my witnesses..."[3] When you're filled with the Holy Spirit, it's hard not to talk about Jesus. I found myself naturally sharing with others the great work God had done in my life.

My girlfriend had a hard time understanding what was happening to me. Late one night she sat in her car in front of my apartment, while I sat on the curb trying once again to help her understand. Suddenly she broke her silence.

"I know what you're doing and why you're changing. You're hanging out with those people who go around saying, 'Praise God, Hallelujah!' all the time."

Immediately I began to deny it. "No, no, you've got it all wrong. These new friends of mine are really cool. They're not religious weirdos."

While I was speaking, I heard a car coming down the street with the radio on way too loud. As it approached, you could feel the bass notes slapping the night air. I thought to myself, *What's that guy doing? It's almost midnight.* The car slowed down as it drew near us and then pulled into my driveway. It was my friend Greg Anthony. Rolling down his window, he stuck his head out and shouted, "Praise God, Hallelujah!"

My girlfriend just looked at me, rolled her eyes as if to say, "I knew that's what your friends were like," and drove off.

Greg jumped out of his car. "Hey man, God told me to come over here."

"I'm sure He did," I said, perturbed but somehow relieved.

## FACING MY FAMILY

Well, the girlfriend thing hadn't gone the way I expected. The next critical encounter was with my family. I knew that after all my emotional and spiritual struggles, the news that I had become one of those "born-again" Christians was not likely to bring me a hero's welcome.

My brother, the skeptic, had decided to study the Bible to find all the contradictions so he could "save" me from being saved. As a lawyer-to-be with a background in psychology, Ben was an excellent debater. Based on my previous experience, the prospect of sitting down with my big brother and defending my newfound faith was not exactly my idea of a good time. He was so confident that he could talk me out of my faith that, before our meeting, he announced to a class-mate at law school, "I'm going home to get my little brother out of this 'born again thing.'" The stage for the showdown was now set.

We met at my parents' house in Dallas, and Ben immediately began to interrogate me. Before I really met the Lord, he had been able to quickly dismantle my feeble efforts at being religious and convince me instead to quit thinking about God. This time it was different. As he began to fire questions at me, I fired back. Gradually the tables were turned, and he began to be the one with doubts. Finally I looked at him and said, "It's not what you *don't* know that is keeping you from God, but what you *do* know." I challenged Ben to pray with me and commit his life to Christ. I actually stood up on my parents' patio and gave an altar call: "Ben, you know what I'm saying is true; now give me your hand—you're going to get saved." Even though it was just Ben, myself and another Christian friend, it was like there were thousands surrounding us. He looked at me as if to say, "I can't believe I'm doing this," raised his hand to meet mine, and we prayed together.

Later that night we found a swimming pool and baptized him. He came up out of the water and said, "You haven't answered any of my questions, but they don't seem to matter anymore." This would be a vital lesson in apologetics that I would use in ministering to people around the world. The real problem is spiritual, not intellectual; it's not people's questions so much that hold them back; it's their will. As Isaiah 59:1–2 says, "The arm of the Lord is not too short to save, nor his ear too dull to hear, but your iniquities have separated you from your God." In other words, the gap between God and man is a moral one. God is holy; we are not. It's not just a matter of God answering our questions, but us answering to Him.

God continued to pour out His grace on my family and, within a matter of just a few months, many more of my loved ones had been brought into the kingdom. The first one was my dad, who told my mother he had asked God years before to show him a miracle. He felt that God had performed this miracle in saving his two sons. He said, "I got down on my knees and asked God to forgive me for my pride and self-sufficiency." Today, after more than twenty years, my dad has faithfully served God and become a true spiritual father as well as my natural one. Needless to say, we got caught up on all those deep, emotional talks we had missed growing up. My brother, Ben, has also maintained a powerful witness for Christ as a successful attorney in Austin, Texas. The miracle of my family's turning to Christ would become a life theme for me: If you reach a young person, you can reach their family. Stepping back and looking at the even bigger picture, if you can change the campus, you can change the world.

## LEARNING TO BE A DISCIPLE

Back at school my friends and I found ourselves experiencing a depth of relationship and commitment that went far beyond anything we had experienced growing up in church. Discipleship was perhaps the one most defining aspect of what was different. We talked about how to conduct ourselves as Christians, how to help lead people to Christ and then follow up on new believers. We became people who longed to grow into the image of the Lord.

Pastor Walter Walker had been discipled by Methodist ministers who had laid a foundation in his life of a passion for Christ and the fire of the Holy Spirit. That foundation had carried him through many obstacles and trials as a minister. I was struck by the determination and character of Walter and his wife, Linda. My friends, Steve Murrell and Greg Ball, had been influenced by a young Presbyterian pastor named Ron Mussleman, whose messages of holiness and dedication had gripped their hearts in high school. Ron's no-nonsense approach rubbed off on them, and they determined that it would rub off on me as well. Because they had all been thoroughly discipled, they were able to disciple me properly.

I heard it said once that a Christian could grow five years in one year, or take five years to grow one year; it all depends on how committed you are. Well, I was committed. I wanted to do everything I could to make my life matter for God.

Several months went by. One night I was having a meal with my pastor at a local fast-food place. Though I would later find out that Walter had sensed for some time that God had called me to full-time ministry, he had never said anything to me about it. Having finished his meal, Walter rubbed his eyes and looked off into the distance. He spoke almost as if to himself.

"You know, the greatest and most meaningful thing I've ever done was to serve God in the ministry."

That's all that was ever said about it—for which now I'm very thankful. In the end, it had to be my decision. I had to hear God without a lot of static interference from other people and their plans for my life. My mind was set when I graduated. I was going into campus ministry.

## OUR EARLY DAYS OF MINISTRY

In January of 1979, I became a campus minister at the University of Tennessee in Knoxville. Later, Steve and Phil would both follow. The ministry we worked with was called Maranatha, one of the few charismatic campus movements at the time. Although I was met with a lot of challenges and hard work, in the end the excitement and sense of destiny outweighed them all. Looking back, I am thankful for all the lessons I learned—even the painful ones.

At first the going was very rough. The ministry in Knoxville was small and somewhat out of touch with the campus it was trying to reach. At times I actually found myself discouraging friends from coming to visit. To put it bluntly, it wouldn't be the church I would attend if I had a choice.

An early test occurred when a series of conflicts with the leader of the ministry left me feeling that it really wasn't worth continuing. To make matters worse, I was living in the back of a storefront and wasn't exactly prospering. People were calling me with attractive ministry opportunities in other places. It began to seem that the best thing to do was to accept one of these offers and get away from the pressure I was feeling.

Even though I wasn't very happy with where I was, I didn't want to miss God's will. I prayed and told God, "If this is what you want me to do for you, I'll do it." Suddenly, a profound peace settled around my soul. I determined to put my destiny in the hands of God, and to keep it there. Things really didn't change all that much externally, but something changed inside my heart. The Scripture verse kept coming to me, "humility comes before honor."[4] My breakthrough in ministry was around the corner.

It wasn't long before I was asked to go back to Starkville and Mississippi State University and spend a month holding down the fort while the regular leaders left on a summer mission trip. Walter,

Greg, Steve and most of the other leaders were going to Canada to help plant a new church. With only eight people there for the summer, there wasn't a lot of risk in putting me in charge. The first thing I did was call the people to prayer. We were going to intercede and give God the best of our time before we went out and ministered to people. Day after day as we prayed, a sense of faith and expectation began to grow in our hearts, and each week our meetings grew larger—from eight students to almost eighty in one month. Many of the young people who were saved and filled with the Spirit would eventually become pastors and leaders. In addition, our ministry to athletes really had its beginnings during that month of breakthrough. It happened in a very unusual way.

One day as I waited to get into a basketball game at the university, the Lord spoke to me about a football player who was standing nearby. "He's been praying for someone to come and talk to him about Me. Go tell him you are his answer." The player happened to be African-American, and I don't think he expected the answer to his prayer to look like me. I felt like Clarence, the angel in *It's a Wonderful Life*, introducing himself to George Bailey, who responded sarcastically, "You look like the kind of angel I'd get." I walked up to him and delivered the message, and the next thing I knew he had given his life to Christ right there on the spot. He invited me to come up to his room in the athletic dorm, and there his roommate got saved. Eventually, many of his teammates were either converted or filled with the Spirit. What happened to those athletes has now spread to campuses and professional sports teams around the world.

Stories like these became commonplace. Over the next few years, we saw many great things happen as we reached out to campuses in many parts of the world. From Florida State to the University of London, we held outreaches and trusted God to do miraculous things. While some of our efforts were comical at times, one thing was absolutely true: we were trying to change the world with all our might. Some of my closest friendships were being formed during this critical time. We spent hours talking about how we could make a difference with our lives. Little did any of us realize that the seeds of those dreams would have to go into the ground and die before they could bear the best fruit.

## A DARK NIGHT OF THE SOUL

A defining moment was coming for us all. I tell this not to point a finger at anyone or dig up past pain. Instead, my hope is to shed the light of grace on these events and help people look redemptively at any negative experience that may have caused them to lose hope and drop out of the race.

One of the great hindrances in fulfilling the Apostolic Mandate is that many of those called to make a difference have been wounded in a church or ministry setting and cannot get beyond it. This may explain why the book, *The Prayer of Jabez*, has had such a profound and widespread impact. Jabez, as most know by now, was born in pain but did not allow his pain to turn him into a bitter person. The Scripture says Jabez was "more honorable than his brothers."[5] It is this nobility that helps us rise above the pettiness of bitterness and allow the love of God to cover a multitude of sins.

Bad experiences can also sensitize us in many different ways. In a positive light, they can make us more aware of what not to do. This is critical when it comes to handling the powerful truths of Scripture. Matters like faith, spiritual authority and spiritual gifts must be handled with care. Experiencing extremes in any of these areas makes you aware of the caution and boundaries that need to be observed when putting these important principles into practice.

Finally, when we understand the sovereignty of God, we come to grips with the fact that the Lord will use imperfect people and situations to bring us into His purposes and/or mentor us. Many people grow up and disdain their past because of the mistakes of their parents or other authority figures. We must recognize that God is still involved in our lives, even in the midst of difficult circumstances. These are the important thoughts I want you to hold in your mind as I relate this difficult part of our story.

As I was describing, many wonderful things were happening in the ministry while, at the same time, storm clouds were beginning to gather. Phil, Steve and I had joined the ministry of Maranatha after becoming Christians and were drawn to it because of the commitment they preached as well as the power of the Holy Spirit they upheld. Though there were negatives, we knew there was no such thing as a "perfect church." The fact that the leaders truly had a heart for God kept us believing that these issues would eventually get worked out. Still, concerns surrounding the ministry began to surface. Many felt that some of its practices were heavy-handed and legalistic. There were also concerns that mysticism had crept in, placing too much emphasis on subjective experiences rather than the Word of God. The latter was a charge leveled against many in the charismatic community from the traditional Church at large. These issues weighed heavily on the hearts of most of the leaders. Attempts were made to bring about reforms and extricate these negatives from the mix. In retrospect, it was a "coming of age" moment for many of us as young leaders to grapple with such important issues.

These issues all came to a head at the end of 1989. The organization was dismantled and all its affiliated ministries released to follow the leading of the Spirit as they saw fit. As relieved as we were that the ordeal was over, the following season would prove to be one of the most difficult of our lives. I'm sure that was the case for many others. Yes, I had suffered heartaches after I came to Christ, but watching a ministry end was deeply painful. This pain is inevitable when churches split or close their doors. When relationships fail or when visions die, it can shipwreck the destiny of many. I've spoken to pastors of churches from many diverse backgrounds and the fallout of ministry failure is always very difficult, especially for the young. In the midst of our situation, I remembered Jesus' words to Peter, "I have prayed for you that your faith should not fail." He concluded with a message of purpose and hope: "Strengthen your brothers."[6]

It has been said that you learn more in failure than you do in success. That may be true, but only if you get up and keep trying to succeed. Deep down, the knowledge that my calling was not from an organization but from God was undeniable. As Hebrews says, "Hold fast to the beginning of our assurance firm until the end."[7] I was holding fast. My whole passion was to simply see the miracle of salvation that had happened to my family and me, happen to as many people as possible. That motivation kept me going, and it kept me encouraging my closest friends to not lose sight of the Lord in the midst of turmoil.

Looking back now, it's obvious that God was orchestrating all these changes for His purposes and everyone's good. In hindsight, many of the organizations birthed in the sixties and seventies during the "Jesus Movement" or the Charismatic Movement, majored in zeal and boldness while minimizing theological training. While reacting to "dead religion," the proverbial "baby" was thrown out with the "bath water." Surveying the landscape of many different church and parachurch movements, the result seemed to be a very short shelf life.

## NURTURED IN THE WILDERNESS

As the year 1990 dawned, it felt like the whole world was getting a fresh start. The Berlin Wall had collapsed and a new spirit of freedom and opportunity was spreading. At the beginning of that year, my family and I moved to Midland, Texas, to seek the Lord for direction during this new season. Russ Austin, a long-time friend and pastor of Mid-Cities Community Church, invited us to come and be a part of his team for "as long as we wanted." Though West Texas looked like a wilderness in the natural sense, it turned out to be a spiritual oasis. The people of his church rallied around us like family. I will always be grateful to that church in Midland for taking such good care of us in this critical season.

During this time, I began to reflect deeply on the lessons of the past. Reading books, talking to Christian leaders and studying Church history confirmed my sense that none of the problems I had encountered were new. I heard somewhere that, "Those who do not learn from history are doomed to repeat it." There was a hunger to not just learn from the mistakes of the past, but to learn how to build spiritually in a way that would stand the test of time. The more I prayed, the more I realized that, in order to prepare for the future, I needed a deeper and stronger foundation both theologically and devotionally. I wanted not just to know more about God, but to know Him in a deeper way. Loving God more always results in loving people more. God is looking for leaders who are not just bold, but gentle and caring when it comes to His Church. As George Whitefield said, "It is not enough to love to preach; we must love those to whom we preach." The Bible describes David as a man after God's own heart. He not only loved God but was chosen to lead God's people because he would shepherd them with "integrity of heart."[8] The Lord loves His sheep and wants them led by those who love them, too.

## BACK TO THE CLASSROOM

With all these things in mind, I enrolled in Reformed Theological Seminary in Jackson, Mississippi. Over the next two years, I would be exposed to some wonderfully gifted and godly men and women who helped me understand the strengths and weaknesses of the Christian faith throughout the generations. I had a fresh hunger, almost to the point of desperation, to find the necessary balance, theologically and practically, that would produce churches and ministries that could bear lasting fruit. This season of concentrated study and reflection was an incredible time of restoration and refueling. I learned as much outside of class as I did inside, through lengthy discussions with professors and other leaders from various theological backgrounds. As I wrote in the book, *New Apostolic Churches*, one of my professors in a candid moment said, "We Presbyterians can build a great fireplace, but we have a hard time building a fire." I responded, "We charismatics can sure build a fire, but we tend to burn things down."

Throughout history there have been countless movements that God raised up to impact the world and fulfill His purposes. At the same time, there has been a cycle of extremism between scholasticism, which in attempting to focus only on the "truth" ends up squelching the life of the Spirit and any supernatural manifestations, and mysticism, which tends to ignore the boundaries of the objective truth of the Word of God and places the emphasis on subjective experiences.

Those who kept the right focus on the Apostolic Mandate and avoided the extremes in either direction were able to last longer than others and produce the fruit of the kingdom in the lives of individuals and cultures. This whole scenario reminds me of a runner in a marathon. Along the way, various people offer you water to refresh you so that you can keep running. For some strange reason, many in the charismatic movement tend to forget the race and chase the person offering the water. They make "the refreshing" the focus. If the enemy can't hinder you from receiving the power of the Spirit, he will attempt to trivialize it by tempting you to major on esoteric expressions that ultimately leave the person emotionally stirred, but unchanged. This pattern is repeated generation after generation.

My hope began to grow that this pattern could be better understood, and many of the mistakes avoided. God had surely raised up men and women to touch their generations, and He wanted to do this in our time as well. The fire began to burn again in me to touch the world. The problem was that I still felt something holding me back—as if my foot was in a snare. Hebrews 12 tells us to lay aside every weight and the sin that easily besets us, and "run with perseverance the race marked out for us."[9] This weight was my reluctance to start building something and not be able to finish it. What discourages most people from attempting great things for God is this very fear: that what is started will not last. Why begin if it's all for naught? As

I began to cry out to God for deliverance, He sent His answer in a very dramatic way.

## SURPRISED BY THE HOLY SPIRIT

While attending seminary, I was invited to speak at a conference where a very famous prophet was also speaking. I found myself sitting at this great conference, listening to this man, and thinking about how ironic my situation was: *Here I am attending a conservative seminary, studying theology and Church history, and at the same time attending a conference on the other end of the theological spectrum.*

As I tried to balance this apparent contradiction in my mind, the man of God broke through my conundrum in a dramatic way. In front of hundreds of people, he abruptly said, "Rice Broocks stand up."

My immediate thought was, *Uh oh, I'm about to have all my double-mindedness exposed.* It would be safe to say that my life passed before my eyes. To my utter amazement, he had no words of rebuke. Instead, it was as if he brought out a huge axe and cut away the things that held my feet in the snare. In essence he said, "God pulled you out of one thing to put you into something else; something that will change the world." What I remember most was this phrase: "The things you've seen in the past will seem like beating the air compared to what I [the Lord] am about to do."

## CONFIRMATION COMES

Paul instructs Timothy, "My son, I give you this instruction in keeping with the prophecies once made about you, so that by following them you may fight the good fight, holding on to faith and a good conscience."[10] It is the incredible combination of the Word of God as well as the gifts of the Spirit—in this case, prophecy—that enables you to fight the good fight of faith and win. My calling was reenergized by this timely word. A second prophecy would soon come and leave no room for doubt that God's plan for me was unfolding.

Ron Lewis and I had launched Campus Harvest, a ministry designed to train local churches to reach students. Our motto was "Revolutionizing Campus Ministry by Mobilizing Local Churches." Each year there were meetings at Duke University that drew hundreds of students from throughout the East Coast. A few months after I received the initial prophetic word, a second word came. I was at Duke helping host a Campus Harvest conference. One of the invited guests was Jim Laffoon, a powerful speaker who was recognized throughout the nation as a respected prophet. As he finished preaching one evening, I came up on the stage to close the meeting. Unexpectedly, he grabbed my hand and began to prophesy, "God is going to use you to tie men's lives together into a team that will shake the world."

Every remaining vestige of uncertainty instantly evaporated. The fear of the Lord came to my heart. To doubt now would be a terrible sin. With a new sense of faith, it was as if my eyes were opened. I was as excited as a kid at Christmas, expectant as to what God now had in store.

In 1994, interestingly ten years after the first "Miracle in Manila," I found myself back in Manila with Phil Bonasso and Steve Murrell talking about world missions and how we could work together. There are times when God's plans are revealed in dramatic ways. In this instance there was no vision, no dream, no audible voice and no cloud. And yet, in some quiet, ineffable way, we knew that the Holy Spirit was directing us to birth a new ministry together. Each of us was very different from the others. Yet our differences in the context of a team would prove to be one of our greatest strengths. Many organizations are founded by a single man with a tremendous vision and gift. But once that man passes away or steps down, the dream tends either to die or to continue on in a half-hearted fashion. But a cord of three strands is not easily broken. We sensed the call for the three of us not only to birth a ministry, but also to model true submission and teamwork.

## MORNING STAR INTERNATIONAL IS BORN

Phil, Steve and I began to reflect on the common sense of destiny and calling we shared. True covenant is not something you can manufacture. Just as the hearts of David and Jonathan were joined together during a tumultuous time in Israel's history, we sensed that God had joined our hearts as well. "If we are going to make this work, we need to build something strong and well defined," Steve said. "We're going to have to put aside our individual agendas, trust each other and build together." Phil agreed. Both of them then turned to me and said, "We'll join together if you will lead us." My moment of decision had come. With the overwhelming sense of God's call on my life, the fact that God had joined me with these leaders, and the compelling prophetic words that had been spoken, I knew I was truly right in the middle of God's will. It was time to put my hand to the plow, to trust that God had indeed called me to reach the world and to do it with this team. Another "Miracle in Manila" had taken place.

That initial agreement we made joined together a group of twenty-five churches that these men represented. Steve's churches were under the banner of Victory Christian Fellowship and Phil's were called Morning Star. After a brief discussion, we decided that our name would be Morning Star International.[11]

Looking back, it's easy to see God's hand at work preparing us "for such a time as this."[12] We knew that if the three of us stayed together and guarded our relationship as a team—if we became and remained a true "cord of three strands"[13]—Morning Star International would prosper in the kingdom of God. And what was clear to us then, is even clearer now. Something that was lost for us had been recovered: the sense of family and relationship that we had developed in the past. And that wasn't all. There was a deeper sense that something not only sacred but very serious on the heart of God had been recovered. The Bible describes the joy that is in heaven when a lost person repents. When a lost coin is found, it is big news. When a lost son is found, there is a party. When lost vision is regained, there is a revolution. For us it was not just relationships that had been recovered, it was God's heart for the nations. It was and is the vision for the Apostolic Mandate.

## OUR MISSION

*To honor God and advance His Kingdom through Church Planting, Campus Ministry and World Missions.*

Focusing our efforts on this mission statement has not limited us; rather it has paved the way for us to touch and impact the culture, as well as the nations, in ways we could never have dreamed. As we approach the ninth anniversary of that memorable day in Manila, we have watched God open doors and confirm His Word in truly miraculous ways. Morning Star International (MSI) now has churches in more than thirty-five nations. As we mentioned in Chapter 1, through the 2010 Initiative, we have set our hearts to plant a church in every nation of the world.

Through Victory Campus Ministries (VCM), we're specifically reaching out to the university community. There are now vibrant VCM outreaches on hundreds of campuses, specifically geared to meet the needs of college students. Young men and women are being raised up to enter full-time ministry by building a support team through our partnership development program. Our ministry to athletes, Champions for Christ (CFC), has grown to prominence through the leadership of Greg and Helen Ball and an incredible team of men and women who serve the Lord in this key area. CFC is having an impact in the sports world at all levels: high school, college and the professional ranks, and in many nations of the world.[14] The motto, "Reaching Athletes, Building Leaders," is truly being fulfilled as athletes become disciples and learn how to advance God's kingdom through their positions of influence.

Victory Leadership Institute (VLI) is the educational arm of the movement and provides excellent biblical, theological and practical training for every believer. There is training for new believers as well as those entering full-time Christian ministry. In keeping with the philosophy that God has a calling for every person, there are five major schools of VLI: the School of Ministry, the School of Business Leadership, the School of Government, the School of Arts and Media and the School of Family Leadership. VLI is now available online so that *anyone*, *anywhere* can get the training they need to do *anything* God calls them to do.[15]

The vision and the values presented in this book embody not just our movement; they are key truths that must be emphasized and embraced if the Church is to fulfill the Apostolic Mandate. Anyone who builds on these foundations, with the blueprint and building materials these principles represent, will grow and bear "fruit that remains." These core values will be discussed in Part II of this book. We hope to impart not just the information, but the wisdom needed to present these truths in such a way that their credibility is not marginalized. In the final section, we will talk in detail about the mission of planting churches and reaching nations—a mission that is the responsibility of every Christian and body of believers. The importance of apostolic ministry and the incredible power it gives to our mission will be presented as well. It is this vital spiritual gift that assembles, coordinates and deploys all the other gifts in the Church for maximum impact. We've certainly seen what we can do without recognizing this gift; now it's time to honor and release this God-given dimension of ministry.

Our prayer is that every church and believer, regardless of denomination or theological leaning, will rise up and commit themselves to the awesome task ahead. I share the ups and downs of our own journey in the hope that the thousands of people who have had some setback or deep disappointment as a Christian would not let it be the final word about their life. Instead they would, like the apostle Paul, shake off the pain and press forward to the higher calling in Christ.[16]

Let us begin with the central message of the Christian faith—the truth that distinguishes us from every other religion and people on the face of the earth: *the Lordship of Jesus Christ.*

# PART II

# VALUES

# CHAPTER 3

# THE LORDSHIP
# OF CHRIST

*If I profess with the loudest voice and clearest exposi-*
*tion every part of the truth of God except precisely*
*that little point which the world and the devil are at*
*the moment attacking, then I am not confessing*
*Christ, however boldly I may be professing Him.*

—MARTIN LUTHER

In his book, *The 100: A Ranking of the Most Influential Persons in History*, author Michael Hart attempts to place history's most important people in the order of their impact on the world. This ranking was not based upon the individual's moral worth or strength of character; he simply sought to recognize the overall significance of their lives and philosophies upon the community of man.

Incredibly, Jesus Christ was ranked third behind Mohammed and Sir Isaac Newton! Hart explained that the Son of God was demoted from the top position solely because of the inability of His followers to obey and implement His teachings. He states:

> Now these ideas [Jesus' teachings in Matthew 5:43–44] are surely among the most remarkable and original ethical ideas ever presented. If they were widely followed, I would have had no hesitation in placing Jesus first in this book. But the truth is that they are not widely followed. In fact, they are not even generally accepted. Most Christians

consider the injunction to "Love your enemy" as—at most—an ideal which might be realized in some perfect world, but one which is not a reasonable guide to conduct in the actual world we live in. We do not normally practice it, do not expect others to practice it, and do not teach our children to practice it. Jesus' most distinctive teaching, therefore, remains an intriguing but basically untried suggestion.[1]

Could this be what Jesus was referring to when He said, "Not everyone who says to me 'Lord, Lord,' will enter the kingdom of heaven, but only he who does the will of my Father who is in heaven"?[2] This separation between what Christians believe and what they actually do, is a far too common characteristic in today's Church. Multitudes are content to profess faith in Christ without the least expectation that it will ever intrude into the reality of their day-to-day lives.

The Gospel has been sliced, diced, homogenized and sanitized— packaged to sell quickly and cheaply. To borrow from an old commercial, modern tastes prefer *Christianity Lite*: "Tastes great; less filling."

Surveying the moral landscape of our culture there are some harsh realities we need to face: there's little difference between the character of Christians and non-believers. What a contrast this is to what God expects of us, "For what partnership have righteousness and lawlessness, or what fellowship has light with darkness…what has a believer in common with an unbeliever?"[3]

Paul instructed the Philippians to conduct themselves in such a way that they may "prove [themselves] to be blameless and innocent, children of God above reproach in the midst of a crooked and perverse generation among whom you appear as lights in the world."[4]

## WELCOME TO "THE HAUNTING TIME"

In attempting to explain the declining influence of the Church in the West, George Barna speaks about "costless faith," the watered down Gospel that allows people to make a decision for Christ—to "cast their vote" for Jesus—without having an attitude of submission to Him as their new Lord and King.

My interpretation of this condition is that we have simply made it too easy to be part of the church. Christianity has no cost in America. In fact, we've made it way too easy to be "born again"—perhaps much easier than Jesus intended…The result has been a transaction consummated with tens of millions of Americans in which the "free gift" of salvation was claimed with no substantive reciprocation—no commitment, no change, no responsibility…We have millions of people who have simply tried to exploit God—people for whom salvation is little more than a fire insurance policy they won't think about until the Devil comes knockin'. In the interim we witness a "born again" population that is indistinguishable from the rest of the nation—and has very limited credibility when it comes to promoting genuine Christianity.[5]

Barna concludes with one of the most succinct statements about our current reality and the subsequent fallout from our failure to obey God: "The American Church is the world's primary exporter of cheap grace. At some point, though, poor products come back to haunt the producer. Welcome to the haunting time."[6]

## THE MOST MISUNDERSTOOD MOMENT IN CHRISTIANITY

Like many other Christians, I've attended countless meetings where a challenge is given at the end of the service and people get up and come forward to the "altar." A deep burden often comes upon me as I look into the faces of these precious souls. Expectation and hope are evident upon some. Others are etched with the harsher emotions: the guilt of immorality, pain from an abusive relationship, the anguish of addiction, the loneliness of abandonment. And not infrequently there are the "repeat offenders," those who have walked the aisle before and are now shadowed by doubt. I can almost hear them in their minds asking the question, "Will it work this time?"

Making the trip to the front of a church service or crusade meeting has become for many the simple mechanism by which people are "saved." Unfortunately, the "altar call" has evolved into an evangelical sacrament, an act that in and of itself is a means of grace. Those responding are led in a simple prayer, given a few Scriptures on assurance, a Gospel of John, and pronounced "saved" to the applause of the congregation. Everyone is out in time to catch the game on television.

And while many people, by the grace of God, are genuinely born again in and around these moments, there are a large number of people who come down "Just as I am" and leave in virtually the same condition. For them, and for the multitudes of pastors and congregations that share this "rite of passage" with them, *the altar call has become the most misunderstood moment in Christianity.*

As a minister, I learned years ago to stop trusting the simple act of raising one's hand, standing up or coming forward as being any guarantee that a person is being changed by God. Of course, I still challenge people to give their lives to Christ and provide them with the opportunity to "confess Jesus before men" by coming to the front of the church, thus allowing them to set up a "memorial stone" they can look back to, to mark the beginning of their journey of faith.[7] But when people do this, I will point out that coming forward is a step in the right direction, not a guarantee that you've arrived.

Jesus said, "When anyone hears the message about the kingdom and does not understand it, the evil one comes and snatches away what was sown in his heart."[9] We must do everything we can to make sure our potential converts *understand*. They must grasp who God is, what they are and what the cross means for both God and them.

## WHAT'S MISSING?

It's a well documented fact that most of the people who respond to traditional altar calls—the percentage hovers at around 90 percent for evangelistic crusades—are not serving the Lord a year later. What are we doing wrong? Why is *mass decision* followed by *mass defection*? What's missing from our message that encourages people to do one thing while believing another? Anyone who really loves God and cares about people should be wrestling with these questions.

It was Albert Einstein who defined insanity as "doing the same thing over and over again, but expecting a different result." What do we have to change to start getting the results that God both intended and deserves?

Well, we can begin and end with the one thing that summed up the totality of Paul's life and ministry: the foundation of the Lordship of Christ.

For I resolved to know nothing while I was with you except Jesus Christ and him crucified.

—1 Corinthians 2:2

For no one can lay any foundation other than the one already laid, which is Jesus Christ.

—1 Corinthians 3:11

## UNDERSTANDING WHO JESUS IS

Jesus Himself asked the question of His disciples, "Who do men say that I am?" Ask that question today and get ready for a torrent of confused responses. For instance, at the University of California at Berkeley, in one day I actually met a young man who claimed to be the real Jesus Christ. Almost an hour later, I met another person claiming to be Moses. Of course, I offered to get them together and they refused. But campuses have nothing on churches when it comes to producing people who are riddled with inconsistent and self-contradictory beliefs. Consider the responses to this question from those who claim to be Christians, and you will be amazed at the answers you get. George Barna, who has been analyzing Christian culture for almost two decades, has commented extensively about the muddled thinking in the Church. For example:

> What may be most amazing, however is that so many people who are committed to the Christian faith and who believe the Bible is an accurate document conclude that Jesus was a sinner.[10]

Nearly half—44 percent—believe that the Messiah was a sinner! As Barna went on to note, this would mean that the Lord needed a savior like the rest of us. Against this heretical nonsense, Jesus declared, "Which one of you convicts me of sin?"[11] He repeated this claim of moral perfection when He spoke of His impending confrontation with Satan at the cross: "The ruler of this world is coming, and he has nothing in Me."[12] The devil had no hold on Christ because Christ had never yielded Himself to sin. And it was this sinless life that gave Him the victory at Calvary and made His sacrifice on the cross sufficient to pay the price for our sins.

For you know that it was not with perishable things…that

you were redeemed…but with the precious blood of
Christ, a lamb without blemish or defect.

—1 PETER 1:18–19

So it is here where we must start; laboring to restore the glory, the
uniqueness, the all-sufficiency, the dominion and preeminence of
Christ, first in the Church and then in culture. The simple confession
of the early Christians, "Jesus is Lord," must not only become our cry,
but our reality.

### His unique role as the only Savior

It's one of the most controversial and hated verses in the Bible; one
more example of just how politically incorrect Jesus could be. To hear
some people tell it, He might as well have said, "It's my way or the
highway—the one that leads to destruction." Well, in a sense…He did.

Jesus answered, "I am the way and the truth and the life.
No one comes to the Father except through Me."

—JOHN 14:6

Multitudes are offended at the idea that Jesus is the only way to
heaven, the exclusive Savior of the world. If all religions are essentially
the same—and this is the *Great Law* in our relativistic age—then one
means of salvation is as good as any other.

The Bible, on the other hand, knows or cares nothing for this plu-
ralistic nonsense. Paul goes so far as to pronounce a curse on anyone
who preaches any other Gospel.[13] What other redeemer could there
be? Who else was sinless? Who else purposefully suffered and died for
the sins of the world? And who else has risen from the dead?
Reflecting on the life and character of Jesus, one is not left with a man
who stands just head and shoulders above the crowd of rival
redeemers. One finds instead a Messiah who stands absolutely and
perfectly alone. When one begins to understand how holy and righteous God is, the amazing thing isn't that there's only one way to God.
The truly amazing thing is that there is *any way* to Him at all.

### The desperate need people have for Him

Ray Comfort, the legendary evangelist from New Zealand, has
pointed out that the failure to understand God's law—specifically the
Ten Commandments—has lured multitudes into a false sense of
security concerning their spiritual condition. *I'm a good, well-
meaning person,* they are seduced into thinking. *Why do I need to be*

*saved?* Preaching the law of God is the God-ordained means by which the knowledge of sin comes; the tutor that leads people to Christ.[14] The law presents both God's holiness as well as the penalty (eternal separation) He exacts for sin—for breaking just one commandment one time. Once people begin to understand the great gulf that is fixed between their sin and God's perfection, they will also understand how great is the salvation they've been offered, and how truly wonderful the Savior, Jesus Christ, really is.[15]

One caveat here: "preaching the law" can call up images of angry Christians carrying clapboard signs, wagging condemning fingers at sinners. Obviously, this is not what I have in mind. There are artful and redemptive ways to make sin "utterly sinful" and to draw out the inborn knowledge people have of God's righteous standards.[16] Being "wise as serpents and harmless as doves"[17] means that we need to find and use them. While the religious and the reprobate may despise our preaching anyway, if the "common people aren't hearing us gladly," we're doing something wrong.[18]

### *Proclaiming His Lordship*

Presenting Jesus as Savior alone, though, is not enough. He is Lord—God incarnate, the Creator of the heavens and the earth. The almighty, eternal Son who took on the form of a servant, humbling Himself to the point of death on the cross. With His resurrection, ascension and exaltation in heaven, He has received a name that is above *every* other. Before that name *every* knee will bow and *every* tongue will confess—both in heaven, earth and hell—that Jesus is *Kurios*—the absolute supreme authority.[19]

It is significant that He is also God *the Word* made man. The opening lines of John's Gospel are clearly meant to take us back to the first words of Genesis, "In the beginning, God…"

> In the beginning was the Word, and the Word was with God, and the Word was God…the Word became flesh and made his dwelling among us. We have seen his glory, the glory of the One and Only, who came from the Father, full of grace and truth.
>
> —John 1:1, 14

As God—the Word made flesh—the words Jesus spoke have ultimate authority and are the source of grace and truth.[20] Jesus declared, "Heaven and earth will pass away, but my words will never pass away."[21] He challenged those who dared to presume to follow Him without obeying Him. "Why do you call Me 'Lord, Lord,' and do not do what I say?"[22] A "Christian" by definition means "a follower of Christ;" someone with the heart-felt willingness to obey His commands and to turn away from evil.

## THE PREACHING OF THE CROSS

Popular author and scholar Dr. John Stott observed, "There is no authentic Christian faith or life unless the cross is at the center."[23] Having the cross at the center of our lives means not only that the death and resurrection of Christ is to be the focal point of our faith; it is the fulcrum upon which our day-to-day existence rests as well.

Stott continued:

> After speaking of His death Jesus called the crowd to Himself and said, "If anyone would come after Me, he must deny himself, pick up his cross and follow Me." That is Jesus moved at once from His cross to ours and portrayed Christian discipleship in terms of self-denial and even death. For we can understand the significance of cross-bearing only against the cultural background of Roman-occupied Palestine. The Romans reserved crucifixion for the worst criminals and compelled those condemned to death by crucifixion to carry their own cross to the place of execution. So if we are following Christ and bearing a cross, there is only one place to which we can be going, and that is to the scaffold.[24]

It has probably been a while since you heard a salvation message that included that kind of challenge. Yet it's the one that Jesus preached. It was the message Saul of Tarsus heard when he was saved and transformed into the apostle Paul.

> This man is my chosen instrument to carry my name before the Gentiles and their kings and before the people of Israel. I will show him how much he must suffer for my name.
>
> —ACTS 9:15–16

This mindset later prompted Paul to write to the church in Galatia:

> I have been crucified with Christ and I no longer live, but Christ lives in me. The life I live in the body, I live by faith in the Son of God, who loved me and gave himself for me.
>
> —GALATIANS 2:20

The renowned Lutheran pastor, Dietrich Bonhoeffer, echoed Paul in a classic work he wrote before being martyred by the Nazis: "When Christ bids a man, He bids him come and die."[25] Dying to oneself must again be preached as the responsibility of all Christians, not just some peculiar elite.

## COUNT THE COST

> And whoever does not bear his cross and come after Me cannot be My disciple. For which of you, intending to build a tower, does not sit down first and count the cost, whether he has enough to finish it—lest, after he has laid the foundation, and is not able to finish, all who see it begin to mock him, saying, "This man began to build and was not able to finish."
>
> —LUKE 14:27–30, NKJV

Over and over again, Jesus called His disciples to surrender everything and follow Him. In the end, no matter how a person hears about Christ, no matter how relevant, "seeker-friendly" or creative the presentation, they must be told the truth. "Just accept Christ" may be a succinct way to market the Gospel, but it doesn't come close to the message of salvation Jesus or His disciples preached. And neither will it produce the fruit of the kingdom in our listeners' lives. As we have said, the failure to preach this message has resulted in a mass of casualties of those who, as Jesus said, "last only a short time."[26] As we survey the landscape of what some have called "The Great Evangelical Disaster,"[27] we find many searching for answers, digging deep into the wreckage to find clues.

## LAYING FOUNDATIONS

Isn't it sad that so many are so willing, and even anxious, to dig down deep to discover why someone failed, but so few are willing to put forth the effort to dig deep and lay a good foundation in a new

Christian's life to prevent that failure from ever happening? Churches spend an enormous amount of time, expense and training on the counseling ministry. We seem to be content with digging around to do the autopsy on people whose spiritual and emotional houses have crumbled, but we place little emphasis on proactively going deep with people in order to lay a solid foundation in the life of believers both new and old.

Jesus described a house that was built without a foundation: "But the one who hears my words and does not put them into practice is like a man who built a house on the ground without a foundation. The moment the torrent struck that house, it collapsed and its destruction was complete."[28] If we know our culture is sitting on a moral fault line, then why are we content to invite people into the kingdom without the determination to build in them a solid foundation from the very start?

Jesus couldn't have been clearer about the importance of these foundations—as well as the disastrous results of ignoring them. He said:

> I will show you what he is like who comes to me and hears my words and puts them into practice. He is like a man building a house, who dug down deep and laid the foundation on rock. When a flood came, the torrent struck that house but could not shake it, because it was well built.
> —LUKE 6:47–48

One of the most important tools that can help you dig down deep is the book, *Biblical Foundations* (a.k.a. the Purple Book). Every new believer and new member is *strongly* encouraged to go through this twelve-part Bible study to ensure that their foundations are secure in relation to some of the core doctrines of the Christian faith. In the introduction of that book, I recount one of the most harrowing experiences of my life.

## THE IMPORTANCE OF FOUNDATIONS

During the summer of 1993, I took a team of college students to the island of Guam in the South Pacific to help plant a church. Checking into our hotel, everyone joked about calling me for help. My room number was 911. I shrugged off the twinge of foreboding that flickered across my soul. Coincidence, I told myself.

Two evenings later I was on the phone when suddenly my room

began to move. A massive tremor shot through the spine of the high rise, lifting my bed and my world and shaking them both like a baby's rattle. One of the strongest earthquakes of the century—measuring 8.2 on the Richter scale—had begun. After the longest sixty seconds of my life, the quaking just as suddenly stopped.

Thankfully our building somehow stood its ground. Everyone in our party, though shaken, was unhurt. We made our way down the stairs and out into the street. There, amid the screams and chaos, we found a very different world from the one we left just an hour before.

It was incredible the way things had changed in that seemingly eternal minute of the quake. The physical landscape had been altered dramatically. Roads were cracked, buildings had collapsed, and the island was virtually shut down. Though miraculously no one had died, the momentary threat of death and the experience of watching life pass before their eyes had left everyone in varying states of shock. The needle on the phonograph of life had skipped, and suddenly everything somehow felt and sounded different.

The next day we toured the island to see the impact of this cata-strophic event. Two floors had collapsed in a new hotel, and it was now leaning like the famous tower of Pisa. Structures had cracked and fallen all over the city. As is the case in the aftermath of every earthquake that causes either loss of life or property, there would be an exhaustive investigation into what went wrong. Were the building codes adequate? Were those codes enforced? Could the damage have been avoided with better planning? The difference between life and death can come down to the foundation and whether it has been laid properly. Just looking at our hotel, I began to thank God that whoever built it had taken into account the known fact that Guam sits right on top of a fault line. They had invested the time and effort to dig deep and lay a strong foundation.

Consistent victory over sin, joy in the Lord and personal freedom, and the ability to impact others for Christ are in large measure the result of a solid and deep foundation. But when the foundation is weak, the building is unstable. If it is weak in one of the essential areas, the whole structure will begin to tilt. It is usually evidence that the essential truths of a strong foundation are missing.

Remember, the higher the building the deeper the foundation must be. Foundation laying is not glamorous because most of what is done will never be seen. That is, until there is a problem.

# REPENTANCE AND FAITH: TWO ESSENTIALS FOR A STRONG FOUNDATION

To many, the Gospel has been reduced to the phrase, "Simply believe in Jesus and you will be saved." While this is true, real faith, the faith that can save you, is always accompanied by repentance—the two are inextricably connected together.

Throughout the New Testament the call to "repent and believe" is made. There are those who say that you must "only believe" and you will be saved. There are others that preach a dedication Gospel that keeps people constantly committing themselves over and over to Christ, never enjoying the blessed assurance that they truly belong to Christ. Is it faith or repentance? The answer is obviously both. True conversion is like a two-sided coin—on the one side is repentance, on the other side is faith. On the one side is turning from sin, on the other is turning to God. In reality, you can't really turn to God in faith without turning from something else. That's why the writer of Hebrews states, "Let us press on to maturity, not laying again a foundation of repentance *from* dead works and of faith *toward* God."[29] Notice the "from-to" pattern. When the Lord appeared to Paul He told him He was being sent to "turn them *from* darkness *to* light, and *from* the power of Satan *to* God."[30] In other words, when the Scripture says to believe in Jesus, it means to turn to Him and trust Him completely, not merely to make mental assent to a set of truths. And by turning to Him, you necessarily turn *from* everything else.

### *Understanding repentance*

Probably the most neglected aspect of the current Gospel message is repentance. In essence, when Christ's Lordship is properly proclaimed, there should be a right response. In the great message delivered at Pentecost, Peter said, "God has made this Jesus, whom you crucified, both Lord and Christ." His listeners were cut to the heart and said, "What shall we do?" Here are people who are asking what they should do, and Peter's reply was: "Repent and be baptized every one of you…"[31]

The term *repentance* denotes "turning." No doubt, millions of people have a valid conversion experience without being pressed on the issue of repentance because the Holy Spirit Himself convicted them of their need to repent. There are also countless times when people "prayed the prayer," but resisted the Holy Spirit because they were not willing to repent of known sin in their lives.

How essential is repentance in the preaching of the Gospel? After the resurrection Jesus met with His disciples to commission them for their ministry as apostles. He said to them:

> This is what is written: The Christ will suffer and rise from the dead on the third day, and repentance and forgiveness of sins will be preached in his name to all nations, beginning at Jerusalem.
>
> —LUKE 24:46–47

Paul declared, "You know that I have not hesitated to preach anything that would be helpful to you but have taught you publicly and from house to house. I have declared to both Jews and Greeks that they must turn to God in repentance and have faith in our Lord Jesus."[32]

Standing before King Agrippa, Paul summed up his ministry by saying:

> I was not disobedient to the vision from heaven. First to those in Damascus, then to those in Jerusalem and in all Judea, and to the Gentiles also, I preached that they should repent and turn to God and prove their repentance by their deeds.
>
> —ACTS 26:19–20

The apostle Peter placed the same importance on repentance: "The Lord is not slow in keeping his promise, as some understand slowness. He is patient with you, not wanting anyone to perish, but everyone to come to repentance."[33] Many a person's house of faith collapses as soon as it is tested. One of the reasons is that they did not have the proper foundation of repentance laid at the very beginning. Everything they build upon it—through Bible studies, sermons, teaching tapes, fellowship, etc.—is likely to come crashing down because a fundamental issue in their faith has been bypassed.

### Understanding faith

One of the clearest statements of salvation by faith is in the Epistle to the Ephesians, "For it is by grace you have been saved, through faith—and this not from yourselves, it is the gift of God—not by works, so that no one can boast."[34]

If salvation by faith is hard for some to grasp, it's not because it is complicated, but because it is absolutely contrary to everything in human nature; we believe that we must earn acceptance and forgiveness by our efforts, our works and our dedication. A solid foundation is laid in a person's life when, from the beginning, they understand that they come before God with nothing to offer. Even if they were to live perfect lives of total dedication from that point onward, it would not atone for the smallest of their sins. Salvation comes only through faith in what Christ has done. Saving faith is more than believing that God is real or even that Christ was His Son. It is laying the whole weight of your trust on Christ alone for your salvation and receiving the gift of grace by faith.

When it comes to the foundation of our faith, there are three load-bearing pillars that have to be planted deeply and solidly. The reformers summed these up with three key Latin "solas": *sola Christos, sola gratia* and *sola fide.* These pillars correspond to three fundamental questions: *Who* saved us? *Sola Christos*—it is by the merits of "Christ alone." If Christ had not died on the cross, we would be helpless.[35] *Why* did He do this? *Sola gratia*—by "grace alone," and without respect to our own righteousness. If God had not decided to save us through Christ, there would have been no hope.[36] *How* do we receive this gift of grace? *Sola fide*—by "faith alone." Remember, real faith means that we have turned to God and away from everything else that opposes His Word.

## THE ABUNDANCE OF GRACE AND THE GIFT OF RIGHTEOUSNESS

Paul wrote, "Therefore, since we have been justified through faith, we have peace with God through our Lord Jesus Christ, through whom we have gained access by faith into this grace in which we now stand."[37]

We must stand strong in the grace of God that brings us boldly into God's presence regardless of what we have done. As a child of God who has put his or her faith in Christ, therefore turning from a sinful life to the grace of God, I am accepted by the Father. Those who lack this understanding have a difficult time living boldly before God. Usually they have a belief system with a mixture of faith and good works, self-righteousness or condemnation. One result of this kind of foundational mistake is that they will be proud and arrogant, inwardly congratulating themselves for their dedication and commitment. Some spiritual houses will lean in the other direction. Instead of being bold, victorious Christians, they spend most of their lives struggling with guilt and spiritual inadequacy, never being good enough or faithful enough, never sure about how God views them. Satan tortures them with condemnation and accusation, so they work harder and harder to feel righteous before God. They have failed to understand that through faith in Christ they have been given the gift of righteousness and are therefore invited to come boldly into God's presence. As Paul wrote, through the "abundance of grace and the gift of righteousness" we "reign in life through...Christ Jesus."[38] Knowing this, we can be secure in the Father's kingdom. This keeps us from feeling that we need to get saved every week and therefore logging "frequent altar miles."

### Not misusing the grace of God

Scripture warns us of those who would use this grace as a license to sin.[39] Grace is defined as God's "unmerited favor." As we discussed, His grace cannot be earned. This doesn't mean, however, that salvation is a free "get out of hell" pass that forgives us but leaves us essentially unchanged.

More than just His unmerited favor, the grace of God is also His nature and presence in our lives. Scripture says that Jesus was "full of grace and truth."[40] We are told that "sin shall not be your master, because you are not under law, but under grace."[41] We are told to be "strong in the grace that is in Christ Jesus."[42] This implies that we are to be involved in the spiritual disciplines of, among many others, prayer and Scripture reading. In fact, after Paul's admonition to Timothy to be strong in the grace of God, he instructs him to entrust these truths to "faithful men who will be able to teach others also."[43] In the same chapter he exhorts believers to aspire to be vessels of honor and not dishonor and then warns them to "flee from youthful lusts and pursue righteousness, faith, love and peace, with those who call upon the Lord from a pure heart." He continues this admonition by saying to avoid "foolish and stupid arguments" because they lead to quarrels.[44] His conclusion gives an amazing insight into the peril facing the person who lives a life of darkness, and then points to the way out:

> Those who oppose him he must gently instruct, in the hope that God will grant them repentance leading them to a knowledge of the truth, and that they will come to their senses and escape from the trap of the devil, who has taken them captive to do his will.
>
> —2 TIMOTHY 2:25–26

If the foundation of the real grace of God is *not* solidly laid in a person's life, they will gravitate to a form of antinominanism (literally "without law"). That is to say, they believe they can be saved by faith without any need to obey God's moral commands. They wind up simultaneously calling themselves Christians and practicing sin.

Scripture addresses these sort of people head on:

> Dear children, do not let anyone lead you astray. He who does what is right is righteous, just as he is righteous. He who does what is sinful is of the devil, because the devil has been sinning from the beginning. The reason the Son of God appeared was to destroy the devil's work. No one who is born of God will continue to sin, because God's seed remains in him; he cannot go on sinning, because he has been born of God. This is how we know who the children of God are and who the children of the devil are.
>
> —1 JOHN 3:7–10

In other words, if you are a Christian, there will be the evidence of a changed life that delivers you from continuous and habitual sin. Those who have not experienced this may be subject to the warning Jesus gave to those who disregard His commandments:

> Not everyone who says to Me, "Lord, Lord," shall enter the kingdom of heaven, but he who does the will of My Father in heaven. Many will say to Me in that day, "Lord, Lord, have we not prophesied in Your name, cast out demons in Your name, and done many wonders in Your name?" And then I will declare to them, "I never knew you; depart from Me, you who practice lawlessness!"
>
> —MATTHEW 7:21–23, NKJV

## JESUS CHRIST—THE LORD OF CULTURE

Once a person submits to Christ as Lord, a miracle takes place—the miracle of a changed life, and that affects everything. History records the dramatic impact of great spiritual awakenings on society.

Somehow our spiritual lives have been separated from our actions and the effect of our faith on the world around us. Politicians are able to profess to be "devout" believers but have views and actions antithetical to the Gospel. This dichotomy that allows people to call themselves followers of Christ without a corresponding change in their behavior is more glaringly obvious when it comes to the absence of any real impact on society.

To call Jesus Lord means that He is the highest authority in the universe. He is called "King of kings" and "Lord of lords." That means He is the King of every earthly king and Lord of every earthly lord. He isn't just Lord and King of church services and potluck suppers; His rule extends to every area of life.

### The fault is with the salt

Jesus couldn't have been clearer as to who is in the driver's seat when it comes to the preservation and sanctification of culture.

> You are the salt of the earth…You are the light of the world. A city on a hill cannot be hidden. Neither do people light a lamp and put it under a bowl. Instead they put it on its stand, and it gives light to everyone in the house. In the same way, let your light shine before men, that they may see your good deeds and praise your Father in heaven.
> —Matthew 5:13–16

Far too often, Christians point their fingers and blame the "meat" of culture for the rot; for the spiritual darkness that causes so many to curse rather than glorify our Father in heaven. Could it be, however, that the fault is with the salt, the blight with the light? There are plenty of examples I could list that would suggest that the answer is a tragic "Yes!"

In 1995, Judge Roy Moore was sued by the American Civil Liberties Union (ACLU) for daring to post the Ten Commandments in his Alabama courtroom. The ensuing case provoked a national debate on the place of religion in politics, law and public life (culture). One of our fellow ministers got involved in the controversy, and eventually produced a video on it. In the end, the real revelation was not that humanists wanted to censor every vestige of God from our national consciousness. Psalm 2 lets us know that this is yesterday's news.[45]

In the famous words of Paul Harvey, the "rest of the story" was the inconsistency of the Church's response. Thousands showed up at rallies, demanding that the good judge be allowed to post the Ten Commandments. One hundred percent of those interviewed vigorously agreed that our nation's laws should be self-consciously based upon God's Word and the Ten Commandments. But there was an almost universal embarrassed silence when they were asked the next question: "What are the Ten Commandments?" In one rally, only one person out of the scores interviewed could name all ten![46] No wonder there is pervasive lawlessness in the Church as well as the culture.

Speaking of the culture, there is no influence on society more powerful than Hollywood and the content of its movies. Once again, upon review, the fault is with the salt. Our ministry's good friend, Ted Baehr from the Christian Film and Television Commission, tells the story of how the church set up offices in Hollywood beginning in 1933. For over forty years they worked shoulder to shoulder with virtually every Hollywood studio to ensure that evil was never glamorized and the "gratuitous profanity, sex and violence" card was never played. Thus began what has been commonly called the "Golden Age of Hollywood" when, as Dr. Baehr likes to say, "Mr. Smith (went) to Washington, It (was) a Wonderful Life and the Bells of St. Mary's rang out across the land."

But during the shaking of values that marked the 1960s, the church for the most part adopted a spirit of accommodation—progressively becoming the salt that "lost its flavor" and was "good for nothing but to be thrown out and trampled underfoot by men."[47] Against the wishes of many in the film industry,[48] the National Council of Churches de-funded and thus shut down the Protestant Film Office. The result? In 1965 the Oscar for Best Film went to *The Sound of Music*; in '66 it was given to the great story of Christian faith and honor, *A Man for All Seasons*. Three years after the office was closed, however, the "best film" was the profane, nihilistic, X-rated *Midnight Cowboy*. The same year also saw intense violence and satanic sexuality injected into the popular culture by *The Wild Bunch* and *Rosemary's Baby*. Surveying the majority of the thousands of films that have been produced in the ensuing generation, we certainly have evolved…down.

### Understanding culture

Renowned Swiss theologian and social philosopher Emil Brunner defined culture as the "materialization of meaning."[49] Using a farming metaphor to explain "culture," the great Roman philosopher Cicero described it as an interpersonal environment that cultivates and nourishes the people who comprise it. A genuine culture does this by instructing people about where they came from, where they are going, in what surroundings they exist and how they are to live.

Put simply, culture orders human experience and gives meaning to life. Its etymological root—the Latin word *cultus*, meaning "care" and "adoration"—shows why at the bottom all cultures are inextricably religious in nature; why, as the renowned theologian Henry Van Til famously declared, "culture is religion externalized."[50]

It was another Van Til, Cornelius, who then declared the ultimate aim of the Gospel in relation to culture: "The biblical ideal or sum of God's will is the transformation of the world, every part of it, into a place of worship or (cultus) for Christ."[51] A tall order? Well, remember that the world, nations and cultures are simply made up of people who can be changed one person at a time by the Gospel. As Christian writer and social critic Herbert Schlossberg says, "The 'salt' of people changed by the Gospel must change the world."[52]

Wherever you are, you are called to help establish God's kingdom there: starting with your home, your business, and then your city and beyond. Everyone is called to use his or her gifts, talents and position in life to reflect God's glory. As you witness a culture that is definitely lost and decaying, realize that one of the primary reasons this is happening is because of our retreat and the abdication of our role as the "salt of the earth," the "light of the world."[53]

As we step out of the shadows and into the arena of this "new lost world," let us do so with the confidence that the Lord will be with us. Though, at times, brave warriors of the Gospel have been devoured by the lions in these settings, their sacrifice has paved the way for enormous victories for those coming behind them. In this day, God has given His Church much understanding in the areas of prayer, spiritual warfare and authority in His Word. If we will put on the full armor of God, not only will we be able to stand in the day of evil, but the enemy won't stand a chance.

## CHAPTER 4

# REACHING THE "NEW" LOST WORLD

*There is enough light for those who desire only to see,
and enough darkness for those of a contrary disposition.*

—BLAISE PASCAL

When one thinks of a "lost world," images come to mind of uncharted lands where primitive peoples dwell and man-eating animals lurk in the shadows. During the Middle Ages, these places were often marked on maps with warnings such as, "Monsters be here." Few people were brave or crazy enough to venture into these perilous places.

When intrepid explorers like Marco Polo did dare to journey into the unknown, trade routes were opened, knowledge increased and the world became a very different place.

That was the lost world of ages past. Even though there remain pockets of unexplored territories and primitive tribes today, a much greater unreached people group has begun to emerge. And it's one that is all around us.

To understand this new lost world, turn on the television and (cautiously) peruse the channels. Program after program, movie after movie depicts a life devoid of God and His truth.

Our next stop...the not-so-friendly neighborhood video store. There ought to be a sign over the entrance, "Monsters be here, too!" Walk down the aisles, and you are bombarded with images designed to appeal to the basest of human emotions. It wouldn't be much of an exaggeration to describe the typical video aisle as a walk down death row.

The journey into the heart of darkness continues regardless of the direction you turn. Universities, for the most part, no longer pursue "universal verities" or truths. Reality has been deconstructed into an amalgam of felt needs, personal narratives and a commitment to absolute tolerance—unless, of course, you're advocating the Christian worldview.

Entering the arena of public policy, politicians are free to quote Freud, Kinsey or Keynes. But dare to reference the Bible—or even the concept of natural law invoked as the foundation of the American Declaration of Independence—and you will find yourself hung out to dry.

From our moral depravity to our culture of death, the West has entered a new dark age. The *new world* that Columbus uncovered has devolved into the *new lost world*. And monsters are now everywhere.

This new lost world has its own creeds: "Do what you like," "Follow your heart" (or "bliss," to quote the great New-Age apostle, Joseph Campbell) and "All paths lead to God." It has its own stable of prophets—university professors, late night comedians and rock bands—all promoting a humanistic mindset that has taken a generation captive.

The music of this new lost world pulses with the spirit of nihilism; the "sounds of war" against the pain and emptiness of lives lived without God. Rappers promote sex and violence while publicly cursing their mothers for neglect. Sexualized teens mainline eroticism to a younger and younger audience. From anthems to suicide and despair to songs that elevate rebellion to an art form, lyric after lyric testifies to the near bankrupt state of our culture.

And while the Church speculates about the timetable of the Lord's return, MTV is capturing the imaginations of millions. As Bob Pittman, founder and ex-president of the popular cable network, boasted, "We don't shoot for the fourteen-years-olds, *we own them.*"[1]

Stroll down the Champs Elysées in Paris or Times Square in New York and you'll get a quick lesson in why these fourteen-year-olds will likely be content to stay lost. The bright lights, captivating imagery and hard-hitting music promise a lifestyle that seems more real—certainly more relevant and exciting—than anything that would ever happen in a church.

Here's the sobering reality: *If we are not reaching them, it's because they are reaching us.* Every Christian should be alarmed at the Church's ineffectiveness in communicating its message. Every minister should be broken over the massive spiritual casualty rate, and stirred to the point of action.

After telling a parable commending the virtues of cleverness and strategic thinking, Jesus went on to lament the lack of these traits on the part of His people: "For the sons of this world are more shrewd in their generation than the sons of light."[2] I believe we could learn a few things from the "sons of this world" about reaching people. We need a new renaissance that releases the creativity and imagination of the great numbers of Christians who really want to do something but haven't been given the opportunity. We need to use every possible means to reach every possible person.

## REGAINING THE CUTTING EDGE

To be on the "cutting edge" means to be of the *avant garde* of popular culture. As difficult as it may be for Christians—and the world—to conceive, the cutting edge of innovative thinking and cultural change is precisely where the Church belongs. Our destiny in Christ is to be "the head and not the tail…above only and not beneath."[3] Our Lord's inheritance in the saints is a people who are walking in the "exceeding greatness of His power"; experiencing God-breathed lives "that overcome the world."[4] He is the Creator, the fount of all power, creativity, grace and truth. And this awesome God has promised to indwell and inspire us as we seek to fulfill His mission to the world.

With all this, the advantage—the cutting edge—has been somehow lost. Much of this can be attributed to indifference, the loss of vision for the Apostolic Mandate. The fear of being "worldly" keeps others caught in a cycle of failure and outdated methods when it comes to their evangelistic efforts.

On any given evening you can see this dilemma played out in living color on the streets of New York. Coming into Times Square, you are taken aback by the powerful images of the culture that engulf you. Millions of dollars have been spent carefully crafting an image of a product or a company, all vying for the right spot and maximum visibility. In the middle of it all, there is often a group of what I trust are well-meaning Christians, standing on a street corner delivering their message in the least palatable way possible. Not to be unkind, but you get the feeling that the prevailing mindset is that louder is better; the more obnoxious, the more anointed.

I'm not saying that there isn't a time to be bold and take a stand. As has been said, "There can be no impact without a confrontation." Yet overall, styles and methods of evangelism should be evaluated for their fruitfulness. More importantly, we need to ask whether they represent Christ in an honorable way.

Jesus said, "Wisdom is justified by her children."[5] The primary by-product of so much of what passes for evangelism today is the sense in millions of hearts that Christians are naïve, judgmental, out of touch and a bit thick intellectually. When the apostle Peter called us a "peculiar people,"[6] that wasn't exactly what he had in mind. We can't just do something in the name of Christ and then justify the poor response with a shrug and a nod to Isaiah's promise that "the word shall not return unto me void."[7]

Hellfire and brimstone are certainly a reality. There will be an ultimate judgment. But just because there's a hell doesn't mean it should be a primary topic when addressing the unchurched. Jesus spoke of it, but often in the context of the self-righteous whose religion had little room for compassion for others. It's this compassion we must recover if the Church is going to regain the cutting edge.

## GOD'S HEART FOR PEOPLE

Over a dozen times in the New Testament we hear how Jesus was "moved with compassion" and began to minister to people's needs. Even amid the heartbreak of His cousin John the Baptist's execution, He "saw a great multitude; and He was moved with compassion toward them, and he healed their sick."[8] About the only time this empathy towards human suffering and need took a back seat was when He was confronted by the self-righteously religious. "Go and learn what this means," He told them. "I desire mercy and not sacrifice."[9]

The first step in "learning mercy" is to *go*. We're never going to develop God's heart of compassion from the comfort of our living rooms. We've got to experience the needs and the suffering of others firsthand.

Anyone who has ever been on a missions trip knows that there are few things that will change a person faster and more dramatically than going to serve others. Multitudes can attest to the overwhelming sense of awe and brokenness they experienced walking into the Holocaust museums at Auschwitz, Dachau or Buchenwald. From ministering to the poor in the streets of Calcutta to serving the elderly at a local retirement home, all Christians have a responsibility to learn and experience one of the keys to an overcoming life:

> I want to know Christ and the power of his resurrection and the fellowship of sharing in his sufferings, becoming like him in his death.
>
> —PHILIPPIANS 3:10

Paul's passion to be "conformed to His death"[10] was not some morbid obsession with being martyred. It represented his desire to die to self and its lusts, to be conformed to the character of Christ, who before He went to die for the world declared, "Not my will, but yours be done."[11] It showed his longing for the capacity to think of others more highly than oneself and the willingness to "lay down one's life" for them.[12] Paul's passion was to have God's heart for people.

We desperately need this heart today. An entire generation is threatened with extinction in Africa because of AIDS. Large sections of Latin America are staggering under the burden of soul-crushing poverty. Throughout the West there are vast multitudes of people who are harassed and distressed by fear, lust and meaninglessness. With all our medical and technological advances, we still cannot heal the soul.

When Jesus saw similar multitudes, "He was moved with compassion for them, because they were weary and scattered, like sheep having no shepherd."[13] His response to this need? To send out laborers—to send us—into this harvest.

Among those He has sent in recent days is my friend Darrell Green, the legendary twenty-year veteran of the Washington Redskins. From time to time, Darrell would go into the inner city of D.C. for charity events. He described what happened one day when he, like Jesus, "saw the multitude and was moved with compassion for them."

"One Christmas we were distributing food, and the Lord spoke to my heart. 'You're helping them today,' I sensed Him say, 'but they're going to be needy tomorrow. What are you going to do for them then?' I knew then that my efforts weren't really hitting the mark."

Darrell responded by establishing a learning center to teach and train young people and minister to their families. Fifteen years later, these Youth Life Learning Centers are popping up all over America.

Their success has been so tremendous that leaders from many nations, including Nelson Mandela, are now asking for these centers to be established in their countries.

Claudio Zolla, a young Christian leader in Peru, was moved with compassion for the youth of his nation. The open broadcast of pornography was fueling the fires of perversion throughout the country. The United Nations estimated that 70 percent of all adolescent Peruvian girls have been sexually abused. Claudio and his team of young people set out to change this. After organizing a coalition, they were able to get the government to declare a "*Día Nacional de Valores*" (National Day of Values), calling the nation to reject immorality and strive instead to become a nation of righteousness. On July 13, 2002, over fifty thousand people assembled in front of the Palace of Justice in Lima to hear Claudio and other Christian leaders call the nation to repentance. Millions more listened by radio. Following the rally, the leaders of Peru lined up to ask Claudio to help train the youth. The impact since has been felt all over Latin America. Another potential "tipping point" in the right direction occurred because someone was moved with compassion and then acted.

Mother Theresa was able to travel the world and speak out against evils such as abortion because she first served the poor and destitute in India. Her acts of compassion earned her the right to be heard. This is why the Church is first called to servanthood. To win our cities, we must find the greatest needs and then find ways to meet them with God's answers.

Years ago, I was asked to speak at a conference on evangelism with Steve Sjogren, a pastor from Cincinnati. He spoke first and blew everyone away with a message on "servant evangelism." His church had developed a unique method of reaching the lost that involved serving the people in their community. A large part of the congregation had been mobilized to perform "random acts of kindness"—free car washes, soft drink giveaways, cleaning the bathrooms of business establishments (including bars), etc. By showing people "God's love in a practical way," the Holy Spirit used them to lead many people to Christ, plant seeds in untold thousands of others, and generate tremendous favor in the community for the Christian faith.

After he spoke I was pretty convicted. I found myself trying to remember the last time I had served a non-Christian in such a selfless manner. The point is, Steve and his fellow believers made an impact on a city with a toilet brush! I was reminded of what the Lord asked Moses, "What is that in your hand?"[14] That simple staff became a tool that God used to perform many miracles and deliver His elect from captivity. We must never forget that our Father delights in using the weak and foolish things of the world to confound the wise.[15]

Was Jesus on the cutting edge of evangelism? Absolutely. The primary reason is that His love for people moved Him to action. It caused Him to be the "friend of...sinners"[16] and a servant to all. We are to follow in His footsteps. As historian Dr. George Grant has written,

> The Bible is unflinching in its declaration: If we are ever to influence our families or our culture to stand for goodness, faithfulness, and kindness, then we must graciously serve the hurts, wants and needs all around us. Just as God has shown us mercy we must demonstrate mercy to others.[17]

## STUDYING THE CULTURE

Every Christian is called first to "renew their minds"[18]—to cultivate a strong relationship with God and a rigorously biblical worldview. Having done that, however, we must then turn our attention to the culture we have been called to redeem and "learn its language." Daniel didn't defile himself with the king's choice food (he was set apart for God), but he became "ten times better" than the king's advisors concerning the affairs of Babylon. He had "knowledge and skill in all literature and wisdom."[19] The apostle Paul was very familiar with pagan philosophy and literature—quoting at least four different secular writers in his New Testament letters.[20] He was a master at entering their lost world and their narrative and finding those "eternity in the heart" moments that he could use as a natural and compelling springboard for the Gospel.[21]

In the same way, we must learn—as the title of my friend Terry Crist's excellent book suggests—*The Language of Babylon*.[22] The harvest fields aren't within the walls of the New Jerusalem; they're outside its gates—often *well* outside. To leave the Holy City and to enter the lost world and speak its language is the very essence of Christianity. In this, as in everything else, Jesus is our ultimate example.

## MAXIMUM IMPACT

Many are still using methods of evangelism that were effective in a bygone era but that lack broad appeal in the twenty-first century. Today's digital generation depends a great deal on iconographic, or image-based, language. Theirs is a culture that often has to "see it" before they can "get it."

Where are the television shows offering this generation an alternative to programs like "Real World" and "Extreme Dating"? Where are the movies that speak to the higher virtues of courage, honor and purity? Sound corny? Out of style? That's because the culture has tipped in the wrong direction.

How powerful is an image? Just ask the famous Hollywood screenwriter, Joe Eszterhas. Suffering now from throat cancer, he has publicly lamented the scripted use of cigarette smoking in movies, such as, for example, his own film, *Basic Instinct*. He wrote, "A cigarette in the hands of a Hollywood star onscreen is a gun aimed at a 12 or 14 year old."[23] A simple cigarette constitutes a loaded gun? If that's true, what about the words the actors say? What about far more potent and seductive things like sexual imagery, violence, rebellion, the glorification of evil and the mockery of God? If a cigarette is a gun, the overall worldview of the film constitutes a nuclear explosion crashing into the mind of the spectator in a fury of forceful images and digital sound.

Think about it. If what you hear and see doesn't impact you, why do advertisers spend millions of dollars for a thirty-second commercial during the World Cup or Super Bowl? Certainly not to make a charitable contribution to the television network!

Years ago people worried that there were covert messages buried backwards in music that would negatively influence listeners. Once again, we miss the forest for the trees. Just listen to the message forwards, look at the cover of the CD, watch the music video or the live performance, and examine the artist's worldview and lifestyle. That's where the impact is.

## THE CENTER FOR CULTURAL APOLOGETICS

Rather than merely curse the spiritual darkness that modern media has loosed upon the world, Morning Star has begun to use these new digital technologies to shine a light. The nexus for much of this creative work is the Center for Cultural Apologetics (CCA). Directed by legendary culture shaker, Eric Holmberg, and staffed with some of the most creative people I've ever met, the Center is producing high quality video documentaries, TV shows, multimedia seminars, high-tech discussion group materials, movie shorts and all manner of other visually oriented tools to open eyes, renew minds and help redeem the culture.

From the new *Red Pill Forum* to the *Shadows of the Supernatural* seminar developed by Steve Hollander, these twenty-first century evangelists and apologists are on a mission: Take any issue where multitudes have been taken captive—sexual ethics, Darwinian evolution, moral relativism, the supernatural, life after death, the fascination with aliens, etc. Next, present the prevailing worldview through potent images and sound, appealing first to the imagination and then engaging the mind. Season with a little humor, perhaps tweaking the logical and moral fallacies inherent in any man-based worldview. Then take the wedge of God's truth and artfully, redemptively but firmly *separate*—dividing light from darkness; exposing the enmity that God has set between His truth and Satan's. And finally, present Christ as the only bridge from the darkness to the light, from the dominion of Satan into the kingdom of God. The strategy is working. Thousands are coming into the kingdom as a result of these tools.

The Center is also developing a new publication entitled *Up to Speed*.[24] Few ministers have the time to stay "up to speed" with all the emerging trends in media, art, philosophy, science and politics. Since CCA has to constantly research these areas anyway, the inspiration came to compile a monthly periodical that provides highlights in all these areas from a Christian apologetical perspective. Why else did God sovereignly permit the development of the internet, computers and telecommunications if it wasn't to ultimately assist a new generation of Daniels in acquiring "knowledge and skill in all literature and wisdom?"[25] The goal of CCA and all of its productions is to keep Christians "up to speed" in reaching our constantly changing world.

## MAXIMUM EFFORT

Paul said, "I have become all things to all men so that by all possible means I might save some."[26] Paul wasn't satisfied with just showing up or saying, "I tried." He wanted to see people won for Christ; so much so that he even offered to give up his own salvation if his fellow countrymen (the Jews) could be saved.[27]

Have we been that determined to gain results?

If the Church were a sports team, the coach would be giving us a strong challenge on "heart." "You say you want to win," he might say, "but it doesn't show by your effort." Even though there are many churches and ministries that possess the fire and the enthusiasm necessary to make a difference, taken as a whole the Church is in desperate need to recover the passion Paul had to see his world affected for the glory of God.

## THE IMPORTANCE OF SEEKING

This is not to say that a lot isn't being done to reach the lost, some of it very shrewd and innovative. A good example is the wave of "seeker sensitive" churches and programs that have been launched in an attempt to become more relevant and effective in reaching the unchurched.

The backlash against this movement has been severe in some quarters, with detractors accusing those who adopt this philosophy of watering down the Gospel to make it more palatable to sinners. While I am sure there are instances where this charge is warranted—where the dosage of the Gospel is so low that there may not be enough "medicine" to help the patient—overall I am reminded of a similar stir Jesus caused when He ate with tax collectors and sinners. His response was that, "wisdom is vindicated by her deeds."[28] In other words, look at the fruit of what has happened!

A key aspect of any evangelistic strategy is simply to have one. Obviously, it needs to be faithful to the standards God has outlined in the Scriptures. But then we can evaluate our strategy by measuring the results. This doesn't mean that you just count the hands that have been raised or number those who have walked down the aisle. But the fruit of true conversion and effective discipleship isn't hard to spot. Lives change, living waters flow and eventually our efforts should register on the Richter scale of leading societal and cultural indicators. If the world's not being turned right side up, there's something wrong with our strategy.

Though it has born some great fruit, my primary concern with the seeker-sensitive mindset is its notion that the unconverted *are really seeking.*[29] Not to quibble, but practically as well as theologically, one would have to question whether this is true as regards the big picture. In certain parts of America, where going to church is part of the culture, there are masses of people who have dropped out and periodically resurface to try church again. Most of the world, however, isn't wired that way. Even in America—in major population centers on the West Coast and in the Northeast—people are far more likely to sleep in or go seeking a good cappuccino on Sunday morning than a relationship with God in a church service. This is even truer in Canada and in Europe. Sunday morning has little to do with the custom of going to church.

The fact is that the great spiritual awakenings taking place in Asia, Africa and Latin America are happening in a spiritual atmosphere that is far from toned down or seeker sensitive. In these places it is the Christians who are the seekers, imitating the One who came to "seek and to save that which was lost."[30]

## JESUS THE SEEKER

Jesus was and is the ultimate Seeker. He sought out those who were lost and at times even seemed unreachable. He told parables about leaving the ninety-nine who thought they needed no repentance to go out and look for the one that everyone knew was lost. The Gospels find Him strategically calling tax collectors, rough fishermen and notorious characters like Zacchaeus. Can you imagine God choosing a woman who had been married five times to bring His message to an entire city?[31] Hardly the ideal vessel one would expect God to use.

Like our Redeemer, we too are to go and bear fruit. We are to seek and save that which is lost. When you are seeking something, really seeking, the search consumes you. Merchants travel the world looking for hidden treasures in obscure markets. Real estate developers live to find a "sweetheart deal." And when someone's child is missing, their loved ones will not rest until they've done everything possible to find him or her.

I will never forget the streets of New York City after 9/11. Thousands of people walked around carrying missing posters of friends and relatives who worked in the World Trade Center. They searched the hospitals and streets, even though they knew the chances of survival were astronomically small. No stone was too small or large to be left unturned.

I have nothing against door-to-door evangelism; I've done some myself. But anyone who has ever gone out randomly knocking on doors knows the futility of knocking on the wrong one. No big deal when it's just one person and it happens infrequently. But when it becomes the rule and not the exception, we have to ask ourselves, "What's wrong?"

There can be a lot wrong when we take evangelistic techniques that may have worked two generations ago and employ them in what has become a very different world. The concepts of truth and sin, for example, were fairly universal when I was a kid. Evangelism that appealed to these two principles was often effective. Today, however, both ideas have fallen on hard times. Informing people that Jesus died to pay the penalty for their sins may evoke little more than a shrug. At the same time, postmodernism's emphasis on narrative and personal experience opens up a number of doors that might not have been as effective fifty years ago.

Both in seeking and knocking, we have to know which doors we've been called to walk through.

## OTHER PRINCIPLES OF EFFECTIVE EVANGELISM

### The Gospel is the power of God

Sooner or later, the Gospel has got to be presented. This doesn't mean that we can't be inductive or discreet. We can use the same type of strategy as our Lord, who spoke in parables in order that those who really wanted to know the true meaning behind some of His more subtle illustrations could get the point. At the end of it all, the Gospel is still "the power of God for the salvation of everyone who believes."[32] In other words, all our strategies should lead to Christ.

### Wisdom

"He who wins souls is wise."[33] It takes the wisdom of God to see hearts open to receive the Word. Sometimes evangelism is like "cracking" a safe. Remember the old movies where the bank robbers would put their ear to the safe and listen for the faint clicking sound of the lock tumblers falling into place? Many times it is an equally delicate process when it comes to the intricacies of the human heart.

Another way to describe evangelism is like untying a knot. Once Jesus told His disciples to go into a city where they would find a donkey and her colt. "Untie them and bring them to me."[34] What a picture of evangelism. They have to be untied and brought to Jesus. You don't untie a knot by simply pulling harder. You have to study it, find the right place to pull and then work with the knot until it loosens. Sometimes ministering to people, I'm conscious of how my job might be to loosen the knot a bit so that the next person God sends will have an easier time. The wisdom of God is needed to help you locate the exact area that needs to be addressed.

### Maintain the right spirit

There are few things uglier than a mean, dogmatic, religious spirit. The angry fundamentalist thing has never really worked but in these postmodern times, it is an unmitigated disaster. "The anger of man does not achieve the righteousness of God."[35] When speaking of Christ, Isaiah prophesied that, "He will not shout…a bruised reed he will not break, and a smoldering wick he will not snuff out."[36]

Our Lord was loved by sinners. He obviously understood that the religious system of His day had offered them very little incentive to serve God. The love of God keeps us compassionate, ever mindful of how patient Jesus was with us. At one university campus, Jim Laffoon was speaking and the leader of the gay and lesbian alliance came to the meeting. Jim's compassion and ministry touched his heart. All he had ever experienced was anger and rebuke from the Christian world. Without condoning the young man's sin, Jim was able to give him the message of Christ and his deliverance.

### Excellence

There are few things more impressive than a presentation that is done with excellence. Because the enemy has broad-brushed Christians as inept bumblers who ignore the facts and are emotionally crippled, it doesn't take much to exceed people's expectations. When someone does their homework, spends the money or exerts the effort in order to do something right, it gets their attention. It's baffling how so many causes outside the kingdom of God are amply funded by those who believe in them. Ted Turner of CNN donated one billion dollars to the United Nations. Bill Gates set aside one hundred million dollars to fund primarily children's health immunization issues. Regularly, there are huge amounts given to universities and foundations for all kinds of causes. It's certainly long overdue for a new wave of investment to bring the Gospel message to a new level of visibility and excellence in the culture.

### *The power of the Holy Spirit*

This is the great equalizer. Regardless of what we lack, we obviously have the power of God's Spirit and His leading us in ways that will confront unbelievers. His supernatural presence and power will transform someone when combined with grace and wisdom. The Holy Spirit can use us regardless of who we are or how little we know. Whether it's praying for healing, discerning spiritual bondage in someone's life or receiving an insight from the Holy Spirit termed a "word of knowledge," these gifts give us an enormous advantage in dealing with the lost.

Once, while walking across a campus, the Lord gave me such a word concerning a young man walking toward me. After a brief greeting, I was able to tell him what the Lord had shown me about him. He was shocked; he hurried back to his room and told his roommate that he had met a guy who really had supernatural power. His friend came with him to hear me speak that night and got saved. His friend's name was Ken Dew, who is now a Morning Star International pastor in New Zealand and is helping plant churches throughout the South Pacific.

## THE MINISTRY OF RECONCILIATION

> Therefore, if anyone is in Christ, he is a new creation; the old has gone, the new has come! All this is from God, who reconciled us to himself through Christ and gave us the ministry of reconciliation: that God was reconciling the world to himself in Christ, not counting men's sins against them. And he has committed to us the message of reconciliation.
> —2 CORINTHIANS 5:17–19

Winning people to Christ is the goal of the ministry of reconciliation. Paul says, "I have become all things to all men so that by all possible means I might save some."[37] Fulfilling this obligation is critical in keeping our heart right with God and our life relevant to the world around us. When the Apostolic Mandate is lost, it is first noticed in this area. In order to win people to Christ, we must have a clear understanding of what salvation means. If we understand our desperate need for a savior and the miracle of Christ's death and resurrection, it gives us the necessary revelation and motivation that men like Paul the Apostle had.

### Reconciliation means forgiveness

In order to be a reconciler, we must be reconciled ourselves. Sometimes no matter how hard we try, we can still end up with people who don't like us. I learned this lesson early on, growing up in a small town. I had only two childhood enemies, but what made things so difficult was that they were both older and bigger than I. No matter how old I got they were always there, one grade ahead of me. Life can be tough as a seventh grader when you've got an eighth grader mad at you.

In those days, before the growth spurt and the weight room, I was as skinny as a rail. Besides the fact that I was not much of a physical threat, I was also up against the law of upper class dominance—which could not be broken. In the small town where I grew up, there was this unwritten protocol about fighting. Even if as a seventh grader you could beat up a guy in the eighth grade, you just did not do it. It would be as if some fundamental order in the universe would be upset, and in such a case, all the other eighth graders would feel obligated to set things right. No kid wanted to face that kind of middle-school retribution, so consequently my fight with Bruce (his name has been changed to protect the guilty) did not go well.

Bruce and I never did make up after the fight. When I was twelve, my family and I moved to Texas, and that was the end of our confrontations. However, I never forgot my middle-school nemesis or the big fight in my front yard. It was probably part of the motivation in the back of my mind that kept driving me back to the weight room until only a few years later I was six feet three inches tall, 230 pounds and bench-pressing over 350 pounds. I didn't know if I would ever see Bruce again and had no intention of starting a fight, but certainly was better prepared if one came.

Years later I was speaking at the University of Southern Mississippi and into the meeting walked Bruce. I was so stunned I almost forgot my message. I wasn't completely sure that he hadn't shown up to finish what we had started—and never did find out exactly why he came. I do know that when I gave the invitation, Bruce came to the front, wanting to get saved.

*Oh no!* I thought to myself. *I CANNOT spend eternity with this guy! Go away; it's too late for you. You've probably committed the unpardonable sin anyway.*

Actually, that's not what I thought at all. Considering how much

I had been forgiven, how could I not forgive this guy? In fact, of all the people who have come forward in my meetings to get right with God, I've never been more thrilled than the night I saw Bruce walking forward to receive the same gift of grace that had transformed my life. After leading him to Christ, we stood there in front of the meeting room and hugged each other, reconciled enemies.

That was a big deal to me, but it seems trivial when compared to the way others have been challenged to forgive. From Elisabeth Elliot serving the very tribe that had killed her husband, Jim, to Nelson Mandela, who emerged from years of imprisonment without a trace of bitterness in order to lead the nation of South Africa, God has revealed the essence of His love through these trophies of grace won through forgiveness and reconciliation. To the natural mind these kinds of acts of forgiveness are incomprehensible. They are routine, however, in the hall of faith in heaven.

How can we not give grace to others, when God has granted so much to us? When one truly understands his sin, even the most pure among us can be overwhelmed by the riches of God's grace in granting him eternal life. And the one who realizes that he has been forgiven much tends to love and forgive others in the same way.

### *Being reconciled produces a passion for reconciliation*

Our reconciliation text concludes that, since we have had the ministry of reconciliation committed to us, "…we are ambassadors for Christ, as though God were making an appeal through us; we beg you on behalf of Christ, be reconciled to God."[38] The most outstanding characteristic of the apostle Paul was not his intellect, his revelation, his faith for miracles or his boldness. It was his passion for others to be reconciled, even as he had been.

He didn't offer up a dry, dutiful invitation. He didn't say, "Here's the truth; take it or leave it." Paul said, "We beg you to be reconciled to God." Paul was no beggar, except in this sense. He begged, pleaded and did everything in his power to persuade people. Put in modern terminology, he might have said, "I'll throw myself in front of a train if you'll be reconciled to God." Actually, Paul went much farther than that. As we have already pointed out, he wrote, "I could wish that I myself were accursed, separated from Christ for the sake of my brethren, my kinsmen according to the flesh."[39] In other words, Paul said he would go to hell if it meant his brethren would come to Christ. What kind of man says something like that? A man with a passion for reconciliation.

As Ed Silvoso writes, "…we must have a passion for the lost. I am not talking about having a keen interest in the salvation of sinners. No! I am talking about an all-consuming passion for the lost ones. I am not talking about subscribing to a program to evangelize people. No! I am talking about a lifestyle through which we devote every ounce of our energy to winning the lost."[40]

## ETHNIC RECONCILIATION IS A WORK OF THE CROSS

The ministry of reconciliation is the only force strong enough to tear down the walls of racism that still exist in our world. Sadly, these same walls still exist in the Church today, as they did in the first century. For instance, the ethnic prejudices of the apostle Peter were exposed when, in Acts 10, he was called to take the Gospel to the house of Cornelius, a Gentile and an officer in the Roman occupying force. Even after receiving a powerful vision, hearing God's voice, seeing an angel and witnessing the outpouring of the Holy Spirit on Cornelius and his household, Peter's ethnic prejudices later resurfaced. Paul had to rebuke him in Antioch for refusing to eat with the Gentiles.[41]

It's important that we understand just how deep the root of bigotry can go in the human soul and the culture it produces. Whenever people start messing around with the status quo, especially the ethnic status quo, opposition is never far behind.

Consider how even after Jesus commanded His apostles to "go into *all* the world,"[42] there was some serious resistance on their part when "all the world" began to come to them. The news of what Peter had done with Cornelius, for example, beat him back to Jerusalem. Upon his return, Church leaders from throughout Judea were there waiting to call him to an account. In defense of his actions, Peter reported, "Look, God poured out His Spirit upon them just as He did upon us. Who was I to stand in His way?" After hearing the story, the leaders "quieted down," took a deep breath and said, "Well then, God has granted to the Gentiles also the repentance that leads to life."[43] The apostles and elders concluded that, notwithstanding their long list of personal objections, this was God's initiative and His express desire for the Church.

These personal objections were no small matter, however. The respective people-groups in the early Church carried a ton of political, social and theological baggage that their forefathers had been packing around for centuries. Given that kind of history, the unity they were able to achieve was both remarkable and unprecedented.

Still, problems continued to emerge. In Acts 6, we see the fracture along the Hebrew and Gentile fault line reemerge around the issue of caring for the non-Jewish widows. When men from Judea took a missionary journey to the churches in Asia Minor, they stirred up such controversy that it almost split the Christian Church along ethnic lines. The first Church counsel had to be convened to calm things down and restore unity.[44] And then in Galatia, as we just saw, Paul had to address a situation where the Jewish Christians were avoiding fellowship with the Greeks.

## THE CHURCH AT ANTIOCH— A MODEL FOR ETHNIC UNITY

With regard to ethnic diversity, the church in Antioch was very different. It was birthed out of the great persecution that arose over the preaching and martyrdom of Stephen—an event orchestrated by Saul of Tarsus. Stephen had been a member of the Synagogue of the Freedmen, a gathering of Greek-speaking Jews and Gentile proselytes. Those who scattered from Jerusalem were not native Hebrew Christians, but people born from all over the Roman Empire. Some men from Cyprus and Cyrene ended up in Antioch. Hearing their preaching, a large number of Gentiles also became Christians. Consequently, from the very beginning, Antioch was very much a multi-ethnic church.

The church in Antioch became a great apostolic center that took the Gospel to the Gentile world. It also became the home base for the man who bore the title "the apostle to the Gentiles," Paul. Together they planted churches that in turn produced other churches—each becoming an apostolic center in and of itself. In time, they changed the world.

There are a lot of factors that contributed to their success. No doubt a major key was their unity. Antioch was a church in which the spirit of reconciliation overcame ethnic and racial divisions.

One of the great churches that has followed this Antioch model is Grace Covenant Church in the Washington, D.C., area, pastored by my dear friend, Brett Fuller. As Brett says, "Ethnic reconciliation is an elementary stage, among the first steps towards the unity God ultimately has in mind for every local church." The Grace Covenant congregation has certainly settled this issue in their midst, so that they can export this harmony to their entire city.

There is no way we can even pretend to be serious about the Apostolic Mandate if we don't confront the issue of ethnic prejudice. It's not something to just start dealing with upon arriving on the foreign mission field. The spirit of reconciliation must be a core value in our hearts and within any apostolic movement. In other words, how can we love other nations abroad if we don't love those same people in our neighborhoods at home?

Ethnic division and hostility exist in every nation on earth, though they manifest themselves in different ways. In America, the issue is primarily between blacks and whites. In India, it is the caste system. In Indonesia, the indigenous Indonesians are pitted against the Chinese-Indonesians.

One common characteristic of all such cultural schisms is a long, often horrible history of offenses that fuels mistrust and bitterness. It's also here where we find the root of ethnic division even among believers. These issues can run very deep and be quite complex. Without the ministry of reconciliation, we can never hope to heal these rifts and establish true multi-ethnic, apostolic churches.

In this, as in every other dynamic of ministry, *the key is the cross.*

Paul wrote about his revelation in the "mystery of Christ…(that the) Gentiles are fellow heirs and fellow members of the body."[45] This mystery was fulfilled in an awesome truth revealed in an earlier verse:

> For he himself is our peace, who has made the two [Jew and Gentiles] one and has destroyed the barrier, the dividing wall of hostility [or hatred]…His purpose was to create in himself one new man out of the two, thus making peace, and in this one body to reconcile both of them to *God through the cross*, by which he put to death their hostility.
> —Ephesians 2:14–16 (emphasis mine)

God's express desire was not only to reconcile Jews and Gentiles to Himself, but also to reconcile them to one another. His goal was and is to bring every tribe, tongue and ethnicity under heaven into one Church; to make them one body. This grand design was accomplished through the cross.

It is one of the greatest failures of the Church in our time that we remain so divided. Christians, particularly in America, need to face up to the fact that our ethnically segregated churches bear tragic testimony to our carnality and the degree to which we have failed to apply the work of the cross and the blueprint of the kingdom.

From a legal standpoint, we can point to civil rights legislation and say that we are well along in the process of reconciliation. (The nature and extent of legal restitution is an ongoing debate.) For the citizens of God's kingdom, however, the expectations are vastly different. Jesus made it very clear that external compliance to rules was not enough. In His kingdom, it's not just a matter of actual adultery; the deeper issue is lust. It's not whether you physically committed murder, but whether you hate your brother.[46] Anyone who does not truly love his brother abides in death.[47] In Christ's true Church, reconciliation isn't fulfilling some outward technicality. It's truly loving one another and becoming one in Christ.

## BEYOND RECONCILIATION

For many, the issue of reconciliation is still the pressing issue. They are struggling with how to make this possible. Certainly, prejudice and bigotry are spiritual strongholds that must be torn down. This deliverance starts in the Church. The Church is the "pillar and support of the truth."[48] If the Church upholds this vital truth and produces an atmosphere of freedom from this spirit of division, then the world will stand up and take notice.

The hope we offer is that there is actually something beyond just being reconciled, and that is the hope of building the kingdom together as family. When men and women of diverse backgrounds and ethnicities walk together in covenant relationships, it becomes a force to be reckoned with. In Nashville, next to prayer, this has been our major focus: building a multi-colored congregation. My relationship with my senior associate, Tim Johnson, who is African-American, is a major reason why we are succeeding. Tim believes we are building a model in this area because, "At every service and in every setting we labor to present this multi-ethnic picture. In a way, you could call it affirmative action. We are aggressive in creating an atmosphere where this message is prominent." The evidence that your strategy is working will be in the ethnic makeup of the congregation. Since making this our focus, we have gone from being a predominantly white congregation in the suburbs of Nashville to one that is now 50 percent non-white; and 35 percent of that number is African-American. Our goal is to have a church where no one is sure exactly what color it is.

### Praying hands billboard

When this happens, the Lord will use you to be a standard bearer in your city and nation. For us in the southern part of the United States, this is quite a calling. In fact, one of the worst features of our city is a large statue of the founder of the Ku Klux Klan that was erected by a private individual in 1998. This eyesore is located right along a major freeway and is a daily reminder of the ugly side of human nature. I drive by it often and always pray that God would remove this memorial to the dark ages of bigotry and racism.

As I prayed one day, I sensed the Lord telling me to raise a banner declaring that Nashville was to be a place of ethnic unity and that the church was the key in making it happen. Out of that came the idea to place billboards around the city that featured a remarkable picture of a black and white hand clasped in prayer. The image had been developed to promote ethnic reconciliation by Paul Daniel in South Africa. The cost of such an undertaking was a serious consideration, based on our budget at that time. Getting the right locations for the billboards would take a small miracle, as well. We came to a critical point where we had to make a decision to proceed or let the whole project die.

The next day was our regular staff meeting. During the time of prayer, some of our ministers who knew nothing about the billboard idea spontaneously shared their sense that the Lord was going to give us a banner to raise over the city. If that wasn't enough, the phone rang. On the other end was Jim Laffoon, one of our key prophetic ministers. Without any knowledge of the issues at hand he said, "The Lord spoke to me and told me to call you right now and tell you that He had given you a banner to raise over the city."

That was it. With the word of the Lord in hand, it was easy to step out in faith. God provided both the money and the placement of the billboards. The most important location was at the international airport. We wanted our message to be among the first things people see when they arrive in our city. Today, those beautiful praying hands are there along with our church's vision statement: "Reaching a city to touch the world." These banners of reconciliation have been raised all over our town. It's difficult for anyone to miss them.

As the Scripture promises, "When the enemy comes in like a flood, the Spirit of the LORD will lift up a standard against him."[49] This standard first has to be raised in our hearts and lives. It would have been a joke to put up these billboards if ethnic unity was not really happening in our midst. The principle is simple: If it works at home, then you can export it! The standard prophetically displayed on these bill-boards is not only the vision of ethnic unity; it is also a call to prayer. The picture of the praying hands and the message on the billboard is a constant reminder of our primary call as the people of God: to pray and work to reach a city that can then touch the world.

# CONCLUSION

The Lord has committed the ministry of reconciliation to everyone He has reconciled to Himself. We must be motivated by His compassion and love the people we are called to reach enough to learn their languages and customs. As the Church, we must rethink every aspect of what we do and evaluate it in the light of the Great Commandment: Are we loving the Lord with all our hearts and our neighbors as ourselves? If we are faithful with these things, there is no way that the world will be able to stop our efforts or withstand the force of our message. As the Bible promises, "Love never fails."[50]

This kind of spirit and heart can be reproduced over and over again if we will pour our lives into the people to whom we minister. This brings us to the epicenter of the Apostolic Mandate, the very process Jesus employed when He was on the earth. If we want to see His glory fill the lives of a new generation, we must pause and study His method for "nation transformation": *making disciples*.

## CHAPTER 5

# THE HEART OF
# THE MANDATE

*I'm not in the business of making steel. I'm in the business of making men. They make steel.*

—ANDREW CARNEGIE

In the blockbuster movie, *Jurassic Park*, dinosaurs are brought back to life and quarantined on a secluded island. A scientist who visits the experimental facility is shocked when he encounters these long-extinct creatures now roaming the land. He asks the mastermind behind the project an obvious question: "How did you do this?"

The film treats us to a fascinating explanation involving dinosaur blood, prehistoric mosquitoes, frogs, recombinant DNA and cloning. Even though it's classic Hollywood science fiction, the ingenious process seems almost believable. After all, with cloned sheep and cattle running around now—and heated debates about the ethics of cloning humans—who knows how much longer it will be before science is able to resurrect beings who are long since dead.

Watching the movie got me thinking. Suppose that someone found the remains of one of the original apostles, or perhaps Moses or Abraham, and was able to extract a suitable quantity of DNA. What would happen if their genetic material was spliced into the genes of someone living today? Would we be able to recreate men and women with the same kind of world-changing faith and character?

Not likely, when you consider that these characteristics are not driven by mere biology. What is possible, however, is another type of replication—using the *spiritual seed* that made these saints the champions they were. And what's incredible is that this seed—the original, full-strength variety—is still available to be grafted into the genetic makeup of our eternal lives, transforming us into mature sons and daughters of the living God. This spiritual DNA is found in the Word of God.

> For you have been born again, not of perishable seed, but of imperishable, through the living and enduring word of God.
>
> —1 PETER 1:23

In fact, because of the cross, Jesus' resurrection and Pentecost, the spiritual seed that has been offered to us has even greater supernatural potential than what was available to Abraham, Moses and all the Old Testament saints.[1] This awesome reality was reflected in a shocking declaration made by the Lord Himself:

> I tell you the truth: Among those born of women there has not risen anyone greater than John the Baptist; yet he who is least in the kingdom of heaven is greater than he.
>
> —MATTHEW 11:11

## DISCIPLESHIP IS THE DIFFERENCE

In light of this promise, why don't we have more "greater than John the Baptist" types walking the earth?

As much as people would love to blame it on the devil or some deficiency of knowledge or anointing that will be revealed only when the Lord returns, the bottom line is simple: We're not doing the things the Lord has commanded. We're not making disciples.

Putting it another way, even if you could clone a champion athlete such as Michael Jordan, Pelé or Tiger Woods, they would still have to be trained and practice as diligently as the originals. "If anyone would come after me," Jesus said, "he must deny himself and take up his cross and follow me."[2]

Victory comes at no less cost for those who would be champions on the field of faith. The same eternal principles that guided Moses and Mark must be imparted to today's disciples. They must still undergo the same rigorous training, learn how to conquer the same temptations, think the same spiritual thoughts, buck up under the same trials and fight the same fight of faith. There is just no other way for the seed of God's Word to reproduce the character and impact of the heroes of old.

Jesus declared that for those who believe in Him, "the works that I do he will do also; and greater works than these he will do."[3] This promise, however, is not a blanket guarantee for just anyone who claims to be a Christian. The Lord made this astonishing statement on the evening before He went to the cross. Just a few days before, He had predicted both His death and the manner in which He would bring forth those who would do these "greater works":

> The hour has come that the Son of Man should be glorified. Most assuredly, I say to you, unless a grain of wheat falls into the ground and dies, it remains alone; but if it dies, it produces much grain. He who loves his life will lose it, and he who hates his life in this world will keep it for eternal life. If anyone serves Me, let him follow Me.
> —JOHN 12:23–26, NKJV

He is the grain that fell to the ground and died. Christians are the new grain that His seed produces—"chips off the old block," so to speak. But notice the qualifier: These are people who have lost their lives in relation to the cares of this world. These are people who are *following* Jesus, something that can only be done with cross in hand, signifying surrender to self.[4] These are *disciples*.

Great leaders and world changers don't just happen; they are developed. The real reason we aren't producing these kinds of Christians *en masse* is because we have failed to obey the heart of the mandate that Jesus gave: "Make disciples."

## DISCIPLES FIRST, NATIONS SECOND

Everything begins and ends with this vital principle. In his book, *The Disciple-Making Church*, Bill Hull makes a simple but profound observation: "Unless the church makes making disciples its main agenda, world evangelization is a fantasy."[5] Anglican pastor and professor of Church growth at the School of World Missions at Fuller Theological Seminary, Eddie Gibbs, put it this way, "To stay in business we must know what we're in business for—and that is making disciples."

The reason for this should be obvious: You can't export what you don't have. How can we expect to fulfill the Apostolic Mandate—to evangelize and disciple entire nations—if we can't pull it off with individual people in our own backyard? The truth is, only a disciple who has been transformed by Christ will have the faith, desire and commitment necessary to go out and attempt to transform other cultures.

Peter Wagner estimates that since the first century, there have been over seven hundred distinct movements that proclaimed their intention to evangelize the world. Subsequent projections by David Barrett, Research Professor of Missiometrics at Regent University, doubled that amount. Whatever the actual number, in many cases these groups accomplished some extraordinary things, but for the most part their results fell far, far short of the stated objective.

I believe I know why. With all these plans for global evangelism, according to Wagner only 3 percent had any kind of disciple-making program as a part of their stated objectives.[6]

This trend continues today. All manner of strategies have been employed by the Church to reach the world—mass crusades, television ministries, revival meetings, conferences, the explosion of Christian music and book publishing, on and on. All of these things are—or at least can be—great things, but if they're not vitally connected to the enterprise of making disciples, in the end they're just spinning their wheels. This sounds harsh but, as Bill Hull says, "The refusal to consistently make disciples causes decline that leaves the Church more defeated than before, and the world does not become evangelized."[7] In other words, to preach Christ without discipleship leaves people to believe that the promise of transformation is false advertising.

Robert Coleman addressed this very issue in his classic work, *The Master Plan of Evangelism:* "Are our efforts to keep things going fulfilling the Great Commission of Christ? Do we see an ever-expanding company of dedicated people reaching the world with the Gospel as a result of our ministry? That we are busy in the Church trying to work one program of evangelism after another cannot be denied. But are we accomplishing our objective?"

He then concluded, "[Jesus'] life was ordered by His objective. Everything He did and said was a part of the whole pattern...The Master disclosed God's strategy for world conquest. He had confidence in the future precisely because He lived according to that plan in the present…Weighing every alternative in human experience, He conceived a plan that would not fail…Nevertheless, when His plan is reflected on, the basic philosophy is so different from that of the modern Church that its implications are nothing less than revolutionary."[8]

## DISCIPLESHIP DEFINED

> We proclaim him, admonishing and teaching everyone with all wisdom, so that we may present everyone perfect in Christ. To this end I labor, struggling with all his energy, which so powerfully works in me.
> —COLOSSIANS 1:28–29

Whether it's Moses discipling Joshua, Elijah passing his prophetic mantle to Elisha, or Paul training Timothy, there is no question as to what Jesus meant when He called His Church to this glorious task. Discipleship is the key to kingdom advancement. I can best define this key as follows:

> **Discipleship** is the process whereby men and women follow Christ, are trained in His Word, grow to maturity and learn to replicate themselves in others.

By definition, the task of discipleship is hard work, as the apostle Paul made very clear: "My little children, *for whom I labor* in birth again until Christ is formed in you."[9]

Like training children in a natural family, discipleship involves the commitment to not only teach information, but also to provide loving confrontation and correction. Being the father of five has only confirmed what Proverbs and twenty-five years of ministry has taught me: The training you provide for a child (whether natural or spiritual) will determine the type of person he becomes.[10]

Discipleship is an absolute command and, like all absolutes, carries with it a penalty for disobedience. The negative consequences are built in. The fact is, discipling is inevitable. Everything we do and are is being absorbed into the lives of those around us, particularly those whose character and destinies are still being formed. Whether we beget an Isaac or, like the high priest Eli, a Hophni or Phinehas (who became so evil, they were called the sons of Belial[11]), discipleship is happening all the time, all around us.

As we've seen, people produce after their own kind. If you are proud and self-promoting or contentious and hypocritical, whatever you are is the kind of disciple you will produce. And that is also the example they will be to the third generation. May God keep us from the pronouncement Jesus made to the religious people of His day:

> Woe to you, scribes, and Pharisees, hypocrites! For you travel land and sea to win one proselyte, and when he is won, you make him twice as much a son of hell as yourselves.
> —MATTHEW 23:15, NKJV

This "imitative" aspect of discipleship was made very clear in Paul's letter to the young church in Thessalonica:

> You know how we lived among you for your sake. You became imitators of us and of the Lord…And so you became a model to all the believers in Macedonia and Achaia.
> —1 THESSALONIANS 1:5–7

Someone who has been well trained in this way is hard to miss, particularly in our rebellious, dysfunctional era. People who from an early age were taught manners, obedience and humility, and who were held accountable to achieve their highest potential, invariably stand out like roses on a thornbush. In the same way, there's a certain aura—the Bible refers to it as an "aroma"[12]—about Christians who have been properly discipled. After only a few minutes of talking to them, you can tell the difference.

## THE HIGH PRICE OF FAILURE

Few people naturally love discipline. Children particularly think that it would be wonderful if they could do what they want: live without boundaries or the pressures to conform to their parents' expectations. As the writer of Hebrews observed, "Now no chastening seems to be joyful for the present, but painful…"[13] People who were not chastened by loving discipline as they were growing up, however, are among the most dysfunctional, insecure, confused people on the planet. They bear stark testimony to the words the Holy Spirit recorded a few verses earlier in the same chapter of Hebrews:

> My son, do not make light of the Lord's discipline, and do

not lose heart when he rebukes you, because the Lord disciplines those he loves, and he punishes everyone he accepts as a son. Endure hardship as discipline; God is treating you as sons. For what son is not disciplined by his father? If you are not disciplined (and everyone undergoes discipline), then you are illegitimate children and not true sons.

—HEBREWS 12:5–8

Tragically, this spiritual illegitimacy is rampant in today's Church and is a primary indicator of the massive breakdown in our disciple-making responsibility. Local churches are filled with people who are not really accountable to anyone. For many it is a case of "cast[ing] off restraint" because there is no vision.[14] Either they or the leadership of the Church don't know—or don't want to know—about the necessity of discipleship. For others it's a case of pure rebellion; refusing to be corrected when confronted with behavior that is detrimental to themselves, their family or the Church.

Many conservative theologians have written about the marks of a true church. Discipline is always listed as one of the essential characteristics. There is perhaps no more stark example of how far we have fallen in this regard than the simple fact that, when confronted with this type of hardcore rebellion—unrepentant adultery, homosexuality, theft, etc.—only a small remnant of churches would even consider following the clear biblical pattern for confronting sin.[15] The only thing that would ever get you put out of most churches today… is daring to believe that there are some people who should be put out of the church!

## THE ENEMY WILL DO OUR JOB

Nature abhors a vacuum. As we have created a void in the area of making disciples, the enemy has come in like a flood. For instance, the fastest growing religious group in America is Mormonism.[16] Despite their heretical doctrine and the bogus claims of their founder, the Mormons have grown for one simple reason: They have proven very adept at making disciples to their particular worldview. Stephen Mansfield, a noted author who lectures on cults and world religions, has observed,

It is well known that, after seasons of spiritual excitement in protestant evangelical churches, cults and particularly the Mormons do their greatest proselytizing. This is because the Mormons have discovered that, after what some call revival, there are many "spiritually awakened" Christians who are left ungrounded in the truth, nor rooted in the things of God. This leaves them untethered and easy prey to cults willing to do what the evangelicals should have done in the first place: "make disciples."

## UNDERSTANDING DISCIPLESHIP

### Net building

We've looked at the analogous relationship between discipleship and the training of children. Matthew's Gospel (7:24ff) also likens it to laying the foundation of a building that will be tested by the storms of life. Another useful metaphor that is perhaps not as commonly understood is found in one of Jesus' maritime illustrations.

When Jesus called Simon Peter and Andrew to become His disciples, He told them that He would make them "fishers of men."[17] Later, He described the kingdom of God as being like a net that is cast into the sea, catching both the good fish and the bad.[18] Elsewhere, we are told that the means God uses to gather fish is the preaching of the Gospel. Significantly, the "fishermen" who do the preaching are those who have been sent, implying again both training and organization.

This "net" the fishers of men use consists of the lives of His people tied together and then drawn through the sea of humanity. It is His army of disciples working to fulfill the Apostolic Mandate

At our church in Nashville, we have addressed this need for an effective net through, among other things, our "Ministry Team" strategy. As I write this, there are approximately two hundred people on this team. Each has been trained to be as effective as any pastor at ministering spiritual "first aid," leading people to Christ and helping lay the basic foundations for discipleship. Most are also small group leaders, providing another natural forum for visitors to plug in relationally with the life of the church.

Among the most strategically important "joints" in the ministry team are what I call the "connectors."[19] These are people who know how to connect the right people together to either meet a need or help fulfill a calling. I am always searching for those who have this knack as well as working to develop this skill in others. Not everyone, of course, is a good connector. This is a trait I expect from every pastor and staff person, however. In the end, there are few things more satisfying than working with a team of people who know each other and the church so well that they have the skill to get people connected.

Typically, as I talk with people who have come down front at church or who I've met around town, I will say something like, "You need to meet so and so." Rather than trying to do all the long-term ministry myself, which in the end is impossible in any church over fifty people, there are others we've trained who can stand in the gap.

### Other "knots" in the "net"

Along with the ministry team, we have in place a number of other programs and materials that make up additional aspects of the "net." From the way we interact with guests after our Sunday services to an extensive small group network, every person is given not only a good understanding of what it means to be a Christian disciple, but also how this local church can best help them fulfill their destiny.

And let me say something here that may be a bit controversial. There's a tendency, I believe, in many of today's churches to demand far too little from our members. What orchestra would permit a musician to play who didn't practice or study the composition? Is there a soccer coach anywhere who would spend all his or her time helping a player who didn't want to train, study or show up for practice? Why is it harder to join and remain a member of the average Rotary Club than the Church of the Living God?

When Naaman came to Elisha and asked the prophet to perform a miracle and heal him of leprosy (throughout the Bible a symbol for sin and uncleanness), Elisha gave him something simple to do.[20] Naaman became offended. He expected some form of dramatic, personal, one-on-two ministry—Naaman on one side and Elisha and His God on the other. He left angry, grumbling about the quality of ministry he had received. Sound at all familiar?

So when I say that we expect people to go through the *Biblical Foundations* book and avail themselves of the other programs that comprise our local net, I mean just that. When someone comes to one of our pastors for help, one of the first questions they're asked is, "Are you in a small group? Have you been through the foundations class and the 'Purple Book'?"[21] If they're not willing to be faithful in the "little things" we have set in place for their growth, there is no scriptural reason to expect the big things to fall in place for them either.[22]

Of course, there is the occasional exception, the genuine emergency or the new believer who perhaps doesn't yet know better. But in the general scheme of things, we've seen that when people are faithful to work with us in laying the proper foundations in their lives, most, if not all, of their problems have a way of working themselves out.

On a related note, not only are disciples caught in the net we've fashioned as a Church, a lot of potential problems are screened out as well. By way of an analogy, I do a lot of flying, and ever since 9/11, that translates into a lot of security checks. More than once I've been checked by a guard that either goes to Bethel or knows the church and me by reputation. To have someone patting you down or running a security wand over your body while referring to you as "Pastor" and commenting on the Sunday sermon is a little surreal. But the first time it happened to me, I was reminded of the "security check" aspect of our net. By walking people through the "scanner" of God's Word, we are able to detect the hidden "bombs" that people carry around, sometimes without their even being aware of them. Whether it's a faulty foundation, an unresolved conflict or a compromised relationship, we are often able to screen them out on the front end and save the individual and the Church a lot of problems later.

Victory Leadership Institute (VLI), our two-year Bible college program, is another vital tool for every believer. Even people who may never be in full-time ministry or even lead a small group are finding that a good understanding of theology, apologetics, history and like subjects have enormous practical benefits in their day-to-day lives as they seek to walk more closely with God. Thousands of people are enrolling worldwide as VLI has opened new branches and gone online.

## THE LOST ART OF DISCIPLE MAKING

The LORD God has given Me the tongue of disciples, that I may know how to sustain the weary one with a word.
—ISAIAH 50:4, NASB

Making disciples isn't only a command; it's an art. Scattered throughout the Bible are principles that help make the entire process more winsome and effective.

### *The importance of destiny*

Jesus began the process of training His disciples by letting them in on the grand plans He had for their lives. "I'm going to make you fishers of men," He told some. "You will see heaven open," He informed others.[23] Over and over again, the Lord encouraged His disciples, sharing with them His vision for their lives, helping them catch glimpses of the heroic men He was going to help them become.

In the same way, looking someone in the eye and calling them into the greatness of their purpose in God is indispensable to the disciple-making process. Without this sense of destiny, few people will have the necessary faith and endurance to stand up before the inevitable trials that come to both test and promote their growth. Prophetic ministry in particular points to and calls forth this destiny, giving the believer a glimpse into their future calling in Christ. Paul specifically refers to these prophecies when he writes to encourage his son in the faith, Timothy:

> My son, I give you this instruction in keeping with the prophecies once made about you, so that by following them you may fight the good fight, holding on to faith and a good conscience. Some have rejected these and so have shipwrecked their faith.
>
> —1 TIMOTHY 1:18–19

He referred to the things that were prophesied over young Timothy as keys to helping him "fight the good fight." Of course, these "words" are always under the authority of *the* Word, the Bible. And their power is often contingent upon living clean before the Lord. But Paul understood that the destiny spoken over his disciple was a powerful tool in Timothy's struggle to reach his finish line.

I've received numerous prophecies throughout my walk with God that have helped me immeasurably. As a young believer, for example, I received a word to be "always ready to pack your bags, because I will use you around the world to evangelize and start churches." At the time, I hardly knew what an evangelist was but the sense of destiny contained in that prophecy had a big impact on me.

Everyone who comes to God carries within them certain sins, insecurities and tendencies that can lead to failure and even self-destruction. Ministry and discipleship can help root out these harmful forces. In the end, however, they have to be replaced with a sense of divine destiny and purpose.

Imagine the emotional anguish Saul of Tarsus must have experienced as he lay blind and alone after his confrontation with Jesus. *I've been persecuting Christ and His Church*, he must have realized. *I'm responsible for the martyrdom of Stephen!* The Lord sent Ananias to him, not only to heal his sight but also to encourage his soul, prophesying to him that he was a "chosen instrument" to bear God's name. Gideon was hiding out in fear of the Midianites when the angel of the Lord called him a "valiant warrior" and launched him into his calling. Jesus looked at Simon, whose name meant "a reed shaken in the wind," and renamed him Peter, "the rock." Without this sense of destiny, none of us will ever get very far. But when we have this vision of victory and do everything we can to cultivate it in others and in the atmosphere of the Church, faith and hope are the inevitable products. Faith can overcome the world, hope is an anchor for the soul—both are indispensable in producing disciples who can fulfill the call to the nations.

### An attitude of victory

> For whatever is born of God overcomes the world. And this is the victory that has overcome the world—our faith.
> —1 JOHN 5:4, NKJV

The Christian message must impart a spirit of faith and victory when it comes to overcoming the power of sin in a person's life. Deep down, everyone who is truly following the Lord wants to experience this freedom from the bondage of evil habits and sin. Though a person will not be perfect on this side of heaven, they can still see victory in a progressive manner in their lives. This one aspect may be the key difference between a young man or woman entering into their destiny or seeing it aborted or subverted. If you don't believe that victory is possible, then why try to resist temptation and struggle to overcome a besetting sin? If we really can't win over sin, then why should we be shocked at revelations of those who really "can't help what they're doing?"

Christ's death and resurrection broke the stranglehold that the enemy had held over man for centuries. "The law of the spirit of life in Christ Jesus has made [us] free from the law of sin and death."[24] In order to access this promise, a disciple must be taught, of course, to put on the full armor of God and pray at all times, all the while believing that victory is possible. This is so important because, *if you lose at something long enough, you'll quit.* This is why so many have given up following the Lord—because of hopelessness in this area. God wants to break the cycle of defeat and raise up a new generation of men and women who will "withstand in the evil day."[25]

### The power of a holy life

Of course, all this talk of victory is mere words if it is not backed up by real obedience and holiness. When Satan comes for each one of us as we square off on the battlefield of life, we must be sure—like the epic Hero who went before us—that he has no hold on us.[26] Paul made this very clear when talking about spiritual warfare, a primary responsibility of all disciples and a vital component for fulfilling the Apostolic Mandate:

> The weapons we fight with are not the weapons of the world. On the contrary, they have divine power to demolish strongholds.…And we will be ready to punish every act of disobedience, once your obedience is complete.
> —2 CORINTHIANS 10: 4, 6

In his letter to the church at Thessalonica, Paul gives a practical example of what this obedience looks like, focusing on the specific area of sexual purity:

> It is God's will that you should be sanctified: that you should avoid sexual immorality; that each of you should learn to control his own body in a way that is holy and honorable, not in passionate lust like the heathen, who do not know God; and that in this matter no one should wrong his brother or take advantage of him. The Lord will punish men for all such sins, as we have already told you and warned you. For God did not call us to be impure, but to live a holy life.
> —1 THESSALONIANS 4:3–7

Note the phrase, "learn how to control your body in a way that is holy and honorable." This means being above reproach in your relationships, treating the opposite sex with purity and never defrauding one another. These words are *non-negotiable*. Paul seems to anticipate the stir that such a standard would produce (and not just in Thessalonica!) so he immediately follows these injunctions with the warning, "He who rejects this is not rejecting man, but the God who gives His Holy Spirit to you."[27]

Few things are more conducive to training true disciples than an atmosphere of holiness and obedience. Conversely, few things are more apt to abort the birthing of leaders than sin, particularly when it's of a sexual nature. (As we will see in the next chapter, the majority of potential disciples and leaders will come from the younger generation. Many will be single. The seeds of emotional and sexual idolatry can germinate quickly and become thorns that "choke out the Word" and cause potential disciples to become unfruitful.) On the other hand, as we teach people what the Scripture says about this vital area, the "word of His grace"[28] will produce an internal change in the hearts of people and a passion for holiness. As Paul wrote to Titus:

> For the grace of God that brings salvation has appeared to all men. It teaches us to say "No" to ungodliness and worldly passions, and to live self-controlled, upright and godly lives in this present age...a people that are his very own, eager to do what is good. These, then, are the things you should teach. Encourage and rebuke with all authority. Do not let anyone despise you.
> —TITUS 2:11–15

Now that's a disciple...and the path by which we will help make them great.

### Spiritual multiplication

Jesus discipled twelve men and commissioned them to go into the entire world, disciple nations and teach them everything He had taught them. As the apostle Paul took his place on the front lines of this mandate, he found several men he could train to take his place. Paul understood the principle of multiplication: reproducing after your kind.

One of his primary disciples was a young man who had been raised by a Christian mother and grandmother. In his last letter to him, Paul passed on his primary key for multiplication: "[Timothy] the things you have heard me say in the presence of many witnesses entrust to reliable men who will also be qualified to teach others."[29] The apostle made reference to four generations of disciples: himself, Timothy, faithful men and the others whom they would then teach. Note also that discipleship involves two things: learning and then teaching what you have learned to others.

When all these cylinders are firing properly, true discipleship happens and the kingdom of God naturally advances.

### *The goal of discipleship is maturity*

Our objective in all this is to see disciples grounded in the faith, building on strong biblical foundations, living lives of holiness and obedience, and actively working to reproduce the life of Christ in others. As we watch them mature, there comes a point when they need to step out on their own and begin the cycle of discipleship and multiplication afresh. The goal of leadership, in other words, is not to raise up people who are overly dependent on you. We are to set them on the road to maturity so that they can stand on their own and help others get to that same place of strength.

It grieves the Holy Spirit when we are clingy or possessive of those whom we have discipled or with those who have discipled us. We should not find our identity in proclaiming, "I am of Paul," or "I am of Apollos."[30] Neither should anyone assert that, "These are MY disciples (and don't anyone forget it)." We are, foremost of all, disciples of Jesus Christ. Pastors and disciplers are stewards to whom God has entrusted the care of His children.

### *Relationships change as disciples mature in Christ*

On a related note, it is quite common for relationships to evolve during the process of discipleship. Initially, for example, it is probably best for one person to be responsible for mentoring a new believer. But as both continue to mature, that relationship can and normally should change to one of mutual accountability.

In the church where I was first discipled, after graduating beyond the foundational stages, people naturally came to a place where they began to encourage and disciple one another. If one stumbled or strayed from their commitment to Christ, everyone in the smaller accountability group shared the burden to help see that person built up and restored.

One of the most powerful atmospheres for spiritual growth is a fellowship of brothers and sisters in Christ, filled with faith and vision, who will speak the truth to one another in love. Paul encouraged the church at Ephesus in this very thing. "Instead, speaking the truth in love, we will in all things grow up into him who is the Head, that is, Christ. From him the whole body, joined and held together by every supporting ligament, grows and builds itself up in love, as each part does its work."[31]

Christian brothers and sisters should serve as mirrors to help us better see ourselves. They help us "grow up in all the aspects" of our lives, particularly in those areas where we are blind. "Lone Ranger" Christians, or those who just haven't been given the opportunity to build strong relationships, invariably don't grow much beyond the limits set by their blind spots.

In the end, even as mentoring relationships mature and evolve, there will always be those we remember and honor. Paul wrote, "For though you might have ten thousand instructors in Christ, yet you do not have many fathers."[32] Though there is no longer a dependent relationship, I will never forget those whom I consider to be spiritual fathers. Cultivating and protecting this sense of long-term loyalty is critical to turning a congregation of Christians into a true spiritual family. Successful discipleship depends upon it.

## PRESERVING THIS VITAL TRUTH

It seems that every powerful truth of Scripture has somehow been subject to the abuse of either neglect or extremism. Either the truth is ignored, and thus the powerful benefits intended to bless God's people are lost, or they are taken to such an absurd extreme so as to cause them to be seen as dangerous. Such has been the case in the areas of faith, spiritual gifts and financial prosperity, among many other valid doctrines and principles. So also has it been in the area of discipleship. A generation ago, this truth was emphasized and taken to the extreme that somehow gave men the total responsibility over others and placed the burden of transforming people out of the hands of God and into the hands of men. While discipleship necessarily involves men and women helping and training others, it doesn't mean that the process is the total responsibility of men to perfect other men in Christ. In the end, it is "God who works in you to will and to act according to his good purpose."[33] We are to preach, teach, pray, correct, train and encourage others, while at the same time not crossing the line of making someone obey God and do as we think they should.

This is a delicate balance to keep, for we are to be active in the process of disciple making. However, we must always remember the boundaries we have in ministering to others. These boundaries are primarily in the areas of decision-making and matters of conscience. After we share the Word with others, it is up to them to decide whether or not to obey. It is also important to distinguish between those things that are biblical commands and those that are areas of conscience. For instance, the Bible commands us to be holy and set apart as a Christian. If in discipling someone you find they are clearly involved in sinful behavior—i.e. adultery, fornication or homosexuality—you must speak authoritatively on the issue. They must stop this behavior immediately and seek God's deliverance and forgiveness through genuine repentance.

On the other hand, there are areas of conscience on which we can certainly share our opinion and yet be clear that a person must seek the Lord, read the Bible and make up his or her own mind. An example would be the type of music someone listens to. I've seen people who won't listen to "Jingle Bells" because someone told them it wasn't a "Christian song." As much as I want to make others aware of what God's Word commands them to do, I am constantly reinforcing the importance of each person grasping truth internally and not merely looking for an external rule to follow. We can recover this vital truth of discipleship if it is handled correctly and wisely. We must be secure, and extremely patient, when our counsel is not heeded. Above all, remember that if you are helping to disciple someone, you are not his or her pastor or spiritual authority. That position or office is held by those who have been proven and are set apart to oversee the Church.

## DISCIPLESHIP—THE ANSWER TO THE LEADERSHIP CRISIS

Everywhere we look today, we find a crisis in leadership. Warren Bennis, founder of the Leadership Institute at the University of Southern California, points out how serious this crisis really is.

> Humanity currently faces three extraordinary threats: the threat of annihilation as a result of nuclear accident or war, the threat of a worldwide plague or ecological catastrophe, and a deepening leadership crisis in most of our institutions. Unlike the possibility of plague or nuclear holocaust, the leadership crisis will probably not become the basis for a best-seller or a blockbuster movie, but in many ways it is the most urgent and dangerous of the threats we face today, if only because it is insufficiently recognized and little understood.[34]

Where are the Churchills and the Spurgeons of the twenty-first century? Instead of Whitefields and Wesleys, we find fifteen hundred pastors leaving the ministry each month due to moral failure, spiritual burnout or contention in their churches. The divorce rate among the clergy hovers around 50 percent, one of the highest of any profession. Approximately four thousand new churches will be planted this year in America, but seven thousand will close—largely due to a lack of leadership. What's going on here?

The answer is simple: We have short-circuited the process God ordained to create leaders. That process, of course, is *discipleship*.

### Leaders come from disciples

Jesus came not only to die for the sins of the world, but to win, train and love a family of individuals drawn from every nation and tongue under heaven. His strategy to accomplish the second part of His divine plan? He chose twelve disciples, trained them to be His apostles and sent them out to do the same. This is the Apostolic Mandate, as well as "the master plan of evangelism." There is no "Plan B," no shortcut or better idea waiting to be discovered. He will have a Bride, a glorious Church without spot or wrinkle, and it will be built one disciple at a time.

Laboring for years, pouring your life into people who may or may not prove to be great leaders, requires a lot of commitment and persistence. You not only have to trust God to raise up leaders, you also have to have faith in the process of discipleship.

Making discipleship and leadership training a top priority is a long-term investment strategy that can at times seem boring compared to the large crowds and revival meetings that many believe are the mark of a successful ministry. But ministries that attempt to add to the Church only by big events, find themselves constantly looking for leaders, advertising for leaders, going out to recruit leaders— because rarely do they raise up leaders. In the end, the inheritance quickly gained rarely prospers.[35] Investing your time, money and effort in the Apostolic Mandate, however, yields compound returns that continue to increase indefinitely.

Those who commit themselves to the Lord's strategy will win the world, not by addition, but by multiplication.

### Leaders are trained in battle

Alexander, son of Philip of Macedonia, didn't receive the title "The Great" simply because he was a great orator or politician. It wasn't granted him by his tutor, Aristotle, because he did so well in his studies. He became "The Great" on the field of battle, eventually conquering most of the known world. His warfare was fought with the "arm of flesh"; ours is fought with the power of the Spirit, but a life and death battle it remains. It's on this battlefield where true leaders often rise to the surface.

This in no way minimizes the critical training that takes place in the classroom. I've already shared with you the impact seminary had on me. I also believe in the importance of our Bible College, Victory Leadership Institute. But underlying all this is the understanding that what goes into your head in the classroom isn't really "there" until it's put into practice in your life. In a sense, it's like sticking a leadership program into your computer's CD-ROM drive. All the information is there and accessible, but the application won't work until you install the program. That installation takes place when knowledge becomes applied in real-life ministry.

Jesus spent a great deal of time training the twelve, but He also sent them out periodically to exercise what they had learned. In the same way, Morning Star tries to create as many missions and ministry opportunities as we can, particularly for high school and college students. It's not uncommon for parents to schedule vacations around their students' mission opportunities. (A word to students about this: If you haven't figured this out yet, I will let you in on something: In the years to come, the odds are that your life is going to get far more complicated and inflexible than it is now. With the responsibilities of job, family, church and community, it requires a supreme effort to get away for even a week-long mission project. The opportunity to serve Christ on the mission field will never be easier than it is now. Devoting a summer, a spring break or even an entire semester to missions not only does a lot for the world and the spread of the Gospel, but there is also nothing better you can do to mature spiritually. In many cases, it's while you're on the mission field that you'll discover your leadership and ministry gifts. "Be all you can be"—serve the Lord on the mission field while you still can.)

### Leaders learn by serving other leaders

Joshua served Moses and later led the children of Israel into the Promised Land. Elisha served Elijah and received a double-portion of his anointing. Timothy served Paul and became his delegated authority to the churches in Thessalonica, Corinth, Philippi and

Ephesus. After deserting Paul and Barnabas on their first missionary journey, John Mark got a second chance and became the servant of Peter. He went on to write down Peter's recollections of Jesus (the Gospel of Mark) and later became the bishop of the church in Alexandria. Peter recommended to young leaders that they have in themselves the same attitude that John Mark displayed:

> Likewise you younger people, submit yourselves to your elders. Yes, all of you be submissive to one another, and be clothed with humility, for "God resists the proud, But gives grace to the humble." Therefore humble yourselves under the mighty hand of God, that He may exalt you in due time, casting all your care upon Him, for He cares for you.
> —1 PETER 5:5–7, NKJV

We hear portions of that passage frequently quoted, particularly the part about "casting all your anxiety upon Him, because He cares for you." While it's a great verse to claim, most people never think about its context. Peter is writing to young men who are wrestling with the issue of rank. "When am I going to be raised up? When are they going to lay hands on me? When am I going to be sent out? When am I going to be recognized as being one of the leaders?" Peter's advice was to calm down, don't be in a hurry and, most of all, don't get proud. Humble yourself, serve those in leadership, and God Himself will raise you up at the proper time.

By serving the leaders in our church, we ourselves end up being blessed. First, we're given the opportunity to learn, to draw from the deposit of grace and wisdom that God has placed in that leader's life. Secondly, the place of service is an important one as far as God working sovereignly and deeply in our lives. He who will be great in His kingdom must first learn to be a servant of all. And third, we are making a spiritual investment that will be repaid to us many times over throughout the course of our lives. This is the principle of reciprocity that is revealed throughout the Scriptures: Give and it shall be given, forgive and you shall be forgiven, judge and by the same measure you will be judged.

No one can effectively lead if people aren't willing to follow him or her with a right attitude. The way you serve your leaders today will determine the manner in which the people you lead will serve and follow you. God will see to it.

### Leaders are coached

There are a lot of people in this world who have been blessed with great ability, but who will never see their full potential realized because they are either uncoached or uncoachable. That is one of the fundamental differences, for example, between guys who dominate on a city basketball court and those who play in the NBA.

Most professional athletes who are determined to compete at the highest level hire their own personal coach. Who knows better than Lance Armstrong how to attack a mountain run on the third day of the Tour de France? Or better than Ronaldo how to execute a free kick? Well, almost no one. But the reason they've become the very best at what they do is because they've realized that no matter how good they become, they can't coach themselves.

The job of a coach involves a lot more than passing on information and patting their players on the back. The best ones are those who can see what needs to be improved and then provide the necessary correction. A good coach also won't let you forget or gloss over the fundamentals. Human nature tends always to want to take the path of least resistance. If there's no one to hold you accountable, most people are unlikely to deal with the hard issues. And a good coach is never satisfied with anything less than your very best. Good coaches will continue to challenge you to reach a higher level and will refuse to allow you to accept anything less.

Some people don't take coaching well because they can't handle correction and confrontation. Whether it is because of rebellion or insecurity, they're easily wounded or offended. Some even remind me of hostages with hair-trigger bombs strapped to their chests. Try to help them get free and you can get blown up in the process.

Effective leadership training, like coaching, is a combination of two fundamental things: Potential leaders who have a teachable spirit and teachers who know how to confront and correct in a way that lifts their students to a higher level.

### Leaders are found in clusters

For reasons known only by God, leaders are often found in clusters around a particular event or person. The 1946 graduating class from the Harvard School of Business produced an unusually high percentage of today's CEOs. From what was essentially a small group meeting at Oxford University in the 1730s came the greatest hymn writer the Church has ever known (Charles Wesley); an evangelist who brought the fires of revival to two continents and literally saved England from social collapse and revolution (John Wesley); the leader of the Great Awakening in America (George Whitefield); the founding governor of Georgia (James Oglethorpe) and several other great men of God. In the same way, John Witherspoon's tenure as the president of Princeton in the late eighteenth century produced an extraordinary number of notable statesmen: twenty-one senators, thirty-nine representatives, twelve governors, three Supreme Court justices, one vice-president and a president.

Though not as dramatic, we've seen that same phenomenon of leadership clusters coming from our ministries worldwide. When trends like these are noted—when the "Geiger counter of the Spirit" begins to really tick—we should take extra care to "mine" that area well.

### Leaders can be women

This may be obvious to some, but it still remains an area of uncertainty for many. It must be underscored that all that is being said about making disciples and training leaders applies to women as well as men. God certainly calls women into the ministry as well as leadership. He has promised to pour out His Spirit on His *daughters* as well as His sons in the last days.[36]

Women are filling vital roles as leaders in every walk of life. They are certainly filling crucial roles in the Church as well. The notion that God only uses men in ministry has slowly been torn down in this past generation, but there still remains for many women an invisible barrier that seems to block their destiny. Our prayer is that what remains of these hindrances will be removed and women in every nation will enter in to their high calling in Christ. This must happen for the Apostolic Mandate to be fulfilled.

### Leaders are instructed in the classroom

In listing the qualifications for a leader, the apostle Paul primarily emphasized character, but also noted the vital importance of knowledge and biblical understanding. Paul wrote to Titus that a leader is responsible for:

> …holding fast the faithful word as he has been taught, that he may be able, by sound doctrine, both to exhort and convict those who contradict.
>
> —TITUS 1:9, NKJV

The centrality of biblical training—especially as it relates to the rigors of discipleship—was also emphasized in Paul's letter to his young disciple Timothy. Note the many references to hard work, discipline, correction and the goal of producing a mature leader:

> Be diligent to present yourself approved to God, a worker who does not need to be ashamed, rightly dividing the word of truth…All Scripture is given by inspiration of God, and is profitable for doctrine, for reproof, for correction, for instruction in righteousness, that the man of God may be complete, thoroughly equipped for every good work.
> —2 TIMOTHY 2:15; 3:16–17, NKJV

In fulfillment of these and other passages, we have spent years developing and fine-tuning the curriculum for our international Bible school, Victory Leadership Institute. This two-year program is designed to give everyone, whether they are full-time students, business people, housewives or potential church planters, a chance to be trained in a systematic way. While we maintain that the classroom is no substitute for hands-on, real-life training, it is an indispensable supplement to the discipleship process.

### Leaders recognize the gift of leadership

There are a number of gifts God has granted the Church to fulfill its mission. Among them is the grace of leadership.

> Having then gifts differing according to the grace that is given to us, let us use them…he who leads,…[let him do it] with diligence.
> —ROMANS 12:6–8, NKJV

Of all the gifts listed in this passage in Romans, there is probably none that has fallen on harder times than that of leadership. This failure has even gotten analysts like George Barna wondering if we can pull out of our present descent into cultural irrelevance. He gave up on a program to help church leaders revitalize their churches when he realized something very disconcerting:

> My strategy was flawed because it had an assumption. The assumption was that the people in leadership are actually leaders… Most [aren't]…They're great people, but they're not really leaders.[37]

I believe this crisis in leadership has been caused in large part by the lack of vision for the Apostolic Mandate. Why should God provide the grace of leadership when we aren't really that interested in accomplishing the task for which the grace is given?

Another related problem is the way leadership is defined in the Church. And here we have another instance where "the children of this world are wiser" than the Church: "secular" organizations tend to be much better at evaluating the mix of motivational gifts and temperaments that define a successful leader. For the most part we have equated the ability to preach and teach with spiritual and organizational leadership. But think about it. Can you imagine a multi-million-dollar corporation hiring a CEO primarily on the basis of his speaking ability?

In his book, *The Seven Habits of Highly Effective Churches,* Barna drives this point home by addressing the difference between the various ministry gifts and true God-inspired leadership. Surveying pastors, he found that, of those who identified themselves as preachers and teachers, only one in twenty also described themselves as being gifted as a leader. What an astounding statistic! That is precisely why most of us are far more accustomed to hearing the Word than we are to putting it into action.

In order for us to fulfill our mandate as a Church, we need to work both harder and smarter. We can't be so naïve as to think that if a person has one ministry gift they necessarily have another. Just because the Spirit, for example, uses a person to perform extraordinary miracles, doesn't mean they can accurately divide the word of truth as a teacher. In fact, many times the opposite is true. And just because a person can preach, teach or evangelize, doesn't mean he can be an effective senior leader of a growing church.

The call to leadership can at times be hard to spot. From Moses to David, Gideon to Joseph, the Bible is replete with leaders who at first seemed unlikely candidates for the responsibility to lead. The Lord looks at the heart; we need to learn to do the same.

In our college days at Mississippi State University, everyone recognized Steve Murrell as a great disciple. He had a lot of character, was a great servant and was very disciplined in his devotional life. But he was soft-spoken and laid back compared to some of the rest of us. None of us at the time ever dreamed that he possessed some of the best leadership skills of anyone in our ministry. A quarter century and a nation later, well, now we can see what God saw all along.

There are a lot of potential Steve Murrells scattered throughout the body of Christ or in the harvest field just waiting to be brought in. One of the keys to leadership training is recognizing them when we see them. Speaking of potential leaders, Jim Collins, co-author of the best-seller *Good to Great* states: "They exist all around us if we just know what to look for. And what is that? Look for situations where extraordinary results exist but where no individual steps forward to take claim for the excess credit. You will likely find a potential [great] leader at work."[38] That's one of the reasons why we try to organize as many short-term ministry opportunities as possible. Leaders tend to be revealed when the heat is on.

## CONCLUSION

While certainly no magic formula, these principles are the heart and soul of our passion for developing godly leaders in every sphere of life. And while we fix our eyes on the prize—a new generation of leaders to whom we can pass the baton of the Apostolic Mandate— we must also remember that finding and training leaders is a process. We must resist the temptation to take shortcuts or to ordain leaders too quickly.[39] As much as we want to reach the world for Christ, we must not yield to the pressure of putting people in leadership before they are ready.

As we are patient and work alongside the Lord in raising up men and women His way, inevitably a great harvest of leaders will emerge. They won't be shooting stars, either. Their position will be sure as they shine as lights in the midst of the darkness they are seeking to dispel.

In the next chapter we'll see where many of these stars are likely to come from. We will examine the greatest harvest field the world has ever seen: the youth of the nations.

# CHAPTER 6

# THE GREATEST
# HARVEST FIELD

*And the first step as you know is always what matters
most, particularly when we are dealing with those
who are young and tender. That is the time when they
are easily molded and when any impression we choose
to make leaves a permanent mark.*

—PLATO

*Give me four years to teach the children, and the seed
I have sown will never be uprooted.*

—LENIN

W hat would you say if given a chance to address an audience
of over one million people? A crowd that size is something
most evangelists can only dream about. But in 1984 that
dream became a reality for me. At the 100th anniversary of Protestant
Christianity in Korea, I was asked to share a brief message following
the keynote address by the pastor of one of the world's largest
churches. From the stage, I saw what appeared to be a sea of
humanity—a million people quietly listening to the testimony of the
incredible things God had done in South Korea.

As the minister before me was finishing his message, a wave of
humility mixed with apprehension rolled over me. Only five years

earlier I had been sitting in my dorm listening to tapes, studying my Bible, trying to learn how to preach like the great men of God who were now with me on the platform. Since then I had begun to minister on college campuses, often before crowds of less than a hundred people. As I looked out at this vast crowd, I remembered the time at Arizona State University when only one visitor had come to hear me speak. The apprehension waned as I sensed the Lord speak to my heart, "You were faithful with that one, now look what I have set before you."

South Korea was in the midst of one of the greatest revivals in the history of Christianity. In one hundred years, it had been transformed from a nation that was almost universally Buddhist to a country where one-fourth of the population now looked to Jesus as Lord and Savior. And what a faith it was! The Korean saints were among the most dedicated intercessors in the world, praying with a fervency and commitment that put the "Christian" West to shame. What can you say to a nation that has so much from which we can learn?

And yet, I knew there was something God had put on my heart to share with them, something they did need to hear. With all the explosive growth of the Christian faith, there was one segment of the population that was going largely unreached. All over the nation, South Korea's universities were experiencing unrest.

I had spent time on those campuses and found the Christian voice and influence so muted that it was hard to discern if there were any believers there at all. And the absence of "salt and light" was evidenced in the overall spiritual atmosphere. You could almost feel that hell was getting ready to break loose.

As we will discuss in a moment, the forces of darkness do have a way of first gaining a foothold on the campus and then metastasizing throughout the society at large. America and much of the world saw this plainly in the free love, free-speech movement that sprang up on the university campuses during the anarchic days of the early 1960s. Whether we're talking about communism or abortion rights, the college campus has been a primary engine for social change. What's taught and embraced at the university level typically becomes mainstream—either through enculturation or by law—within a decade or two.

Understanding this and what it bode for Korea as a nation, a calm resolve came over me as I walked to the podium. I only had a few moments, so my message needed to be short and direct; every word had to count. *What has happened in Korea has shaken the world. Yes, this has been one of the greatest revivals in Church history. But if you don't reach the campuses and the youth of this nation, this revival will be over in one generation."*

The crowd roared as if to say, "We know you're right." Amid all the praise and testimony concerning the good things that God had done, many realized that, if their children were lost, everything they had seen and experienced was for naught.

There is an important lesson in all this. True and lasting revival enfolds the generations and brings heaven to earth, transforming the culture, not just the Church.

> That your days and the days of your children may be mul-
> tiplied in the land of which the LORD swore to your fathers
> to give them, like the days of the heavens above the earth.
> —DEUTERONOMY 11:21, NKJV

In evaluating the impact of spiritual movements and "times of refreshing" worldwide, these are some of the key questions we need to be asking: Are young people being reached? Are the fires of holiness burning in their souls? Are they being equipped to take the Gospel of the kingdom to the next generation?

It's almost as if the enemy is saying, "I'll concede everything except my real treasures—the youth of the world." Where there are no young people, there can be no lasting change.

## THE 13/30 WINDOW

Missiologists have coined the term "the 10/40 Window" to describe the latitudinal boundaries wherein lie the majority of the world's unreached peoples. Most Hindus, Buddhists and Muslims are located in this geographical area. Several years ago, Steve Murrell developed a similar term to circumscribe the borders of another people group that lie within the Church's reach, but for the most part remains unevangelized. The tragic irony of this failure is that there is no other group more open to the Gospel or that is of more strategic importance to the future of both the Church and the nations. Steve calls it the "13/30 Window"—a designation that's not geographic but demographic. It defines the age group of people between thirteen and thirty and, as we're about to see, outlines the greatest harvest field for the Church today.

Consider just two key facts:

◆   Six out of ten people on this planet are under the age of twenty-five, a percentage that is increasing every day. Of that number, nearly half are in the middle school to college age group.

◆   Ninety percent of all professing Christians come to Christ before reaching thirty; seventy-five percent before the age of twenty-five.

With this in mind, you don't have to be a prophet to know that the youth culture represents the Church's greatest potential mission field. And yet, and here we have a question we need to take very seriously, *How many churches do you know that spend 75 percent of their energy and resources on reaching out to and training youth?*

The truth is, this particular field is even more ripe for harvest than these numbers indicate. There are also many emotional and spiritual dynamics going on within youth culture, particularly in the so-called "first-world" nations, that make the Gospel even more relevant and powerful.

Take, for example, some of the fallout from the cultural explosion that was touched off in the sixties. The "children of freedom" that embraced the sexual revolution and the "question authority/follow your heart ethic" of that era, ended up creating a spiritual and psychological war zone for their children and grandchildren. The result? A new generation of high school and college students who, though not always aware of it, are hungrier for God than any generation in recent memory. Historian Michael Hamilton spoke of the neediness that drives this hunger:

> But now the cultural chickens have come home to roost. Too many of the children of freedom are having trouble coping with freedom. They are emotionally fragile, their idea of family is impoverished, they don't trust social institutions (like colleges), they are adrift in moral relativism, they are highly materialistic, and deep down they are not very hopeful that things are going to get better.[1]

Hamilton concludes by quoting *Life After God*, a novel by popular writer and cultural pulse-taker, Douglas Coupland, who coined the phrase "Generation X":

> My secret is that I need God. I am sick and can no longer
> make it alone. I need God to help me give, because I no
> longer seem to be capable of giving; to help me be kind, as
> I no longer seem capable of kindness; to help me love, as I
> seem beyond being able to love.[2]

What an opportunity for the Gospel! Perhaps at no other time in human history have there been more people in a more strategic place wrestling with the very issues that Christians are uniquely qualified to address. And never has there been a greater battle for the life and destiny of that generation. Abortion, relativism, humanistic education, divorce, sexually transmitted diseases, the barrage of "earthy, sensual, demonic"[3] ideas and images that course through the floodgates of popular media—there is almost no end to the satanic arrows that have been flung at the world's youth.

## THE ENEMY HAS TARGETED YOUTH

While we in many ways have ignored the 13/30 window as a harvest field, the enemy hasn't. There has been a concerted attempt to destroy the post-Boomer generation. That by itself should have clued in the Church on what is really going on in the invisible realm of the spirit. In the Bible, whenever God sends a deliverer, all hell breaks out. When the Lord was about to fashion Moses in his mother's womb for the purpose of delivering the Jews in Egypt, Satan inspired Pharaoh to order the execution of all the male Hebrew babies.[4] When the ultimate Deliverer was sent fifteen hundred years later, King Herod did the same in the town where the Messiah was to be born.[5]

On the day of Pentecost, it was announced that God would pour out His Spirit and His "sons and daughters will prophesy,"[6] a sign that this deliverance would come through this group of people. The last century alone, called the "Century of the Holy Spirit" (the Welsh Revival, Azusa Street, the Student Volunteer Movement, the Jesus Movement, etc.), was also the bloodiest century in history (the World Wars and the Jewish Holocaust, the Cambodian killing fields, the Rwandan genocides, etc.). And whose blood was spilled? Primarily the youth who fought the wars and died by the millions. The next stage of deliverance was aborted, held in trust for another generation.

This war that is being waged now against the youth of the world represents, I believe, the enemy's concerted effort to destroy the new generation upon which this sacred trust has fallen. It's critical that the Church recognize the nature of this present struggle...as well as what's at stake.

Jesus came as "a root out of dry ground."[7] The dry ground all around us today, particularly on the high school and college campuses, shouldn't be a source for doubt and skepticism. Instead, seen through the eyes of faith, it can be transformed into a sign that God is preparing a great work. Satan has targeted this generation because he knows a deliverer is about to emerge. The dry ground is about to flourish. But it's going to take a church that is committed to pray, work and fight hard to see this new harvest come forth.

> He who goes out weeping, carrying seed to sow, will return with songs of joy, carrying sheaves with him.
>
> —PSALM 126:6

## GOD'S CALL ON THE YOUTH

God's plan has always had young people at the forefront. Not only have they fought the wars of history, but they will also fight the spiritual battles that will ultimately decide the fate of nations. When God sent Israel to possess the Promised Land, with the exception of Joshua and Caleb,[8] He used virtually an army of teenagers.[9]

God called a young Jeremiah to bring His Word to a nation reeling under the final stages of apostasy. Israel at the time was steeped in rebellion and the religious pride that makes such rebellion possible. The dream that the older men were dreaming, in other words, had turned into a nightmare. And who did God send to wake them up? A person so young that he felt unqualified. To which the Lord replied, "Do not say, 'I am a youth,' For you shall go to all to whom I send you, And whatever I command you, you shall speak."[10]

Paul trained Timothy as an apostle and bequeathed to him his place of authority in the churches he had planted. With all the winds of false teaching and division that threatened the young churches, the Lord again needed a prophetic leader to lead His people. And once again, His choice was a young man. Echoing God's words to Jeremiah, Paul charged his disciple, "Don't let anyone look down on you because you are young."[11] To Titus, another young apprentice whom he left behind to minister in Crete, a rough and tumble port city, Paul exhorted, "These, then, are the things you should teach. Encourage and rebuke with all authority. Do not let anyone despise you."[12]

To again paraphrase the language of Hebrews 11, "And what more shall I say? For the time would fail me to tell of Gideon, Esther, Joseph, David, Daniel, Hannaniah, Mishael and Azariah (more commonly known by their Babylonian names, Shadrach, Meshach and Abed-Nego), Miriam, Jael, Josiah, Samuel, Mary, and at least several of the disciples—all young people that the Father anointed and sent to accomplish some of the greatest works in the Bible." Even at Jesus' resurrection, who was in the burial chamber to announce the Lord's resurrection? "A young man dressed in a white robe sitting on the right side."[13] Even when God sent an angel, it was one who looked young! The same trend has continued throughout Church history. Even as the Scripture promised:

> Your people shall be volunteers in the day of Your power;
> In the beauties of holiness, from the womb of the morning, You have the dew of Your youth.
> —PSALM 110:3, NKJV

Just a few of the countless highlights:

◆  William Booth, founder of the Salvation Army, started preaching in the slums of London at the age of fifteen.

◆  Charles Spurgeon, arguably the greatest preacher of the nineteenth century, started ministering at nineteen. He attracted such large crowds that before he was thirty he had built and was packing out the five-thousand-seat Metropolitan Tabernacle in London.

◆  Jonathan Edwards entered Yale in 1716 at the age of thirteen, and by the age of twenty-one was pastoring one of the most important churches in the American colonies. His sermon, "Sinners in the Hands of an Angry God," helped spark the Great Awakening that brought tens of thousands to a living faith in Christ.

◆  Amy Carmichael was twenty-eight when she left as a missionary for Dohnavur, India. She served for fifty-six years without a furlough in one of the most dangerous and spiritually oppressive areas of the world.

◆ David Brainerd became a missionary to the American Indians at the age of twenty-four. In the five years before he died, he bore a lifetime worth of fruit. His diary later became a classic of devotional literature.

◆ In 1844, George Williams, a twenty-three-year-old businessman, started the Young Men's Christian Association (YMCA) as an evangelistic outreach to businessmen.

◆ John Wesley was twenty-six when he started his Holy Club at Oxford, sparking a revival on the campus that later spread throughout England and America.

◆ George Whitefield was twenty when he became a member of Wesley's Holy Club. In 1739, at the age of twenty-five, he set out on his first mission trip to America where he preached to crowds as large as thirty thousand.

◆ Phillis Wheatley wrote a poem commemorating George Whitefield in 1770 that brought her international fame and launched a literary career honored to this day in American literature. This gifted lady was African-American, a slave and only seventeen when she wrote the words that brought her to the world's attention.

Each of these tremendous young people validates the apostle John's salutation: "I write to you, young men, because you are strong, and the word of God lives in you, and you have overcome the evil one."[14] The glory of the young truly is their strength.[15]

And yet what glory, what strength are we believing God for and cultivating in our youth *now*? Very few churches and ministries are "lifting up their eyes"—they're not seeing the magnitude of the harvest field and the strategic importance of reaching youth. They're not spending the time, money and effort commensurate with the call. And then what outreach to the youth culture they do have often makes far too many concessions to the spirit of the age. It is as if the best we can hope for is that our kids will "just say no" to drugs and premarital sex or turn in their Korn CD for some "sanctified" equivalent.

With encouragement and help, most young people will rise to the level of what's expected of them. When the Church takes a defensive posture and just tries to keep the "barbarians at the gates," that's about the best you can hope to get. But if you challenge and train the youth to change the world, to go out and evangelize and disciple the barbarians, it can happen. Just ask Jacob Aranza.

## THE BEST DEFENSE IS A GOOD OFFENSE

In the spring of 1978, a pastor driving by a junior high in Houston, Texas, felt a strong compulsion to stop. For some time he had been burdened for the school. Drugs, violence, even prostitution were rampant. After meeting with the principal, he was able to persuade him to schedule a time when he could address the school assembly.

When the man of God spoke, the Lord shook the school. In the coming days, over one thousand young people were converted. At one point, the minister collected a garbage bag full of drugs from the newly saved and brought them to the principal's office. The principal committed his life to Christ as a result.

Jacob Aranza was one of the young people touched during this revival. Born in a ghetto of Houston, Jacob had essentially grown up in a nightclub, surrounded by every temptation imaginable. But the commitment he made to Christ was a lasting one because he was properly mentored. The result? Jacob became a world changer. He took the baton from his spiritual father and began to speak in schools. Today he has ministered to over five million teenagers around the world.

The cycle doesn't stop there either. Jacob was able to mentor a young, multi-talented athlete by the name of Kevin Singleton. Kevin, in turn, has ministered to millions of other students. Together they helped birth Victory Clubs, a worldwide ministry to teens. Though not overtly Christian in certain nations for legal reasons, these clubs meet right on campus, helping young people to make a stand for righteousness.

That's a start. But we've got a long way to go.

## WHY CAN'T THE CHURCH SEE
## WHAT MTV SEES?

One of the greatest forces on the planet in relation to young people is Viacom's MTV Network. There is at present probably no greater global force in mobilizing and shaping youth—their values, beliefs and actions—than this media juggernaut. The network reaches over one billion young people around the world and has become, as host John Norris said, "…a sanctuary for teens akin to church and family." Speaking of events like the suicide of Kurt Cobain, Norris explained, "When things like that happen to people of this generation, MTV, really more than any other source, is where they turn."[16]

No matter where you go in the world, MTV is there—usually far ahead of the Church—working to capture the hearts and minds of their young audience. Why can't God's people see this pattern and at least attempt a response? What does MTV know that the Church should understand about young people?

### They're open and flexible

Far more so than adults, young people are often willing to try new things, buck old trends and start fresh ones. Among the greatest put-downs within their culture is to call something "old-fashioned" or "old-school." Whether you are talking about some new idea—a crazy hairdo, extreme sports, body piercing, tattooing—you name it, many will give it a shot. None of this should be misinterpreted by the Church as evidence that they are closed to the Gospel; on the contrary, it is a flashing neon sign that says they are open.

### They're impressionable

The study of the brain has demonstrated scientifically what we already knew practically: Like wet clay before it's been fired in a kiln, children from adolescence to the teenage years are at the most moldable period of their lives. This is why television shows that attract a young audience get the best advertising rates; companies understand that their ads are far more likely to influence the buying patterns of those viewers.

What this means for the Church is both simple and strategically important: *Young people make the very best disciples.* As perhaps one of the best known verses in the Old Testament states, "Train a child in the way he should go, and when he is old he will not turn from it."[17]

### They're idealistic

In 1961, President Kennedy challenged students to give their lives in foreign service, and the Peace Corps was born. Eventually, over one hundred thousand young people volunteered to serve the poor and needy around the world. In a recent poll, over two-thirds of teens surveyed said that their number one goal was to make a positive difference in the world. This romantic optimism, believing that the world should and can be a better place, is one of the greatest aspects of the "glorious strength" that God has deposited in the young. Today, however, there's a catch.

> "I'm going to buy a gun and start a war, if you can tell me something worth fighting for."[18]

These lyrics by the band Coldplay do a good job of describing the problem this generation faces on today's campuses. Though they remain idealistic, postmodernism has compromised the vision of just what is a good cause worth fighting for.

And once again, instead of throwing our hands up in the air in disgust, the Church should be saying, "What an incredible opportunity!" It's time to tell this generation about the One who fought the greatest fight imaginable for them…and then ask them to return the favor.

### *Capacity for faith*

Children have an inherent capacity for faith, an ability to believe what they're told. That's why they must be protected by child labor laws, advertising that promotes things detrimental to their well-being (like the "Joe Camel" cigarette ads) and a host of other predatory forces.

Jesus declares that unless we have the faith of a child we cannot enter the kingdom of God.[19] Elsewhere He warns that if anyone takes advantage of this childlike faith and causes even one of these little ones to stumble, it would be better for them to have a millstone tied around their neck and be cast into the sea.[20]

When God set out to bring the Messiah into the world through the incarnation, He approached a teenager by the name of Mary. Her response will live forever as a perfect expression of faith, "May it be done to me according to your word."[21] Contrast that with the response given by the older and more mature Zacharias when the Angel of the Lord announced to him a birth that was far less improbable. He questioned: "How can I be sure of this?"[22]

Think about it; Jesus gathered a group of disciples from within the 13/30 window (He himself being only thirty-three at the time) and said, in effect, "Go out and take the world." Only a group of young people would have accepted this kind of challenge!

### *They are the treasure*

What does MTV really see in youth culture? A number of years ago, an ad executive was asked why his company targeted the young. He replied. "For the same reason Willie Sutton robbed banks…that's where the money is." How ironic that the enemy likes to portray the Church as only wanting your money. What the Church must see is that the youth don't simply have the treasure; they *are* the treasure. They represent the vast army that can reignite the cause of Christ and reverse the trend of cultural decay. They are the special forces of the Apostolic Mandate.

## GET READY FOR THE ADVENTURE OF YOUR LIFE

A number of years ago I got a call from the producer of the *Montel Williams Show* asking me if I would appear on the popular talk show. The theme was: "Should the church pass out condoms?" This topic was prompted by the Magic Johnson disclosure and the consequent rising panic concerning HIV and AIDS. For a fleeting moment, I thought that this might be some kind of *Candid Camera* episode. So I responded humorously, as if to say, "I know you're joking."

"Oh no," she assured me, "There's a church here in California that's actually passing out condoms to the young people."

I agreed to come on the program under two conditions: that I could bring another guest on the panel with me and that I would receive fifty passes for the studio audience. The audience tends to control the atmosphere for these "discussions," and I wanted to make sure that our side was represented. I gave the tickets to students from our Victory Campus Ministries (the campus arm of Morning Star International) at USC and UCLA.

The show opened with Montel asking if the church should pass out condoms. There were two other ministers on the panel with me, and one immediately responded with a confident air of expertise. "Definitely," he said. "Jesus gave people bread and fish, which was a life-giving act. Of course He would pass out condoms." Except for our fifty Christian students, most of the audience cheered and clapped.

As I listened to the audience cheer, it occurred to me that I was the designated bad guy, playing the part of the prototypical Pharisee—a self-righteous bigot who wants to see sinners die and go to hell. And the good guys? They are the ones that believe everyone is right, except the Christians. Just remove or water down all those absolute truths, commands and standards for moral purity in the Bible, and you're suddenly the guy with the white hat.

When it was my turn to comment, I'm sure I disappointed them by not "playing my part," but instead spoke very compassionately about Magic Johnson and everyone who was battling this horrible virus. I then addressed the issue of what Jesus would do by recounting the biblical story of a woman caught in adultery. Yes, He was compassionate towards her, but in the end, He didn't tell her to go and "be careful." Instead, He commanded her to, "Go and sin no more."[23] One of the other panelists quickly responded, "How unfortunate that Reverend Broocks would bring up the biblical standard for morality as if there's only one." It struck me that here was a minister, supposedly a moral leader, adding to the confusion of these young people by not being clear on one of the most basic truths of the Bible: Sexual immorality is wrong.

And so the conversation went on for a while, the audience cheering their respective champions, until my special guest arrived. Suddenly the entire audience was united in their applause as A. C. Green, one of Magic Johnson's teammates on the World Champion Los Angeles Lakers, walked out on the stage. After the standard greetings and fanfare, A. C. humbly opened up his heart and talked briefly about his faith in Christ and then about all the temptations that get thrown at professional athletes. To the issue of passing out condoms, he responded, "It's not a matter of birth control; it's self-control. If I can play in the NBA all these years and remain a virgin, don't give me your excuses."[24] You could hear the proverbial pin drop. For all intents and purposes, the discussion was over. This instance is a textbook case in how we are called to minister in this postmodern world.

Man's ultimate problem, as has often been said, is not so much with the mind as with the will. "If anyone chooses to do God's will," Jesus said, "he will find out whether my teaching comes from God or whether I speak on my own."[25] Because we want what we want—in theological terms, we desire to be our own gods—fallen man seeks to "suppress the truth in unrighteousness."[26] The antidote to this problem is truth, but truth that is primarily directed at the source of the problem: the human heart. A. C.'s testimony, and the moral authority behind it, formed an arrow of truth that pierced everyone's heart. Oh sure, people still talked and argued, but you could sense that our critics had the wind taken out of their sails.

In this, there's another great advantage that popular culture has presented to the Church. Intellectual "truth" has been so devitalized by postmodernism that it is no longer the barrier to the Gospel it was a generation or two ago. Now we are left with multitudes "in the valley of decision,"[27] looking for answers. In other words, the fields of youth culture couldn't be more ripe for the harvest. And who knows whether we have come into the kingdom "for such a time as this?"[28]

Understanding all this, we need to think strategically and ask ourselves a few questions. Where is the single greatest concentration of young people and potential leaders? Where is the most likely place to find them at a stage in their lives when possibilities are everywhere but the choice as to which path to take has not yet been fixed? Where are they most open to new ideas and have the available time and psychological inclination to be trained in them?

The answer to these questions takes us to what is perhaps the most strategically important mission field in the world: *the university campus.*

## CHANGE THE CAMPUS, CHANGE THE WORLD

No effective strategy for impacting the 13/30 window is complete without reaching out to the university campus. Even a cursory knowledge of history reveals just how important the role of the university campus is in shaping society. Whether it's the stand that students took for democracy in Tiananmen Square in China; the University of the Philippines, where the majority of the nation's leaders have been educated; or the University of California at Berkeley, which became the headquarters of the social revolution in America in the 60's—the campus is the place to be if you want to make an impact on the world.

If you are a student, your college years are the most incredible time in your life to not only make a decision to follow Jesus Christ but to give your all to fulfilling your destiny. As a student, you can make a difference—but it won't be easy. The price of being a world changer is hard work, dedication and, most of all, a huge love for God. It isn't enough to try to hang on and hope that you can make it through four years of college and not lose your faith. You must be a leader.

For Bret, a senior at the University of Southern California, this dawning need for purpose as well as a deep concern over his moral condition drove him to start talking to other students about God and man's quest for meaning. As a member of a fraternity, he wanted friendship and acceptance, but somehow that need was never really met from all the temporal satisfactions campus life offered. Surrounded by people, friends and parties, he began to feel increasingly alone and hopeless.

Bret has spoken openly about his struggles during this time:

> This sense of emptiness and decay got my attention to the point where, one evening, I was literally unable to look at myself in the mirror. At the very same time this was happening, a ministry on campus started a Bible study in the fraternity house where I was living. The people who sponsored the study were radically different from my friends and me. They seemed to have a joy and a peace that transcended their circumstances. I was envious and wanted to find out what it was they had that I didn't.

Bret did find out and today is a full-time Christian minister working on campuses throughout North America.

Ferdie was a disillusioned student in the Philippines, seeking fulfillment in political activism and campus protests. Then he met the Lord. "Seeing real Christians on campus that lived boldly for Christ changed my whole life," he later said. "I realized that real change in a nation must come from the heart. No amount of protest or political promises will do any good, there must be a spiritual revolution." Today Ferdie leads a national campus movement called "Youth on Fire" and ministers to thousands of students in his homeland.

Bret and Ferdie are just two of the thousands of college students who in the last several decades have discovered what the university experience can and should be—a time of discovering truth, developing godly character and being trained to "serve God's purpose in their own generation."[29] In this, they have uncovered a great truth that our modern world seeks to either forget or suppress: that what they're encountering is precisely why universities were created in the first place.

## THE CHRISTIAN FOUNDATIONS OF THE UNIVERSITY

Martin Luther said:

> I would advise no one to send his child where the Holy

Scriptures are not supreme. Every institution that does not unceasingly pursue the study of God's word becomes corrupt… I greatly fear that the universities, unless they teach the Holy Scriptures diligently and impress them on the young students, are wide gates to hell.[30]

Luther would have been happy to send his children to almost any of the schools founded during the first two hundred years of America's history. All but two of the first one hundred and eight colleges were founded explicitly on the Christian faith. Up through the second half of the nineteenth century, non-religious universities could be counted on one hand. College presidents were almost always clergymen until around 1900. A study entitled *An Appraisal of Church and Four Year Colleges* (1955) stated, "nearly all of those institutions which have exerted a decided influence, even in our literary and political history, were established by evangelical Christians."[31]

Looking at the mottos of most schools, it's easy to see just how central Christianity and the Scriptures were to both their creation and purpose.

- **Harvard:** *In Christi Gloriam* (Glory in Christ)

- **Brown University:** *In Deo Speramus* (In God We Trust)

- **University of California-Berkeley:** *Fiat Lux* (Let There be Light)

- **Rutgers University:** *Sol Justitiae et Occidentem Illustra* (Son of Righteousness, Shine upon the West Also)

- **Johns Hopkins University:** *Veritas vos liberabit* (The Truth Shall Make You Free)

- **Columbia University:** *In Lumine Tuo Videbimus Lumen* (In Thy Light Shall We See Light)

- **Dartmouth University:** *Vox Clamantis in Deserto* (A Voice of One Crying in the Wilderness)

- **Amherst College:** *Terras Irradient* (an allusion to Isaiah 6:3: "The whole earth is full of His glory.")

- **Princeton University:** *Dei Sub Numine Viget* (Under God's Power She Flourishes)

We need look no further than Princeton University, unquestion-ably among the ten most prestigious schools in the world, to get a good snapshot of where we were…and how far we have fallen. Established during the First Great Awakening, the college was a direct result of spiritual revival and was specifically founded to train and educate a new generation of ministers to shepherd the emerging nation. Princeton's first president, Reverend Jonathan Dickson, pro-claimed the leading theory of knowledge of the time when he said, "Cursed be all learning that is contrary to the cross of Christ." Princeton's official seal contained the Hebrew Tetragrammaton name of God, *YHVH*; Psalm 36:10 in Latin ("In Thy light we see light"); the Hebrew phrase *Uri El* (an allusion to Psalm 27:1— "The LORD is my light"); and the Scripture reference 1 Peter 2:1–2, a verse admonishing students to desire the pure milk of God's Word.

Today? Well, let's just say that the milk has gone more than a little sour. I'll leave it to Dr. Peter Singer, professor of bio-ethics at Princeton, to confirm this. Concerning the inherent value of human life, Singer wrote:

> We can no longer base ethics on the idea that human beings are a special form of creation, made in the image of God, singled out from all other animals, and alone pos-sessing an immortal soul…If we compare a severely defective human infant with a…dog or pig…we will often find the nonhuman to have superior capacities…. Species membership alone…is not relevant…. Humans who bestow superior value on the lives of all human beings, solely because they are members of our own species, are…similar to…white racists…[32]

Luther was right. As we have ceased to lift high the standard of God's Word and embraced instead men's minds as "the measure of all things," the enemy has come in like a flood. The first thing that has been swept away by this torrent has been the very thing that was sup-posed to be the university's focus—"*Veritas*" or "truth." In his best-selling book, *The Closing of the American Mind*, Allan Bloom, a professor of political philosophy at the University of Chicago, memo-rably documents this massive paradigm shift in Western education: "There is one thing a professor can be absolutely certain of: almost every student entering the university believes, or says he believes, that truth is relative."[33] With rare exception, by the time these same students are finished with higher education, this intellectual vanity will only have taken a deeper hold on their minds. From the scourge of politically correct ideologies to curricula that increasingly either ignores, attacks or supplants the Christian traditions upon which both the university and Western culture rest, Paul's warning to the church at Colossae has perhaps never been more relevant:

> See to it that no one takes you captive through hollow and deceptive philosophy, which depends on human tradition and the basic principles of this world rather than on Christ.
> —COLOSSIANS 2:8

Without question, the new foundation that has supplanted Christ, besides the aforementioned humanism, is Darwinian evolution. Because any epistemology (theory of truth), system of ethics, and teleology (perception of purpose, why we're here and where we're headed) is ultimately rooted in the question of origins, make no mistake about it: this is not some peripheral issue. Don't believe me? Consider the words of an honest humanist:

> Christianity has fought, still fights, and will fight science to the desperate end over evolution, because evolution destroys utterly and finally the very reason Jesus' earthly life was supposedly made necessary. Destroy Adam and Eve and the original sin, and in the rubble you will find the sorry remains of the son of god.... If Jesus was not the redeemer who died for our sins, and this is what evolution means, then Christianity is nothing.[34]

The lines have been drawn, and the stakes are high. The future of our families, our nation and the world hang in the balance. It's time to take back our future. It's time to take back the campus.

## A CAMPUS MANIFESTO: REASONS WHY WE SHOULD REACH THE CAMPUS

Historically, movements that mean business write a manifesto to explain their cause and call the masses to action. In instances such as the Communist Manifesto or the Humanist Manifesto, an agenda was marked out that eventually impacted the world. Therefore, we will do the same for this critical cause and trust God that there will be a mighty awakening to both the rightness and the urgency of our cause. After each of these statements let us declare: "*For this reason we must change the campus!*"

◆ **The campus is where the future leaders of society are located.**

The university is the place where the leaders of our nation are being trained. Virtually all of the presidents, prime ministers, congressmen, bankers, lawyers, teachers, doctors, as well as the vast majority of business leaders, have passed through the college and university system: In short, the campus is the location of virtually all of those in authority in every critical aspect of a nation's culture.

◆ **The campus is where major movements have started.**

Whether it's a spiritual awakening or political upheaval, the campus is the birthplace of change. From the rise of Marxism, atheism, materialistic evolution, feminism and practically every other "ism" that can be named—the beginning was on the university campus. It was seven students from Cambridge who sailed to China and into history. The story of the "Cambridge Seven" is one of the most inspiring in Church history. At the heart of every significant stage in world evangelization, you will find thousands of students who gave all to take the Gospel to the ends of the earth.

◆ **The values of the campus will become the values of society.**

Every worldview began as a thought. These thoughts, whether good or bad, were developed and canonized in the university setting. The university owes its very existence to the Christian worldview. As the ideals and principles of Scripture gave way to the philosophies of secularism and its various offspring, the values adhered to in society followed suit. The only way to have a realistic chance of being "salt" in the culture is to be "salt" in the campus dialectic.

◆ **The campus is where the most available, trainable masses are located.**

There is no other place where so many young people congregate to simply learn, dialogue and plot their futures. Not even the shopping mall comes close. We must give these young people the opportunity to consider the truth of Jesus Christ and the destiny He has for them. The Church stands to gain thousands of new converts, leaders and heroes by engaging in campus ministry.

◆ *The majority of those who become Christians do so during their student years.*

Statistics confirm that the majority of those who become Christians do so before the age of twenty-five. However, the majority of evangelistic outreach is not directed at this age group. We must spend the bulk of our efforts and resources on those who are, without question, most open to the Gospel.

◆ *The campus is where thousands of international students from unreached nations are studying and are very open to being reached for Christ.*

There are thousands of international students studying on campuses worldwide. Many of these students are from nations that restrict the open declaration of the Gospel. By reaching them while they are on campus, we can revolutionize missions in the twenty-first century.

◆ *God has promised to pour out His Spirit in the last days upon sons and daughters.*

This translates to an enormous awakening among the youth of the world. In every nation, God has promised to raise up an a mighty throng of young people who will "volunteer freely in the day of His power." We must be prepared to handle this coming harvest. We will do this by positioning leaders on the college and high school campuses who are prepared to mentor these new believers.

## CONCLUSION

In a parable, the Lord made it abundantly clear that we have a job to do and that we were to do it—*to occupy*—until He returns.[35] As I have said over and over in this book, that job is the Apostolic Mandate—to preach the Gospel and disciple nations. In this chapter, we have seen from where the vast majority of our converts and future leaders are likely to arise. We have no real choice but to "follow the cloud" of God's leading and go where the harvest awaits.

In the next chapter, we will explore the best way to not only bring in this harvest, but also to preserve it.

## CHAPTER 7

# DISCOVERING SPIRITUAL FAMILY

*You are never more like God than when you are living in relationships with God's people and walking in partnerships for the recreation and redemption of God's world.*

—RAY BAKKE

One of the great debates of the twenty-first century will be over the definition of a family. Its traditional meaning—a man married to a woman who then raise children together—has fallen on hard times in certain circles. Some view it as too "limiting" or exclusionary. As different people and groups step forward to announce their new definition, one thing becomes obvious: Giving a set of relationships the title of *family* is deemed the ultimate validation. There's a certain weight, even nobility granted to whatever is called by that name. Family speaks of identity, loyalty, boundaries and, above all, purpose.

So powerful is this concept that everywhere you look, from businesses to sports teams to military units, when a sense of family is achieved the chance of success increases dramatically. In fact, the very term *team* has been so refined as to become synonymous with the term *family* in many organizational settings. A great team works together like a great family. A team has goals; so does a family. They must work together; they must know their roles and not compete against each other. When these key ingredients are brought together on a winning team, the experience for everyone involved is hard to beat—as Peter Senge noted in his bestseller *The Fifth Discipline*:

> Most of us at one time or another have been part of a great "team," a group of people who functioned together in an extraordinary way—who trusted one another, who complemented each others' strengths and compensated for each others' limitations, who had common goals that were larger than individual goals, and who produced extraordinary results. I have met many people who have experienced this sort of profound teamwork—in sports, or in the performing arts, or in business. Many say that they have spent much of their life looking for that experience again.[1]

Among the most prominent aspects of a team or a family are the authorities at the head of it; coaches for a team, parents for a family. Anyone who has grown up in a family or played on a team knows the power and influence these authorities have over their lives: encouraging, teaching, defining and, yes, even correcting when necessary.

I remember a critical lesson I learned while still a child. I had done something bad and, facing the prospect of punishment, tried a combination of emotional manipulation and self-pity to throw my dad off his mark. "Dad," I said, "I wish you could just be my friend." He fired back, "You've got a lot of friends, but you've only got one dad." No one else was willing like my family to correct me and then turn around and love and encourage me. Their loving discipline gave my brother, Ben, my sister, Rebecca, and me a tremendous boost in life.

## THE BREAKDOWN OF THE FAMILY

As the institution of the family breaks down, society inevitably follows. From today's high rate of divorce to the fact that so many decide to simply steer clear of marriage in order to avoid the chance of pain, fewer and fewer people are being blessed and nurtured within this God-ordained structure for producing life and happiness. Mention the concept of "family" and the adjective "dysfunctional" often gets thrown out to describe a state where relationships are strained or fractured and no one seems to be able to fix them. Every family has trials, disagreements, and hurtful things that threaten their relationships. A "functional" family can encounter these obstacles, fix the things that are broken and see wounds healed. A "dysfunctional" family cannot.

As the institution of the family has begun to crack under these pressures, the results have been an increase in single-parent families, turmoil in schools where kids are out of control, the incidence of juvenile crime, and the list goes on. Perhaps even more tragic is the perpetuation of the cycle. Kids raised in these dysfunctional environments are typically unable to maintain long-term relationships when faced with similar conflicts later in life.

The character of the Church is supposed to reflect the character of family. In many countries today, however, the institution of the family has so deteriorated that less than one half of all children grow up in a traditional family. Consequently, many of the members of the Church don't have a good model of what a family is supposed to be like. For them, the terms *family* and *father* don't always have a positive connotation.

## THE CHURCH AS A SPIRITUAL FAMILY

The breakdown of family is evidence of a number of things, one of which is that many have lost the art of building relationships. So a great percentage of people come to church unable to nurture long-term relationships and with a foggy understanding of what a family should be. That's OK. The church is a place for transformation, where God redeems things. However, for the church to be a healthy spiritual family, we can't let our own dysfunctional family background gain the upper hand. We have to model ourselves after the family God has ordained. Best-selling author, Stormie Omartian, writes:

> God is our Father. We are God's kids. That means we who are believers in Jesus are all brothers and sisters. There are too many of us to all live in the same house, so God puts us in separate houses. We call them churches. Our relationships within these church families are crucial to our well-being. How we relate to the other people there will greatly affect the quality of our life in the Lord.[2]

My dad had something in common with the apostle Paul: "For if you were to have countless tutors in Christ, yet you would not have many fathers."[3] The Bible paints the picture of family as the primary backdrop for all the teachings, commands and missions the Church has been charged with. Jesus astonished His disciples by encouraging them to refer to Jehovah as "Father." Paul referred to Timothy as his "true child" in the faith.[4] The apostle John writes, "I have no greater joy than to hear that my children are walking in the truth."[5] In discussing relationships, Paul wrote: "Treat…older women as mothers, and younger women as sisters."[6]

## DISPOSABLE RELATIONSHIPS

When the Lord spoke to Phil Bonasso, Steve Murrell and me in Manila and told us to work together, He made it clear that if we stayed together in our relationships, what we built would stay together as well. As Steve often says, "We don't believe in disposable relationships." But like any other conviction, the call to spiritual family is inevitably put to the test. Phil says it this way: "Walking together in family is incredible but it will be the hardest thing you will ever do." Why? Because taking offense is the enemy's number one way to destroy relationships.

The word *offense* in Scripture comes from the Greek word *scandalon.*[7] The *scandalon* is the name for the part of the trap where the bait is set. Get the picture? The enemy has set traps in your relationships, and the offense is the bait. My question to people who have walked away from relationships after taking the bait is, "Aren't you even curious what's on the other side of offense?" If the enemy has fought so hard to stop a relationship, it's because of the potential threat it represents.

Sadly, break-ups occur in ministry even more frequently than in marriage. As I noted earlier, the Church is "the pillar and support of the truth."[8] If there's a truth that seems to be lacking in society, it's because the Church did not perform its job as a pillar and hold up the truth in that area. The breakdown in Church relationships is now so frequent that many have resigned themselves to it as an inevitable fact of life.

Over the years, I have had the privilege of speaking in many different churches and ministries. For the most part it has been deeply rewarding. But just as a pastor has the joy of presiding over weddings, he must at times preside over funerals as well. There he learns to mourn with those who mourn.

Starting a church is much like presiding over a wedding. There's always a lot of joy and high expectation. Presiding over a church split or closing one down, however, is predictably like a funeral. Once in Canada, I found myself in the middle of a schism that had developed in a fairly large church. Calling the elders of this group together, I was stunned at how cynical the atmosphere was. What was more amazing was that I had only spoken for this group once and yet they had no one else to cover them in this crisis. As we spent hours talking around the room about the issues of concern, one thing began to stick out to me. The so-called issues weren't the *real* issue. All they were doing was covering up the real crisis: a breakdown in relationships.

Sensing that we needed to move beyond theological quibbling, I took a chance and announced that I had the answer to their problems. After hours of airing their grievances, they paused, a little skeptically, and waited for my assessment. "The bottom line is that you folks don't really like each other." Immediately the religious cover-up began. "Well, now, brother, I really have a love for them [speaking of the other side]." "Yes, I love you too, brother." (Anytime you hear a lot of "brother" talk, that should let you know they're *really* mad at each other!) When it all finally came out, that was the real issue. It was a breakdown in relationships. These breakdowns take many forms and can have many so-called "righteous reasons" behind them, but in the end, a "house divided against itself will not stand."[9]

Just as in a natural family, when this kind of division happens in a church, it's the "children"—the youth and their spiritual condition—who usually suffer the most. Often kids from a divorced home have a difficult time trusting others and are more hesitant to marry. In the same way, children from a church atmosphere of division and strife are reluctant to get involved in church commitment. "What's the point?" many would ask. "It's only going to end in pain."

There are painful moments where the best solution is to leave a hurtful or sinful relationship behind. When this happens, it's important that we proceed in a righteous way. I've had to separate myself from people on a few occasions when I believed the trust factor could not be restored. After following the protocol outlined in Matthew 18:15–17 and still finding no resolution, I came to the place of saying, "It is better that we part ways here."

## GOD BUILDS THROUGH FAMILY

The blessing of finding the relationships you are called to walk with and build with far outweighs the risk of heartache from those situations that don't work out. This is why, if we are to recover the Apostolic Mandate, we must recover the apostolic call to love and unity. In family, we find the necessary structures or "wineskins" to preserve the work of God in the lives of His people.

This truth is so vital—and so often ignored—that I need to be as straightforward as possible: God builds through family. He establishes natural and spiritual families and expects us to teach our children properly. A godly dynasty awaits those who will build God's way.

## THE TRINITY REVEALS FAMILY

Because of His very nature, the mystery of God being manifested as three persons—Father, Son and Spirit—and yet one God, speaks of the sweet community within the "godhead." In *Shared Life*, Donald MacLeod writes:

> The fact that we bear the divine image means that we are *made for fellowship*. This is probably the most important point of all. As bearers of God's image, we are made for "with-ness" (i.e. to be with others). As God Himself observed, "It is not good for the man to be alone" (Genesis 2:18). There is a social life in the godhead itself. The Father, the Son and the Holy Spirit live in community and fellowship. The same must be true for us. It is something we see exemplified beautifully in the life of Christ Himself.[10]

Everything about the nature, plan and people of God, as well as the very mission of the Church, is revealed and understood in the context of family.

Did it have to be that way? Yes, because God doesn't do things arbitrarily. All of His actions are consistent as an expression of His eternal nature. Whatever God does, whatever God creates, whatever God builds is a reflection of who He is. God is holy. If the stamp of holiness is not part of a church, it is not reflecting the nature of God and is missing the mark. In the same way, if you build a church or a movement of churches that do not have the spirit of family, then what you have built is missing something very fundamental. And consequently, something is also going to be missing in the members, the ministry and the mission.

## ABRAHAM, THE FATHER OF OUR FAITH

The bedrock of this truth is based on the covenant God made with Abraham. Before Abraham, the world had been rocked by the breakdown of the first family: Adam and Eve's disobedience to God followed by Cain's murder of his brother, Abel. The breakdown continued with Noah's sons. The quest for a faithful family continued. For His purposes to unfold on the earth, God needed someone who would trust His promises and survive the challenges that would await him. But faith wasn't the only reason God chose and blessed Abraham. The Scripture says, "For I have chosen him, so that he may direct his children and his household after him to keep the way of the LORD by doing what is right and just, so that the LORD will bring about for Abraham what He has promised him."[11] Because Abraham was willing to believe God and raise his family right, God said he would become a mighty nation.

## DISCOVERING SPIRITUAL FAMILY

Once you understand the importance of spiritual family, finding that family becomes crucial. Though the process shouldn't be that difficult, many people spend years searching for the right place to fit into the body of Christ. For them, finding the right place can be a pretty incredible experience. Just ask Rick Shelton, the senior pastor of Life Christian Church in St. Louis. "All my life I was looking for where I belonged, where I fit," he said. "Sure, I had a successful ministry and a large church, but I knew that God wanted me to find a larger family in order to realistically change the world. I've told my staff, if we can ever find these types of relationships, it would be like heaven. Well, I found them, and it's better than I dreamed." In becoming a part of the MSI family of churches—as a result of this new synergy of relationships—Life Christian Church is truly making a greater impact on the world.

## GOD BIRTHS US INTO FAMILIES

There are two primary ways God joins people to a spiritual family: He births you into one, or He grafts you in after you've been saved. Obviously, we are "baptized into one Body"[12] when we become Christians. So, we are a part of the universal family of God when we are born again. However, the concept of spiritual family is a matter of discerning what part of that body you are specifically joined to. It's not enough to say, "I am a part of the universal body of Christ" without a connection to a specific local church. God has designed the local body as a place of commitment for every member of the larger body.

Many face the emotional challenge of having been separated from their natural family before they were old enough to remember anything about them. They may spend a good part of their lives searching, trying to find out where they belong and, in a sense, who they are. That is even more common among Christians who go from one church to another, searching for their spiritual family.

Finding a spiritual family is a little different because it is a matter of the working of the Holy Spirit who "has set the members, each one of them, in the body just as He pleased."[13] What may be needed is more insight into the work He has already done. For many, the issue of spiritual family is obvious. They are attending churches where their lives have been changed and would never consider leaving to go somewhere else to look for family. You hear them refer to "my church" and know that, in a sense, they are also saying "my spiritual family." Paul wrote to the Corinthians saying, "I became your father through the Gospel."[14] To his young disciple, Timothy, he said, "You are my 'son in the faith.'"[15] If you're still not clear on this, then check your "spiritual DNA." In other words, in which church do you feel a kindred spirit with regard to vision, faith and devotion to Christ?

It's one thing to simply say that you belong to a church. It's another to have a rock solid conviction about being a part of a spiritual family. That kind of assurance doesn't come from just going to the church of your choice; it comes by revelation of the Holy Spirit as to where He has placed you in the body of Christ. Does it matter if you have that kind of assurance? Yes, because faith and assurance infuses the relationship you have in the church with a sense of purpose and calling.

## GOD JOINS US TO SPIRITUAL FAMILY

There are many benefits we gain when we find our place in a spiritual family. One is protection from spiritual enemies. Not only are the forces of darkness less likely to have an opportunity to attack when Christians are in real unity, but negative emotions like discouragement, loneliness and fear—among many others—are held back as well. Perhaps even more important than these defensive benefits, however, is the manner in which being joined together helps us to advance the Apostolic Mandate. As each of us is part of the body of Christ, each one has a particular calling and function. And it's not just the working parts that cause the body to grow; the relationships between those parts—the joints—are vital as well. A joint is where two parts in the body combine to work together and help cause the body to grow:

> …the whole body, being fitted and held together by what every joint supplies, according to the proper working of each individual part, causes the growth of the body for the building up of itself in love.
>
> —EPHESIANS 4:16, NASB

Secular management books use the term *synergy* to describe what happens when every part and every joint supplies according to its proper function. Synergy suggests that the effect of the whole is greater than the sum of the parts. The Apostolic Mandate is never going to be accomplished by a church or group of churches unless there is a synergistic coordination of the gifts and talents that the Holy Spirit has placed in the body of Christ. Without this unity and proper placement, your gifts will never function according to their proper working order. In that case, everyone loses: the kingdom of God, the world and you.

Just as it is with the placing of an individual in a local church, so it is with a local church as a whole being placed in a broader spiritual family. Our movement has experienced so many examples of this type of joining that it is difficult to choose which story to tell. Three that come to mind are Paul Daniel in South Africa, Sam Webb in Hawaii and Ray McCollum in Nashville. I will briefly discuss the first two in Chapter 10 when we talk about building a global team. For now, let's consider the way Ray and Elizabeth McCollum and Bethel World Outreach Center in Nashville came into the spiritual family of Morning Star International.

### Bethel World Outreach Center
Ray and Elizabeth McCollum founded Bethel in the late 1980s and it grew to be one of the great churches in the Nashville area. In 1992, I was introduced to them through a mutual friend and was later invited to minister at Bethel. It didn't take long for my wife, Jody, and me to fall in love with their refreshing candor and sincere love for Christ.

We quickly became great friends. I have since come to believe that this couple is the cure for anyone suffering from a "religious spirit."

One day, Ray approached me about moving to Nashville to help him build what he called, "A Disciple-Making Church." He said, "I put this phrase on the logo of our church, but I'm not sure how to make it a reality. Will you help me?"

I was finishing my time in seminary, right before the birth of Morning Star International. Jody and I knew something great was about to happen, but we were unsure as to how Nashville was going to fit into our future. After much prayer and deliberation, we took the step and moved. With very little relational history between us, it was truly a step of faith for both the McCollums and us.

It wasn't long after this that the "miracle in Manila" was taking place and Steve, Phil and I were joining our lives together to form MSI. I returned to Nashville and over lunch informed Ray about what had happened and that I would be moving on to either be a part of a Morning Star Church or planting a new one myself. I'll never forget the moment when this conversation took place. He looked up at me and said, "Why not stay here and we will join with you?"

Even though I loved them dearly, I knew it wouldn't be easy. As an independent church with an assortment of relationships that operated as a loose covering, Bethel would have to make some significant changes. Jody and I didn't want to be the source of any pain or discomfort that usually comes with this type of change.

In the short run, the commitment to join the MSI family was more costly than I anticipated. While we've since seen the "adoption" process proceed much more smoothly in other situations, in this case there were many difficult times and painful losses. Scores of people eventually left simply because they didn't like change. Others took off probably because they didn't like me. The biggest problem, however, was adopting the vision. As an MSI church, we were committed to reaching out to the city and its campuses and then to the entire world. More than a few of the members weren't that interested and left. And then there was the rumor mill. It's sad to watch people who've received so much blessing in a church walk away on the strength of little more than a personal whim or a whispered tale from a bitter person with an axe to grind. More often than not, it led them down a dead-end street.

During the storm that ensued, there were times when we wondered if this joining was going to be worth the hassle. But as we pressed past the tribulations caused by people's speculations and the prophets of doom, we found the grace of God resting on our decision. Once the disgruntled people left, the church began to grow, adding both numbers and strength. The new people who joined were grounded in the foundations of the faith and trained to reach their world for Christ. We began a Victory Leadership Institute, and scores of people every year filed into the classroom to learn how to be leaders.

In 1999, sensing that my season at Bethel was coming to an end, I met again with Ray. I told him that I felt my job there was done and I would be relocating. After mulling it over for a few weeks, he came back with a counter-proposal. "Rice," he said, "why don't you take the reigns of Bethel for six months and help take us to the next level?" I was stunned. We had already told our children we were moving and were in the process of looking for a new home. Talk about trying to put a moving train in reverse! In spite of the confusion surrounding the change in plans, we sensed that we should take this extra season and really finish the job in Nashville on a high note. "Six months more and we'll be gone."

Well, a funny thing happened. Almost as soon as Ray stepped out and I stepped in, there was a sense that this rearrangement was the perfect fit. Pastor Ray, one of the finest Bible expositors you'll ever hear, loved to teach, and people flocked to Bethel to hear his messages. But though he persevered in pastoring—wanting to be faithful to both God and the needs of his flock—he didn't really enjoy the role. Being joined to a larger family beyond the local church opened up the opportunity for him to really function in his true office of teacher and to be devoted to that calling full time. He was free to travel, write and teach.

After only the first month of the six-month period, the change in position had liberated him and he knew it. It also was a burden lifted from his wife, Elizabeth, who was first to inform me that they were not going to pastor anymore. She announced, "We aren't going back Rice; it's your turn to stay at home!" What began as a short-term mission became a revolutionary turn in the road for Bethel, my family and me. By becoming the senior pastor of Bethel, the Lord underscored for me and the entire MSI movement the importance of reaching the world by building strong local churches.

The moral of the story? When you discover spiritual family and find those you are called to walk with, you end up discovering your destiny as well. Ray, Elizabeth, Jody and I all found our callings and giftings energized and focused in a greater way. Being the pastor of this great church these last few years has brought me closer to God's people and strengthened my passion for raising up strong families and world-changing disciples. On top of it all, because of the spirit of family that people feel at Bethel, an incredible gathering of leaders has taken place. It can all be summed up by a prophetic word John Rohrer gave me shortly after I became pastor: "You're going to be stunned to see who I [the Lord] am going to bring around you…from all over the world I'll bring you the best!" This has certainly come to pass.

# THE POWER OF A FAMILY

This testimony demonstrates the enormous power and privilege in being rightly placed in God's family. Today, there is a wealth of material published on both the importance of and how to maintain a healthy, natural family. Unfortunately, however, there's a lack of similar material on spiritual family. So let's look at a few of the principles and blessings that await us when we rediscover this vital truth.

### Exponential impact

As we will discuss in detail in the coming chapters, when churches work together in the context of spiritual family, they can accomplish amazing things. They can pool their resources for church planting, wealth creation (i.e., establishing bookstores, hospitals, etc.), starting Christian television networks, movie studios, and so on. Almost anything that the sanctified mind can imagine can be accomplished when the people of God come together in divinely ordered relationships.[16]

### The vision is kept alive

In the book *The Fifth Discipline*, Peter Senge lists several principles that are helpful in understanding the power of family. Senge writes, "One of the deepest desires underlying shared vision is the desire to be connected to a larger purpose and to one another."[17]

Family and vision are linked together. In the end, you really can't have one without the other. People who talk about family but sit around and do nothing will not keep people together for long. On the other hand, vision without family is not only a lonely road, it's a road that in the end goes nowhere. When we walk together in a spiritual family, however, it helps keep the vision burning bright. Every time we come together in a conference or a church service we celebrate our relationships and inspire one another in the calling of God on our lives. On the flip side, this also explains why dreams pass away. Senge writes, "a vision can die if people forget their connection to one another."[18]

### Team learning

Team learning is another principle brought out by Senge that reflects a biblical truth. It means that we're able to take advantage of the size of our family by communicating and listening to one another. For example, a close family looks out for one another and gives the other members the insight they need to succeed. Fathers and mothers help their children and teach them to help one another.

As the Church begins to think this way, learning grows by leaps and bounds. Today, one of our biggest challenges as an organization is to utilize technology so that people who know something in Manila can help those who need to know in Los Angeles. This concept is so vital that it demands more attention than can be given here. I will say this though: Almost as much as we need five-fold ministers, we need those with the skill to help build and promote communication between all the members of the family.

### Family is a model for building great organizations

Because God is the Creator, understanding the way He builds and then following His pattern is the only way we can succeed. Ignoring or breaking His laws is a recipe for failure. Since He primarily builds through families, so should we. Again, Senge's observations are helpful:

> The more I understand the real skills of leadership in a learning organization, the more I become convinced that these are the skills of effective parenting. Leading in a learning organization involves supporting people in clarifying and pursuing their own visions, "moral-suasion," helping people discover underlying causes of problems, and empowering them to make choices. What could be a better description of effective parenting?[19]

### Long-term view

If we could just view the work of the kingdom the way we view our own family relationships, we would eliminate the short-term mindset that blinds so many in today's Church. We've all but lost our vision for the future and, as a result, many callings and dreams are dying.

You might have seen the T-shirt or bumper sticker that declares, "If I'd known I was going to live this long, I'd have taken better care of myself." If the Church had known we were going to be here this long, each generation would no doubt have been more attentive to its responsibilities.

In every instance where one finds a long-term view actually operating in human affairs, there is a long-term vision at work. The cathedral builders of the Middle Ages labored a lifetime with the fruits of their labors still a hundred years in the future. The Japanese believe building a great organization is like growing a tree; it takes twenty-five to fifty years. Parents of young children try to lay a foundation of values and attitude that will serve an adult twenty years hence. In all of these cases, people hold a vision that can be realized only over the long term.[20]

Good parents think about their children's future: how to educate them and prepare them for careers and marriage. And of course, there are the grandchildren to think about. "A good man leaves an inheritance for his children's children."[21] The framework of family provides us this critical paradigm to see the long-term nature of our spiritual relationships. After twenty years or more of walking with the leaders of our movement, there's a sense that we are just now coming into the real promised land of God's purposes. We're seeing our children becoming godly adults and eagerly taking the baton of the Apostolic Mandate that we've handed to them. If we stay together as a family, as well as stay true to the faith, there's almost no way we won't succeed.

### Promoting personal vision

As much as there's a larger family vision, there are individual visions as well. Far from being mutually exclusive, corporate and personal vision feed off of and inspire each other. In any family, every person has their own individual gifts and needs. When God's vision of spiritual family is embraced, a natural excitement arises as a church begins to discover the "treasure hidden in the field"—all the different gifts resident within the members of that local family.[22] The challenge and the joy of the local leadership is developing those gifts and seeing them marshaled together to creatively accomplish the goal of reaching the world.

Senge explains the connection as follows: "This is not to say that visions cannot emanate from the top. Often, they do. But sometimes they emanate from personal visions of individuals who are not in positions of authority. Sometimes they just "bubble up" from people interacting at many levels. The origin of the vision is much less important than the process whereby it comes to be shared. It is not truly a "shared vision" until it connects with the personal visions of people throughout the organization."[23]

# KEYS TO BUILDING FAMILY

### Commitment with a purpose

There are differing levels of commitment among churches, just as levels of unity and purpose vary from congregation to congregation. Some groups unite along very general, universally agreed upon principles that require no great effort or sacrifice to fulfill. Other churches are so committed to Christ and His Lordship that walking into them is like getting caught in a powerful undertow that dumps you at the foot of the cross. In other words, the level of commitment required in any particular church depends upon its vision and mandate.

The greater the mandate a spiritual family attempts, the greater the unity that is required. That was true in the ancient city of Babel. Their vision was to make a name for themselves and to keep their people from being scattered across the earth. God commented on them and their purpose: "If as one people speaking the same language they have begun to do this, then nothing they plan to do will be impossible for them."[24]

Two things are evident from this story. First, just because you're really committed to something doesn't mean you're doing the right thing. These "Babelites" had a purpose and a plan: to build a tower and keep their people unified. The problem was that they were seeking their own glory and not God's.

There are all kinds of organizations, including some churches, which require a high level of commitment. It's not right to demand commitment only for the sake of maintaining your own organization—i.e., to keep people from scattering. If self-perpetuation turns out to be the primary goal, the leaders need to rethink what they're doing and measure it against the purposes of God. Whenever we talk about commitment to a local church and the vision of MSI, it is always in the context of fulfilling God's purposes. For us, that means fulfilling the Apostolic Mandate by planting churches and making disciples of nations.

The second thing that is evident from the Tower of Babel story is that great things can be accomplished if people are united and committed to a common purpose. A house divided cannot stand, but when a people are united "nothing will be impossible for them."

### Be persistent

When I was five years old, I got mad at my parents and decided to run away. I packed my suitcase—with nothing but two pairs of underwear—and set out to make it on my own. I remember thinking, *When my parents realize that I am gone forever, they'll be sorry for not letting me have my way.*

Today, people are just as easily offended and just as naïve about the repercussions of hitting the road. For some, it's almost as if they're just waiting for someone to step on their toes or knock the chip off their shoulder.

Whether we're talking about marriage, an athletic team or working with people in ministry, to build strong and enduring relationships, you have to press through the difficult times. All of us need to make a commitment to persevere in the relationships God has given us. Without this commitment, you'll never get past the disillusionment stage. Few things are more unnecessarily tragic than hearing a disgruntled church member recite his list of grievances, pointing out all the terrible things that have been done to him. He's so easily offended, he never finds out what it's like on the other side of his offense, what blessing might have come upon him if he had settled down and worked through his real or imagined indignities.

In our walk with the Lord, the revelation of God's purpose or the answer to our prayers often comes right after the test of our faith, right after the desire to give up is about to get the best of us. It's the same way in relationships. God's purpose for you in a spiritual family is often revealed right after you're tempted to pack your bags and leave. The fact is, most people discover their calling and destiny in the context of the local church. God designed it to be that way. However, many never find it simply because they do not persevere in a spiritual family.

Now, we don't ever want to create a situation where people stay in a church merely out of obligation. If a real joy and a sense of God's purpose doesn't undergird your commitment, something is wrong and you likely need to find out where else God would have you fit in. At the same time, however, it shouldn't be easy just to pick up and walk away from your spiritual family. If leaving is easy, there's something very fundamental missing from the life and vision of the church.

I learned this that day when, as a five-year-old, I attempted to run away from home. I wasn't gone from home very long before I realized that I had no money, no place to sleep and nothing to eat. Sheepishly, I went back home and informed my parents, "OK, I'm giving you guys one more chance."

## GUARDING THE RELATIONSHIPS

Satan is constantly attacking relationships in the body of Christ. He knows that a people divided lose the power and effectiveness to accomplish their mission. What is our primary defense against the "accuser of our brethren"[25]—with his false doctrines, deceitful people and demonic schemes? It is speaking the truth in love to one another, according to the principles of Matthew 18. We don't "backbite"; that is, we don't say anything about people in their absence that we wouldn't say in their presence. If there is an offense between us and another person, we go to them privately. If that doesn't work, we take someone else with us—not simply someone who agrees with us so that we can gang up on the other person, but a mature and mutually respected Christian who can mediate and help work through the differences. We don't listen to accusations against another brother or sister, whether they are a leader or a new believer. We don't defraud a brother or sister by being anything less than straightforward with them. We always speak the truth in love—out of respect, courtesy and as a matter of personal integrity. We also do it because we understand the nature of spiritual warfare; we don't want to give the devil a foothold in our relationships.

Remember the words of the old song, "It only takes a spark to get a fire going"? Perhaps the greatest danger to our families—both spiritual and natural—are those sparks that fly off our tongues when we speak words that have the power to burn down marriages, ministries and every relationship in sight.[26]

### We have to pass it down

As important as the atmosphere of spiritual family is to everything we do, we have to be careful that our growth and success don't dilute it. As our Father warned Israel, "...and when your herds and your flocks grow large...and your heart will become proud, [don't] forget the LORD your God."[27] We have to be careful to pass on the vision in every church we plant.

There are several reasons we've been successful in doing this. First, most of the new churches we've planted have been led by men and women who have these principles deep in their hearts. Second, spiritual family is not a Morning Star idea. It's the Holy Spirit who does that work in everyone who is willing to receive it. Third, relationships naturally flourish whenever there is dedication to a great cause. As long as we are committed to fulfilling the Apostolic Mandate, the Holy Spirit will keep adding people to the vision, knitting hearts with hearts and maturing the body "as every joint supplies."

### A spiritual family is non-competitive

One of the best examples of how God joins people together is the story of David and Jonathan. Jonathan, the son of Saul, was a heroic warrior. When Saul and the armies of Israel were surrounded at Michmash, Jonathan said to his armor bearer, "Come and let us cross over to the garrison of these uncircumcised; perhaps the LORD will work for us, for the LORD is not restrained to save by many or by few."[28] Without telling anyone what they were going to do, Jonathan and his armor bearer climbed up a cliff and engaged the Philistines in battle. He slew about twenty soldiers, and the enemy camp was thrown into fear and confusion. Jonathan single-handedly saved the nation.

Years later, another young man named David went out alone against Goliath, the champion of the Philistines, saying, "You come to me with a sword, a spear, and a javelin, but I come to you in the name of the LORD of hosts."[29] When David returned, he was brought to stand before Saul and his son, Jonathan. When Jonathan saw the young man standing there with the giant's bloody head in his hand, "the soul of Jonathan was knit to the soul of David. Then Jonathan made a covenant with David because he loved him as himself. Jonathan stripped himself of the robe that was on him and gave it to David, with his armor, including his sword and his bow and his belt."[30]

People aren't really knit together just by being around one another. Jonathan and David were bound together because they saw in each other a boldness of faith and the heart of a champion. Later on, though he was heir to his father's kingdom, Jonathan had no jealousy when he saw that the Lord intended to place David on the throne instead. He became his ally, even when it went against his own self-interest.

Jesus was not jealous when He told the disciples that they would do greater works than He had done. Good parents will always rejoice when their sons and daughters exceed their own accomplishments. In a true spiritual family, where people's hearts are knitted to one another, it doesn't matter who God raises up. We have come to prefer each other over ourselves.

### A spiritual family is not exclusive

One of the biggest temptations among highly dedicated, purpose-driven Christians is to limit their relationships to a very small circle of friends. I have a long list of good friends who are either involved with or are leading other organizations. Over the years there have been many people I've been close to who have been called to go and serve the Lord in other ministries. Nonetheless, we're still on the same team.

It is important to know that God will move people around. The belief in spiritual family doesn't mean that someone can't leave their church or relocate their ministry. The Holy Spirit may move the members of the larger family around as He pleases. I am convinced that if our church or ministry is supposed to be home for a person, they will not only know that in their own heart; they will want it as well. It will be as it was in the story of Ruth and Naomi: after being told to leave Naomi and go back to her homeland, Ruth responded, "Don't urge me to leave you or to turn back from you. Where you go I will go, and where you stay I will stay. Your people will be my people and your God my God."[31]

That doesn't mean that we wouldn't counsel or question someone who wants to leave the church. We certainly don't want people leaving because of hurt or unforgiveness. The motive in talking with these people isn't just to get them to stay, but rather to make sure that whatever healing and forgiveness is necessary has taken place. It is also important not to be ambivalent about our affection for people. I have no hesitation saying, "We want you to stay and work with us." I've even gone so far as to plead with people because I think they might be making a wrong move in their life. But in the end, everyone must develop their own conviction as to what they should do. Unless someone is blatantly walking away from God, they should be blessed and sent out with love. The goal should be to "preserve the unity of the Spirit in the bond of peace."[32]

## THE POWER OF A PRAYING FAMILY

One of the results of building this way is a powerful spirit of harmony. When everyone wants to be united in a spiritual family, an excitement and energy flows. One of the most powerful outcomes of this unity is the promised blessing of answered prayer. As Jesus said, "I say to you that if two of you agree on earth concerning anything that they ask, it will be done for them by My Father in heaven."[33]

This is precisely why the enemy works so hard to "disturb the peace" in the house of God. A house divided will not stand; a house in strife will not be effective in prayer. Remember the admonition that Peter gave to husbands: "Be considerate as you live with your wives, and treat them with respect…so that nothing will hinder your prayers."[34] When the harmony of Christians in a spiritual family is disturbed, prayers are hindered in the same way.

As Stormie Omartian observes in *The Power of Praying Together:*

> One of the most important things about being in a spiritual family is finding power in prayer through unity. Jesus said that if just two of us agree concerning anything, it will be done for us by our Father in heaven. When people in an orchestra agree on what notes to play and when to play them, the results are powerful. When a husband and a wife are in unity, their marriage is strong. And when children are in unity with their parents and with each other, the family stays strong. *It's the same with spiritual family.* When the leaders are in unity, and the believers are in unity with them and with each other, there is a dynamic that adds power to their prayers. Their prayers become music to God's ears, and He answers in power.[35]

Stormie's books on prayer may have sold millions, but the greatest thing about her is the example of her own life. She and her husband, Michael, live what they write about. Their spiritual father and mentor, Jack Hayford, can attest to this and to the fruit of their lives when they were members of Church on the Way. Now that I am their pastor, I can as well.

It's an immutable law in the spiritual world: families and families of churches that walk in unity are effective in prayer. Those that don't, aren't.

## A HOUSE OF PRAYER FOR ALL NATIONS

So what should be a primary focus of prayer, both individually and collectively? Not just unity for unity's sake, or to see our personal needs met. The primary purpose should be touching the world. This was clearly and dramatically demonstrated by our Lord when He walked into the Temple and began to "clean house":

> He entered the temple and began to drive out those who were buying and selling in the temple, and overturned the tables of the money changers and the seats of those who were selling doves; and He would not permit anyone to carry merchandise through the temple. And He began to teach and say to them, "Is it not written, 'MY HOUSE SHALL BE CALLED A HOUSE OF PRAYER FOR ALL THE NATIONS'?"
> —MARK 11:15–17, NASB

If there is any doubt as to what the focus of the Church should be, Jesus settled it that fateful day. We know what He would do; now what about us? Will we become the Church that answers the call to be a house of prayer for all nations?

Many sincere Christians are crying out for revival, for the Lord's manifest presence to come into the midst of their churches or ministries. Be careful what you wish for. The Jesus who will show up if that prayer is answered is not the manageable, meek and mild deity of popular imagination. His passion is for the lost. His zeal is for His Father's house. He is looking for people who will obey His command to pray. And when He comes, He is likely to clear the deck of any remaining trinkets of our self-will and launch us all into the center of His will—praying and then working to fulfill the Apostolic Mandate.

## TEACH US TO PRAY

The disciples of Jesus were eyewitnesses to the most astounding feats of the miraculous power of God, as well as the most anointed preaching ever heard. In spite of this, they are never quoted as asking the Lord to teach them to preach or to do miracles. Their only request was that they would be taught to pray.[36] For some time they had watched Jesus regularly slipping away to pray. Then they saw the powerful manifestations of God's Spirit that followed. No doubt they asked for a lesson in prayer because they had figured out an essential principle of God's kingdom—miracles, healing and words of deliverance flow out of a life of prayer.

One of life's greatest mysteries is how and why God includes us in His plans to redeem the earth. He has challenged us to pray that His kingdom would come and His will be done "on earth as it is in heaven."[37] His desire is that the life, beauty and order of heaven be brought to our world right now, in our generation. He promised that "if my people, who are called by my name, will humble themselves and pray and seek my face and turn from their wicked ways, then will I hear from heaven and will forgive their sin and will heal their land."[38] God isn't expecting all the citizens of a nation to repent before He begins to heal the land. He begins by looking for *His people*, the Church, to humble themselves, repent and pray. The responsibility for the condition of our cities is laid at the doorstep of the Church. In this hour, we need to be making the same request of God that the disciples made: "Lord teach us to pray."

## THE IMPACT OF PRAYER

As with anything in the kingdom of God, faith is the starting point. We have to believe—to *know*—that prayer can make a difference. Without this confidence in the Lord's power and faithfulness in honoring our intercession, it's impossible to please Him.[39] This faith comes as we hear His word and the testimony of His works in the earth.[40] Isaiah asked an important question: "Who has believed our report?"[41] Hearing the promises of God in His Word will build your faith. So will the act of praying, especially as you see prayer answered and hear the report of what is happening through the lives of other people who pray.

All over the world the Holy Spirit is moving, and there are miracles and dramatic signs and wonders taking place in unprecedented ways. In America there are new television channels specializing in almost any interest you can name. There's the golf channel, the food channel, the news channel, etc. There should be a "Miracle Channel" that does nothing but document and relate the tidal wave of answered prayer and divine deliverance that is sweeping the earth. We have a group of medical doctors in our ministry who could have their own show, sharing testimonies from our city alone. Week after week, unexplainable phenomena take place as an answer to prayer. And it's not just prayer up front after a service or intercession being offered up by the ministerial staff. It's prayer by the rank-and-file believers.

As Jesus promised, "He who believes in Me, the works that I do he will do also; and greater works than these he will do, because I go to My Father."[42] This is the era of the "greater works."

### Asia

In China, the Church has exploded from a small, persecuted minority to a mostly underground movement with, according to the best estimates, over one hundred million followers. In meetings with their leaders, testimony after testimony confirms the fact that, in spite of the persecution, prayer has made the biggest difference. Said one Chinese church leader, "You'll never know how powerful prayer is until it's all you have left." The leaders of the Chinese church say that their prayers are now being directed at the Muslim world, asking God to release them as laborers into the harvest in the Middle East.

Korea has many of the largest churches in the world, including one with over a million members. On Fridays, all-night prayer meetings take place in various churches throughout the capital city of Seoul. Christian leaders nationwide attribute the unprecedented growth of Christianity in Korea to this focus on prayer. Pastor Simon Suh, the director of MSI's Korean outreach, explains, "Prayer is the central part of the church's life. From early morning prayer every day to all-night prayer meetings, the Lord graciously releases His power through the intercession of His people."

### Africa

The largest churches in the world are now in Nigeria. In this strategically positioned nation near the center of Africa, crowds of over two million gather to hear the Word of God in mass crusades. Amid the persecution posed by an Islamic majority in the nation, prayer has produced spectacular church growth as well as notable miracles.

The media and much of the world predicted bloodshed as the nation of South Africa dismantled the oppressive apartheid system. Masses of people fled the country in fear, even leaving their belongings behind. And yet, despite the sense of foreboding that gripped much of the population, the church began to pray. All over the nation, the cry went up to heaven to heal the land and preserve the work of the Spirit.

The result was that hundreds of thousands of people were born again throughout the country. Miraculously, the threat of massive bloodshed evaporated, as enormous strides were made in ethnic reconciliation in a very short period of time. The nation emerged with a new unity and worldwide respect. The grace of God fell so mightily on President Nelson Mandela that he was embraced as the leader of all the tribes and became one of the most respected leaders of all time. His is a fantastic testimony of what happens when the Church "first of all [offers] prayers…for all men, for kings and all who are in authority."[43] When the Church prays for leaders as the Bible commands, God answers by either granting them new ones or by giving the ones they have the wisdom and moral strength necessary to lead the people into righteousness.

### Latin America

In a part of the world that has been steeped in corruption, violence and religious superstition, the Spirit of the Lord is moving in dramatic ways. In Argentina, churches of over one hundred thousand are flourishing. Amid the hedonistic culture of Brazil, the growth of Protestant Christianity now outstrips every other religion. The revival has spilled out of the cities into the countryside, leaving new churches in its wake. As the Scriptures promise, "where sin increased, grace increased all the more."[44]

In the nation of Colombia, there has also been significant church growth, with as many as thirty thousand people flooding into some congregations. There have also been many other dramatic answers to prayer. In May of 1995, twenty-five thousand people assembled in a stadium in the important Colombian city of Cali. Instead of a soccer game, they gathered for a time of prayer and national repentance. "The city's now famous all-night prayer vigil—the *vigilia*—had been born. Forty-eight hours after the event, the daily newspaper, *El Pais*, headlined, 'No Homicides!' For the first time in as long as anybody in the city could remember, a 24-hour period had passed without a single person being killed."[45] Today, it is not uncommon for crowds of more than fifty thousand to gather for an all night prayer *vigilia*.

## BECOMING A HOUSE OF PRAYER

Americans tend to wait until they're in trouble and need God's help before they really begin to pray. After 9/11, there was a dramatic spike in intercession as churches all over the country were open for prayer.

Week after week, the government and the media published warnings
of imminent terrorist attacks, and yet a tangible peace seemed to prevail over many people's hearts. And, of course, no significant attacks
came, potential terrorist strikes were exposed and our military had a
level of success in Afghanistan that surprised almost everybody. In
spite of what the "enemy" had planned, their plots and schemes
seemed to be thwarted.

When I became pastor of Bethel World Outreach Center in
January of 2000, the Lord reminded me of all that I had seen around
the world in terms of the impact that can be made when a church
prays. Certainly there was prayer at Bethel before I became pastor, but
I knew that there wasn't enough to adequately "cover" all that the
Lord wanted to accomplish through us. We issued a call to corporate
prayer, targeting Friday nights (after the model of the Korean
church). Along with morning prayer meetings, we began to cry out
for the Lord to use us as a local church to change the nations. A sense
of determination and urgency began to grow in our hearts to see His
righteous rule extend to the nations and the cities of the world, beginning in our hometown of Nashville.

As the amount and the intensity of prayer increased, an amazing
thing began to happen: the church began to grow. In a little over two
years, the church more than tripled in size—no small thing in a nation
where church membership has plateaued, and in many places is even
declining. What was perhaps even more impressive, though, were the
other things that accompanied this growth. We helped plant seven
other churches, sending out teams of leaders to cities such as New York,
Auckland and Seattle. Several new ministries were birthed locally, and
so many doors of favor were opened to us throughout Nashville and its
environs that it was a challenge just to walk through them all. God
began to move among different communities: doctors, the inner city,
athletes and media personalities. We were able to produce television
specials that were viewed by a large portion of the city. Ideas and creative strategies seemed to pour out on us. The scope of what has
happened is difficult to measure, and is well beyond what we ever could
have accomplished through our own strength and abilities. The Lord of
Hosts has definitely shown Himself to be strong on our behalf.

Now prayer is happening all over the city. From the students on
campus to the inner city, we are trusting God to "heal our land" as we
pray.

# CONCLUSION

Just as God ordained the "natural" family, He also instituted "spiritual" family. All His children, even the lonely and disenfranchised, can experience a place of security and power when they are adopted and then placed into His kingdom family. God reveals Himself as Father, especially to the fatherless.[46] In Mark 10, Jesus promised:

> Truly I say to you, there is no one who has left house or brothers or sisters or mother or father or children or farms, for My sake and for the Gospel's sake, but that he will receive a hundred times as much now in the present age, houses and brothers and sisters and mothers and children and farms.
>
> —MARK 10:29–30, NASB

Many have used this passage to speak of *prosperity*, but there's an even greater hope concerning *posterity*. Those who follow God and start out with a lack, as far as family is concerned, will find a multiplication of relationships as they continue on in their journey. The end purpose is that, through family, we might grow up in all things into Christ and fulfill God's purposes in our generation.

Family and prayer go hand and hand because of the potential power that is released through unity and agreement. The end result is a Church that matures into a household of prayer for all nations. In designing, building and leading this house, God has given us gifts and principles to ensure its well-being and eventual success. It is now time to recover one of the most obvious—yet ironically neglected—aspects of the Apostolic Mandate: apostolic ministry itself. We will examine this needed gift in the next chapter.

# PART III

# MISSION

CHAPTER 8

# RECOVERING APOSTOLIC MINISTRY

*The concealing, and the neglect of certain truths, and certain aspects of Christian truth, has always been the chief characteristic of every period of declension in the long history of the Church.*

—DR. MARTIN LLOYD-JONES

O ver one hundred years ago, Charles Spurgeon asked his audience an important question: "Why isn't the Church accomplishing more in the area of world missions?" After a brief pause, he thundered his response: "Because we have not apostolic men, they do not go about their work in an apostolic style, they do not have apostolic churches backing them up, and they have not the apostolic influence of the Holy Ghost!"[1]

All but buried and forgotten for centuries, the concept of apostolic ministry has reemerged as the Church has stepped into the twenty-first century. Dr. Peter Wagner, professor of Church growth at Fuller Theological Seminary, founder of the Wagner Leadership Institute and one of the most vocal proponents of the effectiveness of modern-day apostolic movements, writes, "The New Apostolic Reformation is an extraordinary work of God…that is, to a significant extent, changing the shape of Protestant Christianity around the world…In virtually every region of the world, these new apostolic churches constitute the fastest-growing segment of Christianity."[2]

Although this new apostolic reformation is primarily based in charismatic churches that have been established within the last several decades, it is not limited to nor did it originate with them. Ministers and theologians from diverse backgrounds are increasingly recognizing the recovery of apostolic ministry as a vital missing ingredient in the Church's regaining of its God-ordained influence over culture. Reggie McNeal, a pastor and leader within the Southern Baptist Convention, has written extensively about the revolutionary aspects of this revival of apostolic calling:

> Apostolic leadership seeks to partner with God in His redemptive mission in the world. Leaders of this ilk commit themselves to an agenda bent on transforming the world. This revolution begins with a different way of thinking and doing church.[3]

The renowned Roman Catholic theologian, Hans Küng, has observed:

> The Church least of all can be an end in itself. Everything the Church does must be directed towards fulfilling its apostolic mission to the outside world; it must minister to the world and to mankind. To be a Church and to have a mission are not two separate things. To be itself, the Church must follow the apostles in continually recognizing and demonstrating that it has been sent out to the world.[4]

It was the apostle Paul who gave us a foundational insight into the ministry of the apostle when he wrote to the Ephesians:

> He [Jesus] gave some as apostles, and some as prophets, and some as evangelists, and some as pastors and teachers, for the equipping of the saints for the work of service, to the building up of the body of Christ; until we all attain to the unity of the faith, and of the knowledge of the Son of God, to a mature man, to the measure of the stature which belongs to the fullness of Christ.
>
> —Ephesians 4:11–13, NASB

God appoints leadership ministries in the Church in order to equip the saints for the work of the ministry. We are to be under these "coaches" until we all grow up and reach the measure of the stature of the fullness of Christ.

Regardless of differing perspectives on the end times, all orthodox Christian traditions agree that the Church is commissioned to grow in maturity and spread throughout the world as we wait for the Lord's return. That being the case, each of these five ministries, including that of the apostle, should be functioning *in some way* until the Church fulfills the Apostolic Mandate and matures into the image of the Son of God. The voices of dispensational theology have insisted that these ministries are no longer valid, and therefore the subject of apostolic ministry is moot. Thankfully, men and women are reconsidering these vital truths due to the critical condition of the Church and the crisis that has kept it from failing to recognize these gifts.

## THE APOSTOLIC MANDATE

In the passage we call *The Apostolic Mandate,* Jesus specifically addressed a group of eleven men that He had chosen and trained to be His disciples. He granted them their mandate as apostles when He declared:

> All authority has been given to Me in heaven and on earth. Go therefore and make disciples of all the nations, baptizing them in the name of the Father and the Son and the Holy Spirit, teaching them to observe all that I commanded you; and lo, I am with you always, even to the end of the age.
>
> —MATTHEW 28:18–20, NASB

The key points of this mandate are straightforward, but allow me to restate them:

First of all, His disciples would be empowered to preach the Gospel, not in word only, but according to Christ's authority and by the power of the Holy Spirit.

Second, they were to go into every nation. The Greek word for nations is *ethnoi,* which literally means "ethnicity" or "people-group." They were not commissioned merely to set up a teaching center in Jerusalem. Neither was it sufficient to reach out to the *Diaspora,* the Jews that had been dispersed throughout the Roman Empire. Their mission field was to be every territory and every people-group throughout the entire world.

Third, they were instructed to make disciples of the nations, teaching them to observe all that Jesus had commanded them. This command calls for obedience and action, not just knowledge. The apostles did not set up training schools in the tradition of the Greek schools of philosophy. The new churches they founded in their missionary journeys were created to be centers for practical instruction and discipleship, training God's people from every nation to both know God and make Him known.

Fourth, Jesus promised to stay with them at all times, "even to the end of the age"—in other words, until the job is done and the curtain comes down on the world's stage. One could infer from this promise that some tough times probably lay ahead for the Church.

Lastly, the promise clearly extends beyond the eleven apostles. None of them would be alive when the end of the age comes. So at this point it becomes clear that this mandate is not restricted to the original apostles or to the first-century Church. This calling, sending, empowering and protecting extends to the Church throughout history.

### God is a sending God

It is perhaps the best-known and most cherished Scripture in the Bible: "For God so loved the world that He gave His only begotten Son…"[5] The apostle John revisited this theme of divine love and sacrifice in the first of his three epistles: "He loved us and sent His Son to be the propitiation for our sin."[6]

Giving and sending is a big part of God's heart and a primary demonstration of His love. Any vital relationship with Him is going to reflect this same focus, as Larry Caldwell noted in his book, *Sent Out:* "God is a sending God. No study of apostleship can properly begin without acknowledging that all sending is rooted in the very character of God."[7] It's easy to understand why the enemy wants to stop this "threatening" dimension of the kingdom. What adversary wouldn't want to stop the senders and the ones being sent to defeat their efforts?

## THE ORIGINAL TWELVE APOSTLES

The ministry and mission of an apostle as exemplified by the original twelve called by Christ, is to go into new territories, preach the Gospel with power and authority, and birth new churches. These churches then become bases from which the kingdom of God expands to impact the entire culture, the leaven that, though small, eventually grows to "leaven the whole lump."[8] This mindset was vital to these early churches and provided the apostolic pattern that caused them to grow from a small band of beleaguered believers to the most influential force in the Roman Empire.

The words *apostle* and *apostolic* come from the Greek word *apostolos*, meaning "messenger" or "one who is sent." The Latin equivalent, *missio*, provides the etymological root from which we get the English words *mission* and *missionary*. So at a basic, semantic level, to be apostolic means to simply function as a missionary in planting churches. And we know from both the Bible and Church history, this is precisely what the first apostles did. From John in Asia Minor to Peter in Samaria to Paul (and later Peter) in Rome, the early Church saw a flurry of apostolic activity once the fire of Pentecost—and later persecution—kicked the Church into gear.

The missionary efforts of the original eleven and Paul, however, could not directly account for the spread of Christianity and new churches throughout the Roman Empire. The good news of the Gospel soon became every Christian's business, spreading by word-of-mouth along the Roman highways and through day-to-day conversations. Soon the churches that had been founded by the apostles became apostolic themselves, reproducing and starting new congregations throughout their respective regions. Like leaven in a loaf, the multiplication began and continues to this day. And wherever anointed leaders oversee the planting and building of these new churches, the ministry of the apostle, as defined by Paul, is alive and functioning in its full capacity.

## THE UNIQUENESS OF THE TWELVE

While there are many similarities between modern-day apostles and the original twelve, there are also a few important differences.

Consider Jesus and His first followers. Though many who heard the Lord later became disciples, He had a special relationship with a select few. Mark writes in his Gospel: "And He went up on the mountain and summoned those whom He Himself wanted, and they came to Him. And He appointed twelve, that they might be with Him, and that He might send them out to preach."[9]

Christianity is unique among all religious traditions because the essential underpinnings of the faith—among them the life, death and resurrection of Jesus Christ—are historical events that can and indeed have been validated by numerous eyewitnesses. Wherever we find the apostles preaching the Gospel in the New Testament, we also find them validating their message with the declaration, "And we are witnesses of these things…"[10] This was a primary validation of their apostleship: the ability to provide an eyewitness account of the foundational events surrounding the Christian faith.

When trying to decide who should replace Judas Iscariot, the remaining disciples raised this very qualification:

> Therefore it is necessary that of the men who have accompanied us all the time that the Lord Jesus went in and out among us—beginning with the baptism of John until the day that He was taken up from us—one of these should become a witness with us of His resurrection.
> —ACTS 1:21–22, NASB

The unique authority of the original apostles rested on the fact that they were eyewitnesses who could personally validate each element of the faith. How firm a foundation that is—one based in truth, not myth and legend! In John's revelation, written on foundation stones of the New Jerusalem "were the twelve names of the twelve apostles of the Lamb."[11] It was on the basis of this authority that the words spoken by these men were accepted as Holy Scripture.

While the place of the original twelve is completely unique, in other ways there's great continuity between them and the apostolic ministries that have operated down through the centuries.

Who were the New Testament apostles? We commonly speak of the "original twelve" and, as we have established, they deserve special honor. If we restrict our list to them alone, however, our theology of apostleship will be incomplete. The fact is there are as many as twenty-two people called apostles in the New Testament. They range from obvious examples such as Matthias, who replaced Judas, and Paul, to less prominent men such as Barnabas, James and Silas. The husband and wife team of Adronicus and Junia were also numbered "among the apostles."[12] Some claim that Timothy, Titus and several other New Testament leaders bear the same title. And then there is Dr. Luke, author of the two longest books in the New Testament. Though nowhere explicitly called an apostle, the "beloved physician"[13] who was a disciple of Paul's, has been recognized by Christian denominations down through the ages as having been an apostle. Regardless of the exact number, it's clear that more than the original twelve bore the title. Those who had been sent and graced with the call to birth new churches held the office as well.

## CHARACTERISTICS OF MODERN-DAY APOSTOLIC MINISTRIES

As we've seen, Ephesians 4:11 tells us that the five-fold ministry gifts Jesus gave the Church will continue *until* we reach the unity of the faith. Even as the office of pastor, teacher or evangelist remains vital and necessary for the healthy growth of the Church, so the apostle and prophet, rightly understood, are indispensable to the fulfillment of the Apostolic Mandate. The task that has been set before us is a daunting one, requiring all the courage, sacrifice and skill we can muster. Shutting down any ministry gift because of fear or faulty theology isn't an option. We need, quite literally, "all hands on deck."

At the same time, let us remember that today's apostles have no authority whatsoever to speak or write *ex cathedra* (infallibly). They are under the authority of Scripture just like any other believer. Every word they preach and everything they do is to echo the cry of both the Bereans in Acts 17:11–14 and the leaders of the Reformation: *Sola Scriptura*—that is, "Scripture alone." As the apostolic gift helps build local churches, it is the plumb line of the Bible that ensures that their walls are straight. As the apostle Paul wrote:

> According to the grace of God which was given to me, like a wise master builder I laid a foundation, and another is building on it. But each man must be careful how he builds on it. For no man can lay a foundation other than the one which is laid, which is Jesus Christ.
> —1 CORINTHIANS 3:10–11, NASB

There is also some confusion as to the place of signs, wonders and miracles as a primary test of apostolic ministry. In his letter to the Corinthians, Paul writes,

> God has appointed in the church, first apostles, second prophets, third teachers, then miracles, then gifts of healing…All are not apostles, are they?…All are not workers of miracles, are they?
> —1 CORINTHIANS 12:28–29, NASB

The healthy, faith-filled church is often graced with people who have been anointed with the gift of healing and miracles. These same people can also be blessed with the ability to teach, evangelize or pastor. But their primary gift is motivated by a passion to see people healed, and it is empowered by the Holy Spirit along these lines. This does not necessarily mean that they are apostles.

In the same way, the apostolic gift should be accompanied by the miraculous. That was certainly the case with Peter and Paul. But these signs and wonders are secondary to the primary focus of winning souls and planting healthy churches. Miracles, healings and deliverance from evil spirits then are a means to that end, a demonstration that the kingdom of God has come and is spreading one soul and one new church at a time. Let's look at a broader picture of what apostolic ministry produces when it is in operation.

### New disciples

In keeping with the Apostolic Mandate, the first order of business is—you guessed it!—making disciples. Since we have dealt with this in detail, we will simply underscore its importance here. A primary manifestation of apostolic ministry is grace to win souls and then father them in Christ. Obviously, all believers can do this, but it should be the burden of the apostolic to ensure this is happening in the Church. Paul referred to this facet of his ministry as a primary badge of his apostleship. For example, in his letters to the Corinthians, he challenged those who sought to subvert his position and lead those whom he had birthed:

> For though you might have ten thousand instructors in Christ, yet you do not have many fathers; for in Christ Jesus I have begotten you through the gospel…If I am not an apostle to others, yet doubtless I am to you. For you are the seal of my apostleship in the Lord.
> —1 CORINTHIANS 4:15; 9:2, NKJV

Therein lies the real secret to Paul's apostolic authority with regard to that church. He was their spiritual father because they had come to Christ under his ministry. As we will see in a moment, this was Paul's *modus operandi*, to go "where Christ had not been preached."[15] Obviously, people who became believers in these places would be his converts, his children in the Lord.

The respected scholar F. F. Bruce, notes this pioneering aspect of apostolic church planting:

> The work of an apostle was to preach the gospel where it had not been heard before and plant churches where none had existed before. When those churches had received sufficient teaching to enable them to understand their Christian status and responsibility, the apostle moved on to continue the same kind of work elsewhere.[16]

### New leaders

If the apostolic gift is working properly, the fruit will not only be new lives, but also new leadership; new leaders who in turn produce new life. The pattern of God-ordained creation is once again realized: "the [good tree] yields fruit, whose seed is in itself according to its kind."[17]

At an international conference in 1985, a minister approached me and asked if I could help him hire a youth pastor. His small church plant had exploded to over ten thousand members in just five years. Now he could be seen on Christian television and had become one of the most influential ministers in North America.

I was stunned by his request. Here was a man leading one of America's largest churches, and, after five years, he apparently had raised up no spiritual sons to fulfill this responsibility. Ecclesiastes says, "Then I looked again at vanity under the sun. There was a certain man without a dependent [literally, "without a second"], having neither a son nor a brother, yet there was no end to all his labor."[18] When the way you build leaves you without spiritual sons or daughters or strong relationships, there is no end to your work, and it produces a sense of disillusionment and discouragement. This is the very heart condition that is the "beginning of sorrows" for many called to the ministry.

I responded to the request for a youth pastor by encouraging him and his ministry team to pour their lives into the hundreds of young men who had flocked to their church. "In six months," I said, "You could have a hundred youth leaders."

My advice was dismissed as "unrealistic."

Today the church no longer exists. Could there be a link between that church's failure and the attitude of the leaders toward making disciples? I believe so.

James C. Collins and Jerry I. Porras conducted a study of large corporations over the last one hundred years and published their findings in two books entitled *Built to Last* and *Good to Great*. The authors commented on the characteristics of what they called "visionary corporations"—companies that had continued to grow and prosper through changes in society, trends in business and the turnover of leadership. Two of the most common characteristics of these visionary corporations were: 1) the emphasis on promoting and maintaining corporate culture and values, and 2) that each succeeding generation of leadership came from *within the company*. It was extremely rare that a senior leader was hired from outside the organization.[19]

Jim Laffoon, who serves on our apostolic team, has rightly observed, "Those who don't birth sons will try to buy them." No expanding organization—and that especially includes ministries—can maintain its vision and values by simply hiring leaders from someone else's field. Bringing people in from the outside should be the exception and not the rule. As in Jesus' day, the harvest is plentiful, but the laborers are few. We must raise up new leaders. Jesus showed the way by pouring His life into a small group of men who were in time sent out as apostles. The apostle Paul trained Timothy to be a church planter like himself. Then he commanded Timothy, as we have seen, to "entrust these [things] to faithful men who will be able to teach others also."[20]

Phil Bonasso, one of the founders of our ministry and noted pastor for years, is a great example of this principle. Hardly a month goes by that he isn't sending out someone to plant a church or work in some area of ministry. And the leaders he sends out tend to produce the same kind of fruit.

There is no better way to gauge the health of a congregation than by looking at this "rate of multiplication." A local church that is producing new converts, making and training disciples and releasing new leaders will necessarily be one where, to use the Reformational formula, "the Gospel is rightly taught and the sacraments are rightly administered."[21]

### New churches

This task is so foundational to our destiny in God that we've devoted the next chapter, "The Most Effective Form of Evangelism" (Chapter 9) to it. But allow me here to be as direct as I can about this vital calling: Birds fly, dogs bark and *apostles plant churches*.

Jim Laffoon put it this way,

> As we see throughout the Book of Acts, apostles are
> anointed church planters. Although each apostle can
> receive a different measure of the apostolic office, most of
> the ones I have met have received a grace from God to
> plant strong, healthy local churches. Whether they are
> planting the churches themselves or assisting others to do
> it, they have an anointing to bring a supernatural power
> and efficiency to this vital task.[22]

Without new churches being planted, there's no real evidence of an
apostolic grace. Yes, there can be a network of churches organized
around a mega-church or some respected leader or leaders. There can
be great benefit to belonging to these types of organizations and affil-
iations. But conferences and gatherings of Christians by themselves
cannot take the place of practical vision and vital, three-stranded
cord relationships[23] that result in leaders being trained, new churches
being planted and the Apostolic Mandate being fulfilled.

Churches that do make disciples and train leaders will inevitably
end up planting new churches. Everything that is living and healthy
reproduces. As new churches multiply, they become a family of
churches that have a common "spiritual DNA" and mission.
Protecting the mission and these "family ties" then becomes a great
responsibility, particularly when other congregations want to be
grafted in. It can be difficult, even destructive, to bring "orphaned"
churches into a spiritual family when they haven't been birthed and
nurtured in the common mission and value system of that family.
People are so desperate to be part of something that is moving (hence
a "movement"), that they will jump on anything (like a boat leaving
Cuba) that is going somewhere, even if they're not sure what its destination is.

In studying the fracturing of many movements over the past few
years, this lack of agreement about values and direction has been a
major cause. Like an airline pilot announcing the plane's destination
before takeoff so the passengers are sure they're on the right plane
(and have the chance to get off if they're not), leaders must make the
vision clear from the beginning to preserve the unity and direction of
the church—if not, disaster looms. There are times when established

churches are grafted into Morning Star International or into any other church or organization, for that matter. For us, this is not a matter of simply "signing up." There is a customary "courtship" process where the prospective leaders seek God as to whether this is truly a divine joining. And, of course, there has to be a "no holds barred" commitment to the Apostolic Mandate as decreed by Christ and as processed through the personality and theological presuppositions of the particular movement.[24] Let me say it again: both the vision and unity of the ministry have to be preserved at all costs. If we join together, it is not just to *be together*, but to cooperate in expanding God's kingdom.

### New territories pioneered

In his letter to the Romans, Paul explained why he had never visited Rome:

> I aspired to preach the gospel, not where Christ was already named, so that I would not build on another man's foundation; but as it is written, "They who had no news of Him shall see, and they who have not heard shall understand." For this reason I have often been prevented from coming to you.
>
> —ROMANS 15:20–22, NASB

As "the apostle to the Gentiles," it might have seemed odd that he had never been to the capital of the Gentile world. But here Paul explains that he had been "hindered" from visiting because his highest priority had been to take the Gospel into unreached territories. Pastor and renowned author, John Piper, observes:

> Paul's conception of his specific missionary task was that he must press on beyond the regions and peoples where Christ is now preached to places like Spain, and to peoples "who have never been told of Him." God's missionary "grace" for Paul was to be a foundation-layer in more and more places and peoples. His aim was not to reach as many Gentile individuals as he could but to reach as many unreached peoples as he could.[25]

If Paul was alive today, his primary focus would likely be the "10/40 Window"—a missiological term that describes the geographical territory bounded by the tenth and fortieth parallels. These two latitudes enclose an area of the world with the least exposure to the Gospel, encompassing the majority of the world's Muslims, Buddhists and Hindus. With a population nearing four billion, the 10/40 Window includes fifty-nine countries—both sovereign states and non-sovereign dependencies. This region should be an area of primary concern for apostolic ministries. Tragically, such is not the case at present. For example, the second largest religion in the world, Islam—with a billion followers and growing—only receives between one and two percent of the church's missionaries. This must change.

In addition to territories that have had little or no Gospel witness, there needs to be a greater concern for areas where Christianity was once pervasive but is now fading or all but gone. There are regions of the United States and most of Europe that are in desperate need of reevangelism and the founding of new apostolic churches.

In our twenty-first century "global village," the Church also needs to focus its attention on areas bounded not so much by geography as by ideology and culture. It has been well noted, for example, that in terms of influencing people and shaping worldviews all around the planet, there is no terrestrial locale more strategically important than a small area in Southern California called Hollywood. Instead of merely "cursing the darkness," a well-lit candle set upon "a lampstand [so that] it gives light to all who are in the house" is well overdue.[26] Christianity at one time used to set the standard for all the arts. Besides poor theology and laziness on our part, what's really keeping the Church that serves the Lord of all creativity from once again discipling the nations in the arena of the arts?

The apostle Paul plowed a deep furrow down the middle of the cultural center that was the Areopagus in Athens.[27] Today, he would find the same forum on the college campus. Internationally, the university and its environs are all but untouched by their respective local churches. This, too, must change.

Ministering to university students, especially on some of the larger, more liberal campuses, can seem a bit intimidating. That by itself should be a good indication of just how important this mission field is. Jesus told us that the strongman guards his treasure until someone stronger comes and takes away the armor in which he trusts.[28] The armor of intellectual pride that guards the gates of the university can be far more easily stripped away than Satan and the world would have us believe. With its feet planted firmly in the air, moral relativism (the prevailing worldview on the campus) is all bark and no bite. The flimsy walls of pseudo-intellectualism, erected to keep out the Gospel and "protect" millions of young people from the call of God, are teetering on their sandy foundations. Like the Berlin Wall, their collapse is inevitable. The captives will be set free. MSl has targeted these university cities for future church planting in anticipation of this great revival among the world's youth.

### New unity in the body of Christ

When properly realized, apostolic ministry can unite both Christians and local churches around the common cause of the Apostolic Mandate. As Peter Wagner observed:

> The unity necessary in a given city for effective spiritual warfare must begin with unity among pastors and top Christian leaders. The pastors of the local churches are the spiritual gatekeepers of the city, and as such they have divine authority. Apparently Satan knows much better than many pastors that, 'by uniting we stand; by dividing we fall." In city after city, Satan has succeeded in keeping pastors divided and thus maintained the authority of whatever strongman he has assigned to the city. For good reason, the thing these territorial spirits fear the most is the unity of pastors, and through them the unity of the Body of Christ.[29]

Anyone with a genuine passion to reach the entire world will view other believers and congregations as allies. Churches without an Apostolic Mandate—whose vision doesn't extend beyond their own growth—tend to see other churches and leaders as competitors. Unity is compromised, and with it, spiritual power.

Along the same lines, we must be careful to avoid the "I am of Paul, I am of Apollos" syndrome.[30] There is but one Lord, one baptism and one Church of the living God. At the same time, however, there are many local families within the universal family of God. It is precisely these local congregations the Lord is speaking of when He declares that "He sets the solitary in families."[31] In the same way that setting people in local congregations is critical for their growth and development, it is vital that churches have apostolic covering if they are going to mature into the world-changing force the Father intends them to be.

In this necessary tension between the universal and the particular—a tension which Francis Schaeffer (among others) pointed out is ultimately resolved in the Trinitarian nature of God—it is the responsibility of apostolic leaders to work with one another to prevent divisiveness and to facilitate the "the growth of the body for the edifying of itself in love."[32]

### New strategies

With the goal of reaching the world firmly in place, fresh strategies are needed to accomplish the task. I believe the Lord of the harvest has much more for us than the occasional breakthrough. The wisdom and understanding necessary to build momentum, trigger exponential growth and impact, and produce a church that is able to transfer this success across generations is available if we will just seek the face of God.

When Paul received a vision to go to Macedonia, it was clearly a groundbreaking endeavor. Taking the Gospel expressly to the Gentiles was a new strategy, one that took several discussions with the other apostles before it was finally endorsed. In the same way, there are those throughout history who have studied the nations, waited on God and then walked into a new mission field as the Holy Spirit opened the door.

One of the key strategies God has given us as a ministry is to focus on college campuses when starting a new work in a city or nation. As we saw in Chapter 6, the campus is a tremendous field when it comes to the potential harvest of leaders who can be won, trained and then sent. Today, Victory Campus Ministries (VCM), our campus arm, is reaching thousands of university students worldwide with the Gospel. Included in this strategy are the historically black colleges and universities (HBCUs) in America. The African American Resource Ministry (AARM), led by Brett Fuller from Washington, D. C., is currently reaching out to these campuses.

Several years ago there was a slogan that was used to endorse higher education for African-Americans: "A mind is a terrible thing to waste." Well, wasting the calling on a man or a woman's life is even worse. We have a profound sense that God is going to raise up from within the black culture a "Joseph generation"—a legion of leaders whose ancestors suffered because of man's evil intent, but whose seed is predestined by God "for good, in order to bring about as it is this day, to save many people alive."[33] Slavery and kidnapping were and are an abomination.[34] But those who came to America in chains will one day produce a generation who will set the captives free.[35] The African continent in particular is waiting on this glorious day.

*Super Church Plants*

When apostles meet, it should be to pool their insights and consider ways to maximize the opportunities opening up around the world. Consider, for example, the hundreds of apostolic movements like Morning Star that exist worldwide. If only ten of them agreed to target and plant a church in a strategic city such as London or Tokyo, think of the impact! Imagine fifty to two hundred people from each movement moving to a city. With the hundreds and even thousands of churches in some of these apostolic streams, this is a very achievable goal.

These "super church plants" would consist of full-time workers, a worship team, and those relocating to find jobs. All of them would be trained and prepared to minister. Remember, these movements wouldn't even have to work together except to respect, encourage and pray for one another. Ten networks sending this number of people would have a dramatic and immediate impact. Now imagine a hundred movements targeting a city. With a measure of this kind of strategic thinking, we could revolutionize the major cities of the world in the next few years.

### New power, new miracles

I use the adjective "new" in connection with miracles for one reason: we need a fresh outpouring of God's power if we're to overcome the forces of darkness entrenched in many of the world's nations and cities. Take for example the Islamic stronghold of Iran. As a direct result of the miraculous healing of a child, a door was opened and Morning Star was able to plant a church there. Dr. "Z," a leader of the home church movement in China, spoke at our MSI World Conference in 2001 and attested to the power of signs and wonders in helping start churches throughout this communist country. Today, there are an estimated ten million people who have become believers through these churches alone. In almost every nation where we start a new work, something miraculous happens to open doors, establish churches and bear witness to Paul's testimony: "For our gospel did not come to you in word only, but also in power, and in the Holy Spirit."[36]

One of our leaders, Ken Dew, prayed for a child whom God miraculously healed, marking the birth of our new church in New Zealand. Cancer has been healed, hearts have been made whole (physically and spiritually), and blind eyes have been opened. The powerful testimony of the reality of miracles occurring throughout the world should make us hungry, as well as desperate, to shake off the chains of doubt and realize that Jesus is the same "yesterday, today, and forever."[37]

For years, many denominations have resisted God's supernatural power. Doubt and unbelief have run rampant throughout much of the western Church. Thankfully that has begun to change. It is increasingly common now for all types of churches to pray for the sick to be healed. Dramatic signs and wonders throughout the earth—especially in regions like Asia, Africa and South America—have created a hunger for an outpouring of God's power in the West. These authentic miracles are not gimmicks to attract attention to some man or ministry, or to build mailing lists for fund raising. They are to point people to the living Christ.

Charles H. Kraft, professor of anthropology at Fuller Seminary, observed: "I came to believe that the primary reason for the amazing growth rate of the Pentecostal and charismatic churches was quite simply their ability to address people's need for spiritual power."[38]

Meeting needs and ministering in the power of the Spirit was an integral aspect of Jesus' ministry. With no fanfare—in fact, He some-times told people to keep their healing a secret—Jesus simply exercised the authority His Father gave Him. Later, He very purposefully granted the same power to His disciples, telling them at another point that they would do the things He did—and even greater things.[39] Finally, He closed out His earthly ministry by instructing them to teach their own disciples "*everything*" He had commanded them.[40]

Echoing his colleague Charles Kraft, Peter Wagner writes in *The New Apostolic Churches*: "I noticed that the churches worldwide that seemed to grow the most rapidly were, for the most part, those that outwardly featured the immediate present-day supernatural ministry of the Holy Spirit."[41]

As we seek to advance the kingdom into new territories and throughout the campuses of the world, these gifts of the Spirit should flow freely. God promises us that in the last days He will pour out His Spirit on all flesh and that our sons and daughters will prophesy.[42] The last days have only grown later since Peter announced the fulfillment of that promise on Pentecost. The Spirit is still being poured out. And young people are volunteering freely in the day of His power.[43]

It's important to keep in mind that, if you have a heart of unbelief concerning these things, no amount of testimonies or doctors' verifi-cations will satisfy you. I have always been amazed by the Pharisees' request for a sign from Jesus. This after an almost constant stream of healings, exorcisms, miracles and even resurrections! Our Lord responded with the dire pronouncement, "You won't get a sign."[44] Here, as well as in the story of the beggar Lazarus, Jesus was observing that there is a certain kind of doubt that no evidence can satisfy.[45] We must all take great care that the seeds of this type of doubt don't take root in our hearts.

## APOSTOLIC TEAM MINISTRY

The concept of "five-fold" ministry is no longer, to quote the Athenians atop Mars Hill, a "new doctrine" or a "strange thing to the ears"[46] of most ministers and theologians. But the outworking of these offices, particularly as they relate to one another, is often a little skewed. Like tends to attract like, and so pastors are prone to see everything through a pastoral lens, preferring the company of other pastors, for example, to prophets. Many evangelists focus on evangel-izing, going from meeting to meeting, crusade to crusade, winning souls but then often seeing them fall through the gaping holes in a church's system for follow-up and discipleship. On and on it goes.

Writing to the church in Corinth about the dynamics of the body of Christ, Paul observed that all the members of the body were not autonomous but had a mutual dependence upon one another. The Lord designed it that way.

> God has placed the members, each one of them, in the body, just as He desired.... The eye cannot say to the hand, "I have no need of you"...On the contrary, it is much truer that the members of the body which seem to be weaker are necessary; and those members of the body which we deem less honorable, on these we bestow more abundant honor...whereas our more presentable mem-bers have no need of it.
>
> —1 Corinthians 12:18, 21–24, nasb

Paul was warning the Corinthians not to get puffed up about their own particular gifts and callings, and not to be jealous of how God has placed others in the body. All of us are important and are mutu-ally dependent upon one another.

Too often those with particular gifts seem to congregate among themselves—eyes with eyes, ears wanting to fellowship with other ears. And guess what those "ears" talk about when they get together?

How poorly all the other parts of the body hear! May God forbid! His design is for all these gifts to function together as a team.

### The dream team

When the five ministries work together in partnership and harmony, they become God's "Dream Team." Obviously, people with different gifts see things from a different perspective. In the end, there is victory in this "multitude of counselors."[47] When five technologies came together in the building of the DC-3, a new airplane wasn't the only result; an entire new industry was born as well.[48] In the same way, as the five ministry offices come together, not only will the local church become stronger, but the strategy of fulfilling the Apostolic Mandate *through that local church* will also be dramatically enhanced.

With this in mind, it would be tempting for a pastor to run out and start looking for the people endowed with the gifts he lacks. For most, this search is unavoidable. In most churches there are already persons with various gifts and ministries that the pastor relates to. Often these relationships become better defined and mutual trust is developed as people work together to build the kingdom of God through the local church. We are in agreement that the Lord blesses different expressions of church government and covering. At the end of the day, if a leader lives a life of integrity, it will carry him through, despite the lack of particular gifts around them. However, as you faithfully walk with God, He will bring you into the relationships you need; relationships that will provide covering and prevent the Church from being blown about by "every wind of doctrine."[49]

### Guarding against the pitfalls

In speaking of this need to be covered or protected, Paul constantly warned about false apostles or those who would use this title to illegitimately gain influence in the churches. Here was a man who served the church at Corinth unselfishly, and yet they considered him weak because, "I was not a burden to anyone…You gladly put up with fools since you are so wise! In fact, you even put up with anyone who enslaves you or exploits you or takes advantage of you or pushes himself forward or slaps you in the face. To my shame I admit that we were too weak for that!"[50] Today, the powerful office of apostleship has its counterfeits: those apostles who are "self-proclaimed" and use the title of apostle or their anointing to manipulate leaders into submission. The apostle Paul did refer to himself as an apostle primarily to those he had birthed into the kingdom, to the churches he had planted, and to those who were in danger of abandoning the faith for false teaching or immorality. His heart was broken not because a church had given him a small honorarium, but because they were flirting with sin and apostasy.

The apostolic heart is ultimately a father's heart for churches and their leaders. This is one of the defining marks of those who possess this calling. As has already been mentioned, Paul appealed to his role as a father repeatedly. He didn't just demand this respect, but earned it through his actions. From birthing them into the kingdom through his preaching to, at times, coming and ministering at his own expense, he proved he was a true father with a pure motivation to help them succeed. As he would write, "Children should not have to save up for their parents, but parents for their children."[51] Like a good father, he was concerned for their well-being—almost to the point of being overprotective when it came to guarding the people of God from those who would take advantage of them. Even though I'm raising a concern, I believe there are many apostolic leaders around the world who have pure hearts and right motivation, and these more than outnumber the more questionable variety.

### The apostolic team in operation

One of the dilemmas I face in this book is to present the concept of apostolic ministry, and its importance in our quest to recover the Apostolic Mandate, without getting bogged down in too many details that might be applicable only to Morning Star churches or those built with similar values. Instead, my intention is simply to highlight biblical principles of apostolic ministry. Every church has to find out what works for them according to their own conscience and resources; however, certain New Testament principles stand out as to how the apostles worked in partnership to plant churches and establish them with a godly government that would ensure their protection and enhance their chance for success. Whether it's setting in elders (Acts 14:23; Titus 1:5), overseeing the planting of new churches (Acts 8), establishing them in the faith (Romans 1:11), giving mandates for the Church to follow (Acts 16:4–5), protecting them from false doctrine (Galatians 6:12–13) or mediating conflicts (Acts 15), the apostolic team had and should have an ongoing relationship with local churches. The very motive behind the majority of Paul's epistles was to speak to the churches, encourage them, correct them and help them build an immune system against the perils of this age and the viruses that would attack the body.

## CONCLUSION—BE CAREFUL HOW YOU BUILD

We would do well to keep in mind the admonition that the apostle Paul gave to all who would dare build upon the cornerstone that is Christ:

> According to the grace of God which was given to me, like a wise master builder I laid a foundation, and another is building on it. But each man must be careful how he builds on it. For no man can lay a foundation other than the one which is laid, which is Jesus Christ. Now if any man builds on the foundation with gold, silver, precious stones, wood, hay, straw, each man's work will become evident; for the day will show it because it is to be revealed with fire, and the fire itself will test the quality of each man's work. If any man's work which he has built on it remains, he will receive a reward. If any man's work is burned up, he will suffer loss; but he himself will be saved, yet so as through fire.
>
> —1 CORINTHIANS 3:10–15, NASB

Apostolic ministry lays the foundation of Christ's Lordship and the vision and values of His kingdom. We all then build upon that foundation. It is our belief and prayer that the principles outlined in these pages will produce the kind of building materials that will endure, that will survive not only the tribulations of this present age but also the holy fire of the day of judgment. In the end, this will be the conclusive test of whether the way we are building is God-inspired. After all, as Paul wrote, "it is not the person who commends himself that is approved, but the one whom God commends."[52] That is our ultimate stamp of approval, the only one that matters.

## CHAPTER 9

# THE MOST EFFECTIVE FORM OF EVANGELISM

*The most effective form of evangelism is planting a church.*

—PETER WAGNER

M ost people probably wouldn't consider a football player an obvious choice for a church planter. But Mark Brunell did a lot more than just run drills and study playbooks while he was in college. He also became a Christian and a serious disciple. By the time he arrived in Jacksonville to help lead the Jaguars, he was a minister disguised as an NFL quarterback.

Mark and his wife, Stacy, began reaching out to their teammates and their families. Men like Tony Boselli, the six-foot, seven-inch, 320-pound left tackle (who, incidentally, had McDonald's name a hamburger with three pieces of meat after him), came to Christ and began to be discipled. Together with his wife, Angie, he formed a core group with Mark and Stacy that began to quickly grow as more and more players were impacted by the Gospel. Friends and neighbors began to respond as well.

Under the oversight of Champions for Christ director and MSI apostolic team member, Greg Ball, the move of God was carefully nurtured until it became obvious that God was birthing a church. Russ and Debbie Austin, pastors of Mid-Cities Community Church in Midland, Texas, responded to the call and moved to Jacksonville to serve as pastors. Today, Southpoint Community Church is a thriving congregation of more than eight hundred fifty members.

The grace of God? Absolutely. Something that just happened? Absolutely not. While Mark was being discipled, he was trained with the vision for church planting as a core value. Greg continually presses the point: "The goal of everything we do in reaching athletes is to train them to be leaders and teach them the importance of being in a local church. We also teach them that if there is no local church with similar values, we need to plant one."

Wherever there's a spiritual harvest, it can only be maintained through the planting of new churches. Mass crusades, healing revivals and Christian broadcasting by themselves are not enough. There's only one thing in this world the Lord said would prevail against the gates of hell: His Church.

Though there are thousands of churches planted around the world every year, sadly, there are also thousands that close their doors. It's an alarming trend that in some parts of the world, including the United States, more local churches actually die than are born. Reversing this trend must be among our top priorities. As I write this, our ministry is planting an average of one church per week somewhere in the world. The goal in the next four years is to plant one per day. We dream of the day when we are training so many new disciples and leaders, that the time frame is reduced to one per hour. If McDonald's can open up a new restaurant every eight hours[1]—offering nothing but fast food—what's to stop us when we can offer new life?

No one has studied the dynamics of church growth more than Dr. Peter Wagner. After investigating most of the various techniques and movements around the world, Wagner cuts right to the bottom line: *"The most effective form of evangelism is planting a church."*

This is the heart and soul of the Apostolic Mandate. Planting churches, as we've seen, is the very essence of what it means to be apostolic. Larry Caldwell writes, "Apostleship indeed is the gift of cross-cultural church planting that God is using and will continue to use in reaching the unreached billions in today's world."[2]

## REBUILDING THE CITIES

As we survey the cities of the world, the needs we encounter can be overwhelming. Crime, poverty, injustice, disease, drugs, racism, homelessness…the litany of misery seems endless and beyond the scope of any human remedy. And it is.

By the grace of God, however, we can and must face the challenge. Consider one simple fact with profound implications as to fulfilling the Apostolic Mandate: In 1900, 8 percent of the world's population lived in cities. Today, that number has swelled to approximately 50 percent.[3] Cities and urban areas are gaining an estimated sixty million people a year—over one million people a week![4]

Ed Silvoso writes, "Cities are central to God's redemptive strategy. The Great Commission begins with a city, Jerusalem—and culminates with another city—the new Jerusalem.…In order to fulfill the Great Commission we must reach every city on earth with the Gospel."[5]

Because of their many problems, most cities can appear as daunting fortresses, giving ground only begrudgingly to the work of God. Small gains at best dot the moral landscape. If spiritual revival caused the crime rate in any city to drop noticeably, it would be front-page news. And that's precisely why revival needs to be our goal. Slogans and "spiritual bandages" aren't going to heal the wounds of poverty (spiritual or material) and hopelessness.[6] These places must be rebuilt as the Scripture promises:

> They will rebuild the ancient ruins and restore the places long devastated; they will renew the ruined cities that have been devastated for generations.
>
> —ISAIAH 61:4

This passage follows the great promises of deliverance and healing that take place when the Holy Spirit is poured out and the Gospel is preached. It's interesting who the primary audience is: the poor, the broken-hearted, those in captivity and those who mourn. It will take hard work and the investment of more than a few years. But in the end, beauty will take the place of ashes, the garment of praise will abolish the spirit of heaviness.

### City transformation

The power of the Spirit is the source of all real change and transformation—both of an individual soul and of the life and character of a nation. "Be faithful in little things," God said, "and I'll make you faithful over much."[7] If one person can be transformed by the grace of God, then so can the second and the third, on down the line. Once the fact of individual change is established, then the possibility of the family, the neighborhood and, yes, even the city and nation being transformed becomes possible as well.

Church planting must target all areas of the city with this power, from the wealthy to those who are burned out and forgotten. As we systematically do this—street by street and home by home—we enter the eternal purposes of God and the provision necessary to fulfill His mandate.

Following the pattern of Darrell Green's Youth Life and Learning Center in Washington, D.C. (see Chapter 4), we opened a similar facility in downtown Nashville. Located in a large apartment complex, the three-thousand-square-foot center provides after-school care for a large group of children who live in the complex. Over $250,000 was invested to make it a first-class facility and a beacon of light and hope to the community.

The mayor of Nashville and many other dignitaries attended the grand opening to applaud our efforts. The head of the Tennessee Department of Education was so impressed by what she saw, she agreed to serve on the advisory board. Looking at the excellence and hope emanating from our modest facility and the impact it was already having on the city, I thought about how much had been accomplished with just a little effort. I also realized how much more needed to be done; there were scores of other areas like this one with no witness at all from the Church. Rather than stop and pat ourselves on the back, we're determined to press ahead and work to plant similar facilities where possible. Most people will never see the love and the blessings of God unless we bring it to them.

### The nations in the cities

As God works in and through His people, there are certain patterns that emerge. One common pattern goes like this: God commands us to do something and then "hides" the resources and the blessings we need for the work within the task itself. If we will diligently obey the Lord and keep His commandments, all these blessings will come upon us and overtake us.[8] Elsewhere God tells us that He gives us "the treasures of darkness" and the "hidden riches of secret places."[9] These treasures are often people, in darkness because they have not yet been redeemed, their talents and resources hidden because they have not yet been developed. Could it be that all we need to touch the world is waiting on us as we commit to reaching out to the cities of the world? As missiologist Ray Bakke explains, "Yesterday's cities were in the nations; today all the nations are in our cities." He then goes on to describe the "fuse being lit…for a Twenty-first Century Pentecost."[10]

Fulfilling the Apostolic Mandate entails targeting the cities of the world, both small and great, with a strategy that goes beyond merely holding church services. Everywhere you look there are gaping holes and needs crying out for attention. As we make our plans and pray over these areas that God would call us to, let's remember something very critical: As much as we should have a vision for the world, we must have a vision for the city we are called to. Church planting is the "Ground Zero" of city transformation.

## DISTINCTIVE TYPES OF CHURCH PLANTS

With the burden and call to reach the nations by reaching the nations' cities, let's look at some of the different methods that that can be utilized to plant these new churches. In the years since planting the initial church in Manila with Steve Murrell, our apostolic teams have been privileged to work with God in birthing scores of churches in other cities around the world—congregations that themselves have grown into church-planting churches. While each experience has had its own unique aspects and challenges, there are a number of principal lessons we've learned over the years. In a broad sense, here are some of the strategies implemented in this process.

### *Transplanted congregations*

Once the kingdom of God gains a foothold in a nation through the planting of a new church or churches, the end result, as Jesus declared, should be like that of a mustard seed. Though its beginning may be small and in some eyes a bit insignificant, eventually it grows to become the largest tree in the field, bringing everything around it into its shade.[11] If we're not seeing these types of results, we shouldn't doubt God or His Word. We should examine the way we're doing things.

From the Enlightenment on, the seminary has been the primary mechanism by which the mainstream Church has trained its leaders for the work of ministry. Today many people have begun to question its validity as an adequate method for discipling, training and equipping ministers. Whatever its limitations may be as conventionally practiced, in theory at least, the concept of "seminary" is precisely where we should be focused. In his 1828 *Dictionary of the English*

*Language,* Noah Webster defined the word *seminary* as, "a seed-plat; ground where seed is sown for producing plants for transplantation; a nursery; as, to transplant trees from a seminary."

What a profound description of what church planting should be! Instead of focusing our efforts on broadcasting seed, we should be transplanting healthy seedlings. Our prayer should then be that these seedlings take root, mature and, in turn, produce new seed. From there a new seed bed—a new seminary—can be established where seedlings can be cultivated and sent out to those other nations on the horizon that Jesus wants to subdue for His glory.

Steve Murrell and his leadership team in Manila have learned many valuable lessons about church planting in relation to this "seedling" paradigm. He observed,

> A number of years ago we did an evaluation of how effective we had been in the several dozen churches we had planted. There were many congregations that had grown explosively and some that have never gotten off the ground in years. We realized that the pastors who were struggling were associated with our third wave of church planting. In an attempt to advance the kingdom more quickly, we did not plant churches, we just planted a person or a couple. That was a mistake. Not only did the churches struggle to get established, it took a heavy toll on the individuals we sent. After looking closely at the results, we determined never to ever do that again.

Steve isn't alone in this. Around the world, new churches either fail or struggle for the same reason—a person or a group of people were planted instead of a seedling congregation. In metropolitan areas, our most effective church plants have been where we've taken a minimum of twenty people—and sometimes upwards of a hundred—and strategically sent them as a team into the heart of a city.

### Scattered seeds can take root

While most of the churches we've planted are the result of targeted and diligent effort, there are those wonderful moments when the Holy Spirit blesses the random seed that gets scattered as we're about our Father's business. Both the Bible and Church history provide examples where great churches have arisen from these humble and serendipitous circumstances.

Among the more notable examples is the story of Philip and the Ethiopian eunuch. At the direction of the Holy Spirit, Philip traveled south of Jerusalem to a place in the desert on the way to the old Philistine city of Gaza. Arriving there, he met his divine appointment: an official in the service of Candace, the queen of Ethiopia. Philip led him to Christ and, when they happened on a small pool of water, baptized him as well. Then, in one of the more intriguing moments in the New Testament, "the Spirit of the Lord snatched Philip away; and the eunuch no longer saw him, but went on his way rejoicing."[12] Philip's ministry to this man was apparently done. Not God's, however. Under His sovereign hand of blessing, this interesting character became a missionary to his people.[13] Christianity blossomed in northern Africa and many churches were planted due, in part, to his ministry.

Another example can be found in Athens several years after Paul's address to the Epicurean and Stoic philosophers atop Mars Hill. Paul's reason for being in Athens at the time was to simply wait for his apostolic team to catch up with him. Provoked by the rampant idolatry of the city, however, Paul began to preach in both the synagogue and in the "free speech zone" that was the Areopagus. After receiving a mixed response, Paul moved on to his intended destination, Corinth. The biblical account, however, concludes with these words: "But some men joined him [Paul] and believed, among whom also were Dionysius."[14] Well, the seed that Paul sowed was far more fruitful than he might have realized at the time. According to Eusebius, the bishop of Corinth in the second century and the primary historian of the era, this same Dionysius became the first bishop of the church in…you got it—Athens.[15]

We've done a lot of seed sowing around the world ourselves, and we've been blessed in a few instances to see churches come "spontaneously" into existence as a result. Ten years after I ministered in Japan, for example, I got an e-mail from a young man who began by reminding me that I had led him to the Lord. The main reason he wrote, however, was to tell me about the church he had since planted there!

Larry Matsuwaki, from Hawaii, attended an MSI Conference in 1995 where he heard the vision for planting churches. He responded by saying that he felt called to go to Singapore. At the time there was no infrastructure in place to send him. He ended up going on his own. In Singapore, God stepped into the gap and helped Larry as he began to reach out to his fellow students and neighbors. In time, a church grew out of his efforts that today is attempting to impact the nation, particularly its youth.

When things like that happen, it's a wonderful and also humbling reminder of the fact that it is the Lord who builds His Church. As you might expect, however, in the "school of discipleship" God fashioned this world to be, these types of unintentional consequences are few and far between. It's the hand of the diligent that will ultimately rule.[16] Consequently, if you really want to be part of the apostolic mission to plant churches, you can't count on merely scattering seed. You're going to have to plan, stay focused and work hard.

### The "come and help us" scenario

> And a vision appeared to Paul in the night. A man from Macedonia stood and pleaded with him, saying, "Come over to Macedonia and help us."
>
> —ACTS 16:9, NKJV

This type of church plant hits close to home for me because of the way God used my older brother, Ben, to help start our church in Houston, Texas. For some time Ben had been part of a group of Christians who met once a week to study the Scriptures, pray and encourage one another. At the same time, Leo Lawson had started a student group at the University of Houston that was growing. These two groups would meet together from time to time and, slowly but steadily, grew both in numbers and in resolve to see a new church plant. The legendary persistence of Leo Lawson, along with that of my brother, finally paid off. With the help of Pastor Ron Lewis in North Carolina, his senior associates, Elliot and Olivia Warren, were sent to Houston to be the pastors. The church today is growing and making plans to plant other congregations as well.

In Vancouver, British Columbia, Greg and Debbie Mitchell were long-time friends of a member of our leadership team. They made the trek to Nashville, and then to several of our conferences, and became convinced they were to help plant an MSI church in Vancouver. Because of their relationship with the ministry, we knew their character was strong. All that was needed was a time of training and impartation from the apostolic team to get them on the same page in regard to our vision and values. Approximately a year later, a new church was planted in that key Canadian city.

This has become a common occurrence as leaders, as well as groups of believers, have called and asked us to come to their city and begin a new church. We're always excited about these opportunities and ready, as God leads, to send in a member of our leadership team to explore the possibilities. It is not uncommon to find a divinely opened door for our particular ministry family to help plant a new church.

For those leaders who will work with us in starting a new church, attending the VLI Graduate School of Church Planting and Pastoral Ministry is a requirement. Hosted by David and Sandy Houston, a pastoral team with over twenty years of experience in planting and cultivating strong churches and leaders, this program features teaching from many of the leaders of MSI.

### Small group expansion

Many of our churches in Asia grew out of transplanted small groups. An existing church would move a small group to a new location for an informal mid-week service. When that meeting grew to a hundred people in regular attendance, they would start meeting as a church on Sunday mornings.

At the University of the Philippines in Manila, Pastor Manny Carlos took twelve people and started a small group. The plan was to start a small group or cell every time the group doubled. Within nine months, Manny had ten small groups and began meeting on Sunday mornings as a new church. Five years later there were five hundred people in his congregation, half of them university students. It's important to also point out, particularly when so much church growth in some parts of the world is through transfers, that 85 percent of the increase in Manny's church came about through conversions.

### Apostolic sending churches

King's Park International Church in Raleigh-Durham, North Carolina, began as a campus ministry that then matured into an apostolic church. Today it has an effective outreach to four major university campuses in the area. They've also planted new churches in Greensboro, near the University of North Carolina, and in Greenville, the home of East Carolina University. And recently they sent a team to plant a church in Boston, Massachusetts, led by Wayne and Sharon Mitchell. Home to six of the finest schools in America (Harvard, M.I.T. and Boston University among them), the best and brightest of the world's students come to this city to be trained as leaders.

In the last ten years, King's Park has made missions and church planting one of its foremost priorities. Following the collapse of the

U.S.S.R. and the new openness in the Russian satellite nations, Tom Jackson led a team to scout out the land. As they tend to do when the harvest is ripe, doors supernaturally opened—in this case to the Ukraine. A quickly planned university outreach there saw many students and atheistic professors dramatically converted. In response, King's Park sent a team of young people, led by Jeff Bullock and Mike Watkins, to plant a church in the city of Lviv. As I write this, eight churches have been planted in cities across western Ukraine. Another dynamic church, led by Jeff and Ana Bullock, was planted in Krakow, Poland.

During this same period, the Raleigh-Durham congregation also participated in successful church plants in Guam, China and Korea. These churches, in turn, have had a dramatic impact on unreached people groups throughout their areas; often in circumstances where western missionaries have proved ineffective. In all this, King's Park International has lived up to its name; it is truly an *international* church. Founding Pastor Ron Lewis likes to think of it as a "suburb of heaven."

Have you ever attended a conference where the internationals present have carried their national flag in some type of processional? I have, numerous times—and it never fails to move me. I'm sure there are many reason for this, not the least of which is, as Ron Lewis noted, it provides a glimpse into heaven: nations gathered before Christ, every knee bowed and every tongue giving glory to Him as Lord. Well, that is the sense you get when you attend King's Park. Flags are everywhere, representing the thirty different nations in the church.

Every week the congregation comes together to intercede for the nations. Of course, there's a special grace, a divine connection, to those nations who have a representative in the congregation or where King's Park has helped plant an MSI church. The number of those nations is always growing, and they have become what Jesus described as His Church: "A house of prayer for all nations."[17]

### Corporate church plants

When you take a part of your congregation to establish a church two hours down the road, it's not likely that you'll get much help from churches on the other side of the country. When planting a church in a large city a time zone or a continent away, however—and if you're smart—you'll start looking around for other churches with which to partner. More often than not, that's how we set out to start a new work. The worship team comes from one church, the pastor from another. And then any number of churches will get involved in sending outreach teams and helping support the church financially through its critical first year.

Our church in Guam, for example, began when a group of Filipinos from our church in Manila moved there and began ministering to people. Sensing the potential harvest, the apostolic team made the decision to support them in starting a church. Taylor and Elizabeth Stewart, campus ministers at Duke University, teamed with people from several churches from around the world and relocated there. Today the church is firmly planted and reproducing itself through new church plants.

In addition to the regional church planting efforts of local churches, we also work together internationally to strategically plant churches each year. For this to work, churches and committed members of the MSI family must utilize their gifts and talents as the Lord determines. One of the ways we coordinate this effort is through the MSI website: www.everynation.org. Sections of the site are dedicated to planting churches and MSI members and friends can keep the apostolic church-planting team updated on areas of the world to which they feel called, as well as the gifts and talents they can use to serve. These are sections entitled *The 2010 Initiative* and *Who Wants to Change the World?*

The power of a movement is seen in its ability to work together corporately to plant churches. When you train people throughout the world with the same basic values and vision, when they get together to work on a project like this, it's as if they already know each other. Building together works because they're working from the same blueprint and with the same tools. That's the power of unity.

## NEW YORK CITY

This was precisely our strategy for New York City. Shortly after the terrorist attacks of 9/11, a small group of leaders from our churches in Nashville and Raleigh-Durham met in New York City. Walking the streets, talking and praying with people who had suffered personal loss or who were devastated by the specter of sudden death and inexplicable evil, the burden we felt for the city only continued to grow.

On our second day there, we met a producer from one of the major networks who was a believer. Gesturing to the sea of missing-persons

204    <small>EVERY NATION IN OUR GENERATION</small>

posters and broken people all around us, she made an observation that echoed in our souls. "This city is the most atheistic city in America, but it's open to God now. But I don't think there's enough spiritual help to go around."

Later, Ron Lewis and I sat down to discuss what to do with her challenge. Our plates were already full and this was New York, after all—perhaps the most proud, sophisticated, secular city on the planet. Did we have sufficient forces in faith, money and personnel to pull this off, or should we "ask for terms of peace" and just pray for the city?[18] In the end, our confidence in the Lord as well as our commitment to the Apostolic Mandate made the choice obvious. How do you best bring the grace of God to serve a city? You start a church.

After talking with other members of our apostolic team, the decision was made. We were going to plant a new church in the spiritual center of the city, right in the heart of Manhattan. The following Sunday, I stood up in our church in Nashville and announced our new adventure. "I don't know how we're going to pull it off," I said, "but by the grace of God we're going to plant a church in New York City." After the service, a man came up and told me of his affiliation with a historic theater right off Times Square on 44th street. I laughed when he told me its name—the "Lamb's Theater"! And his was not the only "sign and wonder" we experienced that night. People freely volunteered and financial resources began to stream in as well. Enough, at least, to get us started.

Within just four weeks of the World Trade Center collapse, a new church was born. Morning Star Church of the Nations was opened just off Broadway and West 44th street. We affectionately called it "The Miracle on 44th Street." Meetings were held on Sunday nights so that small ministry teams from other MSI churches could attend and support the new work. Bethel in Nashville committed to flying the worship team in every week, as well as relocating some staff to serve there permanently. Kings Park in Raleigh-Durham did the same. Help also came from our churches in Lawrence, Kansas; Austin, Texas; Manila, Philippines; Cape Town, South Africa; and Harare, Zimbabwe. Due to the expense and challenge of such a project, we had to approach this city from our ministry-wide strength. (Let me say that, though we are off the ground in New York City, we still need this attitude and help from around the world to see this important church reach a "safe cruising altitude." Today, the call still goes out to come to this strategic city and to leave no stone unturned in finding and referring people to come and be a part as well.)

Week after week, people came who had heard about the new church from friends in other cities. The buzz started making its way through New York as well. An employee of a well-known comedy club came to "check out the show," and ended up giving her life to Christ. Her cynical boss, after weeks of ribbing her, decided to finally see for himself…and walked out a new believer as well. Soon people from every walk of life were strolling through the doors on West 44th Street and into an encounter with the living God. One of the highlights came when the network producer whose off-hand comment had helped start the church walked into the Lamb's. During worship she began to weep as she encountered the power of the Holy Spirit. She joined the church that night and has since been discipled and trained. A year later, she has become a true leader as well as a light to her network associates.

## UNITING THE NATIONS

Flying out of New York after one of my routine visits to minister at the Lamb's, I looked out over the city and a new burden began to rise up in my soul. A lot had happened in the year since the church had been planted, but I sensed that we had only begun to lay the foundations for a much larger vision and work that the Lord wanted to accomplish. Not to sound melodramatic, but as the plane circled the city, the word of the Lord came to my heart: "I want you to gather leaders from the nations of the world and bring them to this city."

It suddenly occurred to me that beneath our plane at that moment stood the United Nations, a secular organization created after the Second World War to foster international unity and peace. While I appreciate what the United Nations is trying to accomplish, as a Christian I knew that there could be no real peace without Christ. Where was the Church's equivalent to the United Nations in this great international city?

That moment sparked a new dimension of our New York vision which we call "Uniting the Nations." Initially this strategy will draw Christian leaders from the nations that lost people in the World Trade Center.[19] Imagine Christian "ambassadors" from these countries moving to New York and reaching out to the people from their nation who live in the area. Then imagine these nations coming together to worship God and receive His word. There isn't a church like that anywhere in the world. What a prophetic picture of the kingdom of God and the way the Lord can take what was meant for evil and redeem it for good.

The ambassadors from these nations will spend at least one year in New York. Our prayer is that, as the years go by and the momentum grows, more and more nations will be represented in this city that many have called the "capital of the world." The program is coordinated by Lynn Nawata, a Japanese-Canadian and former corporate executive who not only speaks five languages but also has the character and determination necessary to help make this vision a reality. If you know of anyone who would be a candidate for an ambassador or could in some other way fit into the "Uniting the Nations" strategy, please get in touch with her through the website.[20] There will be a special leadership program sponsored by VLI to train this new wave of international culture-shakers as well as to help develop the necessary financial support.

The "Miracle on 44th Street" must not be limited to the churches in our MSI family uniting to reach this key city. *We cannot do it on our own.* The real miracle—this vision of "Uniting the Nations"—will involve the body of Christ at large working together to make the vision a reality. So many great things are possible if we will think strategically and work with a global, united vision. As strategies like these come forth, the Church has the opportunity to learn how to work together and reap a greater harvest of lasting change all over the world. As a movement, we look forward to helping other movements with similar strategies that will affect the major cities and nations.

## OTHER STRATEGIES FOR CHURCH PLANTS

Within MSI, all roads lead to church planting. Even though it may not always seem apparent, you can be assured that whatever we do is leading up to planting a church somewhere, somehow. Other tools and strategies mentioned throughout this book all have the same aim—to make the following approaches to church planting work.

### Campus outreach

Some of our strongest churches began as outreaches to university campuses. The Morning Star Church of Tallahassee, Florida, for example, was started by Chip and Hope Buhler and Ron and Cindy

Miller. Their first one hundred and fifty members were mostly students from Florida A&M and Florida State University. The churches in Raleigh-Durham, North Carolina, and Los Angeles, California, also began as an outreach to the campuses in their respective areas. While they have continued to focus on reaching university students and faculty, they are now established community churches with members from every other part of society as well. Churches have even been started as an outgrowth of reaching high school students. Franco and Mary Lou Gennaro began a Victory Club ministry at a high school in Murfreesboro, Tennessee. Through the teenagers, they eventually began to reach into the lives of their parents. Today, a vibrant community-wide church is the result, now pastored by Ron and Nancy Moore.

### Athletic outreach

I began this chapter by mentioning how football players who were trained in our Champions for Christ program were instrumental in starting our church in Jacksonville, Florida. Something similar also happened in Phoenix, Arizona, when a core group of on-fire athletes began to break through a lot more defensive lines that what they found on the football field. The next thing we knew, another door was opened to start a church. Troy and Denise Johnson were sent out from our church in Nashville to pastor the new work. Today there is a strong and growing congregation in Phoenix that has also begun to reach out to students at Arizona State University in Tempe. At present, there are several other cities where a core group of athletes with their families and friends are building toward starting a church. In a culture where athletes have so much influence, finding and developing true disciples from within their ranks makes a great deal of strategic sense.

### Inner-city ministries

The Youth Life Learning Centers pioneered by Darrell Green have birthed not only new life and hope on the mean streets of the inner city, but churches have been spawned by them as well. In Washington, D.C., the impact of the Learning Center on the lives of children and their families resulted in another apostolic center. Under the leadership of Donnell and Marianne Jones, City of Light Covenant Church is not only reaching out to the residents of northwest Washington, but also to Howard University, one of the premier African-American campuses in the nation.

### Medical missions

Another church-planting approach—and one that has been partic-ularly useful in nations that are more antagonistic to the Gospel—is the avenue of medical missions. A few years ago, for example, we sent a team to Myanmar (formerly Burma) to minister to physical needs. Out of that grew a new church that is staffed entirely by indigenous leaders. Not to be outdone, this Burmese congregation also shares a vision for becoming an apostolic center, birthing churches that will reach their nation and then the world.

Throughout Asia, Latin America and Africa, doors are wide open to anyone who can offer medical and humanitarian assistance. Here in Nashville, Dr. Steve Robinson has joined our pastoral staff and is leading MSI Medical Missions. Working with doctors and nurses throughout the ministry and with medical missions organizations sponsored by our churches in the Philippines and Southern Africa, Steve and his valiant volunteers are demonstrating the love of God while opening doors for church planting in Colombia, Zimbabwe, Latvia, Costa Rica and Peru. In order to reproduce doctors like these—medical professionals with an apostolic, church-planting heart—we have started outreaches to medical colleges as well.

## ESTABLISHING LOCAL CHURCH LEADERSHIP

Regardless of the methods used to plant a church, it is the job of the apostolic team to oversee the process. In the last chapter we gave a list of the responsibilities of the apostolic team, not only in the supervi-sion of churches as they are birthed, but also in the ongoing covering of established congregations. It cannot be emphasized enough how important it is to have clear lines of authority spelled out in times of peace, so that, should conflict come, it can be resolved quickly. This is true regardless of what form of government a church possesses. Simply put: *Make sure that there is an agreement among the leaders as to who will be called in from the outside to settle any disputes. This one principle will spare churches from hitting the impasses that cause them to fail.*

The spheres of authority and the distinction between the extra-local team and the local team of elders must be clear. The local elders or leaders are an indispensable part of the life of that church, but they should not be the final court of appeals when it comes to issues that could affect the life and ultimate health of the body. The fact that an apostolic team, or extra-local group, sets in local elders, points to their accountability to this oversight as well. It is a clear principle of authority in any institution of any kind: to have authority, you must be under authority. That covering not only protects the people of God, it also protects the leaders. Many times, tragedy is averted and the best possible solution to a difficult situation is found when experienced leaders are called in to help the local leadership team.

Once a church is established, the pastor and elders are responsible for all aspects of the church: from the congregation[21] to the strategy for reaching their city; from the finances to the nursery. It's a high calling, worthy of "double honor."[22] The Bible warns that there is a stricter judgment[23] and that necessary qualifications must be met to hold that office.[24] It is this kind of character and integrity that will enable the church to be faithfully led, as well as fed.

## WORKING TOGETHER

Though the spheres of authority and the way they function together are briefly laid out in these pages, the secret of making all this work has taken us half a lifetime to figure out. Simply put, the key is *trust*. As we discussed in Chapter 7, trust in relationships is what constitutes and sustains spiritual family.

It is critical that everyone clothe themselves in humility toward one another. It is vital that we fix our eyes together on our corporate mission and destiny. When these vital components are in place, fruitful ministry results. And that is why the enemy's primary tactic is to "accuse the brethren."[25] When he can compromise trust and fray the bonds of love, spiritual barrenness results. As long as local churches stay independent and unconnected, there will never be any serious threat to Satan's hold over a nation.

One of the seeds that the enemy sows to prevent unity at an extra-local level is the idea that these relationships will become hierarchical, rigid and controlling. Once again, we give up on a powerful avenue of blessing because of failures and weaknesses in the past. The solution to these potential problems is not to reject authority, but to reject unbiblical expressions of authority. Leaders must be able to exercise "control without being controlling."[26] And most of all, there must be a common vision that cultivates a sense of teamwork and camaraderie.

We should learn what secular companies have discovered: the

power of an organization that is built horizontally and not vertically. Leaders lead from the core of the organization and not just from the top. Their primary responsibility is to maintain the vision as well as the core values. In a sense, this is precisely what Paul implemented when he told Timothy, "keep the pattern, guard the deposit."[27] At the same time, there are multiple centers of influence that thrive throughout the organization, any one of which can come up with innovative ideas and solutions. It is an illusion, and an obstacle to growth, to think that all breakthroughs will flow from the top down. When everyone embraces and owns the vision, that's when it really gets exciting. And that's when the power of God truly begins to flow.

## CONCLUSION

*Every joint supplying…every part doing its share…growing up in all things into Him who is the head*…What would we be able accomplish if the Church truly became one, if we were to approach the measure of the stature of the fullness of Christ? God has promised that He will bring it to pass. His gifts to the Church—apostles, prophets, evangelists, pastors and teachers—have been given both the charge and the grace to transform a congregation into an apostolic center, an outpost of heaven that is colonizing the planet through church planting.

It is critical that we note, however, that the job will not be done by those gifted for this five-fold ministry. Their ultimate job is to equip "the saints for the work of ministry"[28]—to produce a people who "all know the Lord, from the least of them to the greatest."[29] This is this kind of glorious Church that will be a "light to the nations."

## CHAPTER 10

# A LIGHT TO
# THE NATIONS

*The Holy Ghost would never suffer the imputation to rest upon His holy name that He was not able to convert the world.*

—CHARLES SPURGEON

Y ou could see it in their eyes and hear it in their voices. Compared to the uncertainty, panic and fear that followed 9/11, Dayna Curry's and Heather Mercer's calm and loving demeanor seemed out of place, almost shocking, to the millions who followed their saga. After a harrowing captivity and rescue from the Taliban in Afghanistan, they spoke to the world of their love for their captors and their deep desire to return to that troubled land as soon as possible. "Our hearts are with the Afghan people," they said repeatedly. "Our dream is to return and see them set free!" The interviewers were incredulous. The most disarming sight of all was the light that shone from their faces and the hope that radiated from their words. I couldn't help but think of Stephen when he testified in the Book of Acts and how those watching were, "…fixing their gaze on him" when "all who were sitting in the Council saw his face like the face of an angel."[1] This radiance is what Isaiah prophesied when he said:

> I am the LORD, I have called You in righteousness, I will also hold You by the hand and watch over you, And I will appoint You as a covenant to the people, As a light to the

nations, To open blind eyes, To bring out prisoners from the dungeon And those who dwell in darkness from the prison.

—Isaiah 42:6–7, NASB

With this great promise in front of us, we need to ask why we are not displaying this heavenly light that the nations of the world so desperately need. Sadly, we have to conclude that, while there are many hindrances throughout the world, *what ultimately keeps the Church from advancing into the nations is the Church itself*. There is nothing that can stop the light of God's Word if those who preach it are willing and sacrificially obedient. Frankly, much of the Church has been neither. As Andrew Murray said, "The worldwide proclamation of the Gospel can be accomplished by this generation, if it has the obedience and determination to attempt the task. There is not a single country on the face of the earth to which the Church, if she seriously desired in our time could not send ambassadors of Christ to proclaim His message."[2]

Once again, the absence of light in a nation points to the lack of our presence there as God's people. What is so ironic about this is that these nations have been given to us and represent our inheritance in Christ. We lack so many of the treasures of our inheritance because they are hidden in places we refuse to go.

## THE NATIONS ARE OUR INHERITANCE

Ask of Me, and I will surely give the nations as your inheritance.

—Psalm 2:8, NASB

The Lord won the battle for the nations at His crucifixion and victorious resurrection two thousand years ago. In sending us to preach the Gospel, Jesus commissioned us to claim what rightly belongs to the Lord Himself and has been bequeathed, in turn, to us. Again and again in the Bible, the promises of God point to the Lord's ownership of the nations and how He has destined them to return to Him in worship.

All the ends of the earth will remember and turn to the LORD and all the families of the nations will worship before

You, For the kingdom is the LORD's and He rules over the nations.
> —PSALM 22:27–28, NASB

Beginning in Manila in 1984, Steve Murrell started preaching this message to young disciples: "The nations are your inheritance in Christ." He would say, "If you really want to follow Christ, you need a Bible and a passport." To date, the church in Manila has planted churches in seven nations. This is just one example of how there is an inheritance in the nations for those willing to claim it.

Jesus told a parable about a king preparing a dinner. No one he invited was willing to eat.[3] Many in the Church today are not unlike these people. The food we need to eat is what comes from obeying His command to reach the nations. Jesus taught us to do this by example. He reached out to a Samaritan woman who in turn brought an entire city to faith. Then the Lord said,

> My food is to do the will of Him who sent Me and to accomplish His work. Do you not say, "There are yet four months, and then comes the harvest"? Behold, I say to you, lift up your eyes and look on the fields, that they are white for harvest.
> —JOHN 4:34–35, NASB

A good example of this principle is illustrated in a spontaneous outreach that began in the Middle East. Our church in Manila had sent some believers to a certain city in this region of the world to begin to reach out to the Muslim world. This particular city was prosperous in comparison to other Arab cities, and relatively open to western culture and commerce. Through our ministry there, two Filipino women, who were already married to Arab men, became Christians and were discipled. Not long after, one of them had to move with her husband back to his homeland, an Arab nation with a fundamentalist Islamic government. There this Filipino Christian met a female cousin of her husband's, a woman grieving because her child was dying and the doctors could do nothing to help. The Christian encouraged the woman to go and pray for her baby, using the name of Jesus Christ. As you might expect in a Muslim culture, the woman was very hesitant about using the name Jesus. But with her child dying, she was willing to try anything. Not only was the baby healed, but the woman also had an extraordinary encounter with the

Lord. She was so overwhelmed that she gathered over thirty of her relatives, including the husband of the Filipino woman, and told them about the miracle that had taken place at the name of Jesus Christ.

What happened next was similar to the "Gentile Pentecost" that took place in Acts Chapter 10. Just as in the house of Cornelius, the Holy Spirit fell upon them all and everyone in the house was saved. The result is a new church, planted in one of the most closed nations on earth. Later, an MSI pastor flew into the city where this young congregation had formed, carrying a suitcase full of Bibles and outreach tools for its thirty members. The immigration officials searched almost every piece of luggage coming into the country—but not the one that contained the Bibles.

This is not the only Arab country where something this dramatic has happened and, over the last few years, we have seen similar things in other supposedly "closed" nations. Obviously, there is no way we could have planned an outreach like this. Jesus is the Lord of the Harvest and He has plans we can't even imagine. If we were trusting only in our own initiatives, the task would be impossible. But with God's plan working, and with our willingness to serve, all things are possible.

## CHURCH OF THE NATIONS

It all comes back to how we think of Church. When we have a vision for the nations and pray for God to redeem them, an amazing thing often happens: The nations come to us. Into your church in London might stroll the future church-planting leader for an African nation. Into a Manila congregation might walk the future leader of the church-planting team to India. Why would God bring these people to you if you have no vision or method for the fulfillment of their destiny? The Church should be the on-ramp to God's love and purposes for the people groups of the earth. Whenever you enter a local church, you should feel like you have stepped into another dimension of ethnic diversity and international vision. The Church should reflect the kingdom of God on earth as it is in heaven. It should be a place where the heart of God who "so loved the world" is revealed and where "every tribe and tongue and people and nation" are assembled.[4]

That kind of atmosphere is demonstrated in a magnificent way at His People Christian Church in Cape Town, South Africa. In the midst of the turmoil of apartheid, that church has been an example to the nation of what the kingdom looks like: thousands of every color and ethnicity worshiping God in one place. This is a true picture of what worship and community will look like in eternity.

Several years ago, then-President Nelson Mandela happened to pass by their meeting, which was taking place at the University of Cape Town, and briefly looked in to see what was going on. When he saw the vast multi-colored crowd, he asked an usher to inform Pastor Paul Daniel that he was present and would like to greet the congregation. What a shock it must have been for Pastor Paul to see the president of the nation in the back of the meeting hall. Of course, President Mandela was immediately escorted to the stage where he told the crowd in essence: "This is what our nation needs! You are our hope. If the Church can give the example of ethnic unity, the people will follow."

## THE CHANGING FACE OF THE CHURCH

This type of diversity is a broad phenomenon, one that has been building for years. In the parts of the world that have been the least evangelized, some of the greatest gains are now being made. Thanks largely to the foreign missions emphasis of the nineteenth century— the greatest era for missionary activity in Christian history—the demographics of the Church at the beginning of the twenty-first century look very different than they did a hundred years before. In 1900, 77 percent of all Christians still lived in Europe or in North America—almost eight out of every ten. Only 11 percent of the Church was in Latin America; 6 percent in all of Africa and Asia combined. However, the "mustard seed" of God's kingdom[5] planted by these missionaries in what has come to be known as the "developing world," began to take root and flourish. The year 1982 marked a historic turning point. Since that year, for the first time since the second century, the majority of Christians in the world are neither Caucasian nor Western. By the year 2000, 56 percent of the Church was located in Africa, Asia and Latin America. Missiologist David Barrett projects that by 2025, this group will comprise 65 percent of the Church of Jesus Christ. Once again, God has turned the kingdoms of this world on its head.[6]

Another significant transformation over the last century is the type of churches that make up the body of Christ. In 1900, charismatics/

Pentecostals accounted for about one half of one percent of all professing Christians. Today, one out of every four church members
internationally is a member of a Pentecostal or charismatic church.[7]
David Barrett's projections are that by 2025 the ratio will be one out
of every three. This represents an astonishing transformation within
the Church, as historian and author Philip Jenkins has noted: "Since
there were only a handful of Pentecostals in 1900 and several hundred
million today, is it not reasonable to identify this as perhaps the most
successful social movement of the past century? According to the current projections, the number of Pentecostal believers should surpass
the one billion mark before 2050. In terms of global religions, there
will, by that point, be roughly as many Pentecostals as Hindus, and
twice as many as there are Buddhists."[8] This confirms what Scripture,
history and church-growth experts worldwide attest to: *When the
Word of God is preached and where the gifts of the Spirit are honored
and responsibly operate, the Church will win.*

### A Closer Look at the Numbers

Although the heartbeat of this book is the Church regaining its
focus and influence, there is some encouragement in the statistics
concerning the present state of Christianity throughout the world. A
closer look at the numbers reveals, however, the good news with the
"not-so-good" news.

The good news is that from 1900 to 2000, the number of people
who profess faith in Jesus grew from 558 million to almost two billion; a 358 percent increase. There are probably more Christians alive
at the beginning of the twenty-first century than all the Christians
who lived and died from A.D. 33 to 1900. Christianity remains the
largest religion in the world, 1.6 times that of Islam and 2.4 times
larger than Hinduism. The not-so-good news is that the number of
Christians, as a percentage of the world population, has not changed.
In 1900 Christians represented 34.4 percent of the population, and
that percentage has remained remarkably consistent for one hundred
years. In 2000, it was still about the same, 33.4 percent.

Unfortunately, this means that, as as a percentage of the popula-
tion, we aren't really doing any better than the Muslims. Patrick
Johnstone, in *The Church Is Bigger than You Think*, states that ". . . the
Muslim percentage is about the same today as it was 200 years ago."
Yet for Muslims, the reason for growth is different: "Present Muslim
growth is more through a higher birth rate than through conver-

sions."[9] The real test is to come, as Christians and Muslims square off over many parts of the world. Can we learn the lessons of history and fight this holy war in the Spirit instead of using the arm of the flesh?

## UNREACHED PEOPLE GROUPS

To sharpen this point a bit, let's consider the matter of unreached people groups. An unreached people group is a tribe or ethnic group that does not contain enough Christians to reach that group without outside help. Missiologists use varying statistics on exactly how many of these groups there are, but *it may be that there are as many as 1.7 billion people spread among eleven thousand unreached people groups on the earth today.* This represents an astonishing need and only heightens the importance of the Apostolic Mandate: Go where the Gospel is not heard and the nations (literally "ethnicities" or "tribes") are not discipled.

In looking through the research that has been done on the state of the Church worldwide, that data can leave you somewhat dazed and confused. Amidst a sea of information, you find yourself asking a simple question: Are we as the Church winning or losing the battle? Some shrug off the question, point to their Bible and exclaim, "Not to worry; the back of the book says 'we win.'" Yet for the serious Christian who is trying to be faithful to the Lord's call in his or her generation, the real condition of the Church and its mission is a critically serious issue; one that needs to be addressed.

The story behind the numbers is this: *Christianity is declining in North America, all but dead in Europe and booming in Africa, Asia and Latin America.* These facts raise a couple of important questions. How do we reverse the trends in what was once the cradle of Christendom? And what can we do to prevent the nations that are experiencing an outpouring of the Spirit from slipping into a similar pattern of decline and apostasy?

## AN MSI WORLD TOUR

The answers to these questions are found in the example of William Carey. He made a map of the world and studied it carefully to determine the most strategic means of global harvest. This type of strategic thinking is vital if we're going to keep track of our inheritance. As I mentioned in Chapter 2, it was while studying a world map that the

Lord spoke to my heart about planting a church in Manila. A lot has happened since then. Let's take a moment for a brief tour of some of the significant gains the ministry of MSI has made as of 2002. Perhaps by doing so, we can gain insight into the methods of future victory.

### Asia

As we have discussed throughout this book, the Word of the Lord is "growing mightily and prevailing" on the continent of Asia.[10] By far, this is our most heavily evangelized area of the world. In the Philippines, our church-planting efforts are led by Steve Murrell and his Filipino apostolic team. We have a similar church-planting movement in Indonesia, led by Frans Wowor and an Indonesian leadership team. Again, when we plant a church in a nation, our goal is to raise up indigenous leaders and ultimately see them lead a movement of church planting within their own nation. Using this method, we have birthed strong churches in China, Singapore and Malaysia. On the forefront of the church-planting frontier for MSI, without question, is the nation of China. We already have training centers in ten of the 30 provinces there and have begun a VLI School of Church Planting.

### Africa

Traditionally known in the West as the "dark continent," Africa is slowly beginning to lose this reputation and becoming instead a continent of light. Our major outposts there are in South Africa, including, of course, the apostolic center in Cape Town. Led by Paul and Jenny Daniel, the church has inspired a church-planting movement throughout Africa that has now spilled over into Europe. Bill Bennot and his wife, Connie, have been vital instruments in planting the church in Johannesburg and in facilitating church plants throughout the continent. In Zimbabwe, Tom and Bonnie Deuschle have raised up a thriving outreach in Harare that has stood strong in the midst of very difficult circumstances. Overall, churches have been planted in Namibia, Sierra Leone, South Africa, Zambia and Zimbabwe, with others planned in the near future for Botswana, Kenya, Liberia and Uganda.

Our Bible school in South Africa is producing leaders at a pace that is exceeding our means to support them. For less than $500 per month (U.S.), you could help sponsor a church planter in Africa. We mention this financial need for Africa primarily because so much has been taken from her—without giving back—over the past 500 years.

Now is the time of restoration for Africa; now is the time for the Church to rise up and call her blessed.

### Latin America

Peru has been our primary beachhead in South America. Franco and MaryLou Gennaro spent several years there raising up an apostolic center, and in 1996 they handed the leadership to Claudio and Dunia Zolla. The church in Lima is thriving and has planted numerous congregations. It has also adopted and trained scores of new churches. MSI has planted churches in Colombia and Costa Rica, and is working to assist church planting in Cuba. Latin America represents a huge open door, with comparatively few laborers to meet the need. Our hope is to see tremendous growth in this area by the year 2010. In order to do this, we must train a new generation of Spanish-speaking leaders.

One way to accomplish that is to launch an effective ministry to Hispanics in North America where there has been an enormous influx of Spanish-speaking peoples. Many of our churches now have special church services in Spanish. Our foundational Bible study materials, as well as Victory Leadership Institute courses, are all available in Spanish. As I've emphasized throughout this book, if you need leaders, you must first make disciples. To make disciples you must first reach them for Christ. The increase of Latinos in North America is a sign from the Lord to the Christians of the United States and Canada that it's time to get very serious about reaching our brethren in the southern hemisphere. Certainly reaching those who have come to our shores is a great way to start.

### The South Pacific

Several years ago, a new sound of worship began to come out of Australia that has touched the world. Great churches with passion for the nations have sprung up as well. As we have mentioned, Ken and Renee Dew from MSI were sent out to raise up a work in New Zealand. Within a year, David and Christy Spring from Nashville joined them and have started a church in Melbourne, Australia. One of the most beloved couples in our movement, Luther and Nenette Mancao, moved from Manila to Sydney, Australia. The result has been a synergy that is accelerating the outreaches of all these ministries as well as drawing other churches into this spiritual family. Our first MSI conference in the South Pacific was held in 2001. The need of the hour is for musicians and campus workers to give at least two years of their lives to bolster these new works. In the days to come, islands in the South Pacific, like Samoa, are targets for church planting.

### Europe

Once thought to be a land of unremitting spiritual darkness, signs of life are beginning to spring up throughout Europe. The collapse of the Berlin Wall in 1989 brought in a vast army of ministers, crusades and Gospel materials. Thankfully, in the midst of this "soul rush" some great new churches were planted. In Western Europe, the nations of England, Ireland and Germany now have growing movements.

For MSI, the churches in London, England, and Innsbruck, Austria, pastored by Wolfgang and Allie Eckleben and Sean and Trudie Morris respectively, are flagships for our movement that have already planted other new churches. In Eastern Europe, Bob and Sharon Perry and Jeff and Ana Bullock have started works in Latvia and Poland. Each year, MSI hosts a conference in Europe to help generate a synergy among the European nations, both East and West. Seeds have been scattered all over Europe, particularly in Germany, Italy, Spain, France and Russia. In the coming years, church-planting teams will be assembled and then sent to every one of these important nations.

### The Middle East

Somehow this part of the world gets overlooked in terms of strategic planning for churches. Just because a nation forbids the Gospel from being legally preached, doesn't mean that there isn't a way to minister to the people for whom Christ died in these countries. Remember that the Gospel was considered "illegal" throughout much of the first three centuries of the Church's history. It was amid this persecution that God raised up a mighty people, purified by trials and ready to lay down their lives for the cause of Christ. (Obviously, we must use discretion in relating the testimonies of the Lord's work in these areas.)

Starting in Israel, God's Church, though small, has grown significantly over the last few years. The few evangelical works that were planted there a generation or so ago have reproduced and now there are many congregations dotting the landscape where the Messiah once walked.

The largest church in the Middle East is in Egypt. Thousands of people have been dramatically converted through its ministry. The revival there actually began on the garbage dumps of Cairo and then spread like a wildfire. The prayers of God's people are tearing down this "titanium curtain."

MSI now has ministries in Iran, Kuwait and the United Arab Emirates. Plans are being made to begin a work in Tel Aviv by 2004. As we continue to reach out to the men and women from these "closed nations," the Lord continues to make a way in the wilderness.

One of the greatest ways to reach these countries is to minister to their people when they visit our country. Whether you live in Manila or Manhattan, the nations of the world have come to the great cities of the world. If you reach them when they visit your homeland, when they return to these restricted nations the Gospel will have already gained a foothold.

### North America

Another encouraging sign for us as a spiritual family is the church planting going on in Canada. This great nation is unique among other western countries, in that it has never experienced a nationwide revival. We are praying and working hard for that to change. Led by Canadian Bert Thomson from his home base in Nashville—where he assists me in many vital aspects of the ministry—we are seeing a new generation of gifted leaders emerging in this strategic nation. As Bert points out, "Canada has unsurpassed favor worldwide as evidenced by its passport, which is the world's most accepted. This openness to Canadians, combined with the nation's commitment to multi-culturalism, makes it a strategic country for unlocking the destiny of other nations."

Brant Reding of Calgary and Greg Mitchell in Vancouver, along with Bert, are spearheading a nationwide call to radical commitment among the youth, as well as a bold strategy for starting new works across the nation. Core groups of believers have formed in Montreal and Toronto and are on their way to becoming new churches. Again, the apostolic dimension of "advancement on purpose" is bringing new life to this nation.

In keeping with the 2010 Initiative, we have made it a faith goal to double our churches in the United States by the end of 2004. Remember, if you are from Asia, the ends of the earth not only represent Africa but also America. As the nations of the earth flock to America's cities, where there is little or no outreach geared to reach these masses, America is becoming one of the world's great mission fields.

## RECOVERING A GLOBAL IMPACT

As we near the end of this book, I want to discuss the final stages of becoming a worldwide force for Christ's kingdom. We've looked at a whole range of principles and practices that are essential to building strong disciples, planting healthy churches and promoting effective evangelism. We've examined our responsibility to disciple the nations, including the great challenge of reforming popular culture.

Now, to gain the momentum that will lift us out of the gravitational pull of the ordinary and into the extraordinary purposes of God, let's concentrate on a few final keys that will propel us toward the goal of recovering the Apostolic Mandate.

## THE BIG PICTURE OF GOD'S KINGDOM AND PURPOSE

What is unfortunate about much of Christianity in the developed world is that many of our ideas about God and His purposes pertain only to the individual. We tend to understand His purposes in terms of how He wants to bless us and help us with our chosen pursuits. His kingdom is interpreted as the blessing of righteousness, peace and joy in our daily lives. These concepts have some truth in them, of course. But, in the end, they are but very small pieces of a timeless and expansive puzzle that encompasses God's heart for the world.

"Seek first the kingdom of God and His righteousness,"[11] means infinitely more than merely being blessed and seeing my children prosper. Seeking God's kingdom means getting involved with the plans and purposes that flow from His heart. One of the most loved and quoted verses in the New Testament is Romans 8:28: "And we know that God causes all things to work together for good to those who love God, to those who are called according to His purpose" (NASB). Again, this purpose doesn't simply refer to an individual's life, but rather to God's purpose for the Church and the world.

It's pretty common these days for people to wonder about what God "is saying now to the Church." I agree with Steve Murrell that God is saying primarily the same thing He's been saying for two thousand years: "All authority has been given to Me in heaven and on earth. Go therefore and make disciples of all the nations."[12]

People love the idea that when they seek first the kingdom, all the things that the world seeks will be added to them. They also love the idea of God causing all things in their lives to work together for good because they are called according to His purpose. But if we're really serious about claiming the promises of those verses, we need to be every bit as serious about the qualifiers. What really is this kingdom we are to seek? What are the purposes of God and how do we really fulfill them?

From the time I became a Christian, I have always sensed that God's purposes and His blessings were a part of my life. However, as I have become progressively more committed to His purposes for the nations, I have seen His hand move through my life in ways that are beyond anything I ever expected.

## THE CHURCH AS A MISSION BASE

An effective missions initiative must begin by redefining some traditional ideas, particularly those involving the local church. While the truth is immutable, the Church's approach to a whole range of cultural distinctives is not; we do need to change with the times in certain areas if we are to be a relevant witness to the world. Again, there are many essential characteristics modeled in the New Testament that we have to tenaciously hold on to; otherwise, we'll wake up one day and find ourselves way off course. We don't need new and improved concepts of world evangelism nearly as much as we need to realign the local church with its fundamental mission, the Apostolic Mandate. David Barrett and the Global Evangelism Movement report that 70 percent of money and effort invested by Christians go to people who already profess to be Christians. Only 5 percent of our total missionary activity is focused on the unevangelized world, those who have never once had a chance to hear the good news of the Gospel.

The mission of the universal Church, as well as the local church, is ever expanding. The mandate Jesus gave His disciples was to go to Jerusalem [the city], then Judea [the state], Samaria [the bordering nation], and to "the remotest part of the earth."[13] We shouldn't overlook our neighbors in our efforts to reach out to the rest of the world, but neither can we focus exclusively on our city, our state or our nation. Every church, at every stage of growth and maturity, has to be connected with God's heart and vision for the whole world.

Several years ago, I was spending some time with one of our Asian pastors. He shared with me that he felt a little insignificant, given the fact that his new church plant at the time was still small and struggling. I determined to impress upon him how nothing could be further from the truth. "You are the Morning Star missions headquarters in this country," I said. "You have an apostolic mandate to go into all the world and to make disciples, and this is your headquarters!" Eventually he got the message. Later, he put a sign on the door of his humble office that read: "MORNING STAR WORLD MISSIONS DIRECTOR." Wherever you find yourself—in your family, your job or your neighborhood—consider yourself the missions director in that place.

This has to become the attitude throughout the Church as well. Regardless of how a church has defined itself, or what words it has placed on its sign, in the sight of God and according to His Word, it is to be a "world outreach center." Scholar Patrick Johnstone notes: "The local church is the launch pad for missions... [it] is pivotal to the whole missions enterprise, and it should be the 'seed-bed for missions'... Only as the local church sees its reasons for existence as missions—whether local, national, trans-ethnic or international—can it really be a truly biblical church."[14] Pastor Ted Haggard, author of *The Life-Giving Church*, agrees: "Life-giving churches don't exist for themselves, but for those who don't know life Himself, Christ. God has spoken that same message to lots of people. That's why many life-giving churches are missions churches."[15]

## BUILDING A GLOBAL TEAM

Sam Webb had been the leader of Grace Bible Ministries in Honolulu for almost twenty years. Besides having multiple congregations there, the Grace Bible Churches had spread from the Hawaiian Islands to Guam, Japan and other parts of Asia. We had heard of Sam and Nancy Webb as people of integrity with a tremendous heart for the lost and the world. Their movement of churches had been courted by several denominations and fellowships, because of this integrity and the strategic position of their outreach. We were very blessed and honored to have them as our guests when Sam and his team began attending our annual world conferences.

What a shock it was after one conference when he approached me and requested a meeting with our leadership team. He and several of his leaders joined us at a restaurant and Sam began by saying that they had been praying for quite some time about God joining them to a larger team. "We know that we have gifts and strengths from the Lord, but we also know that we need help from other giftings if we are going to fulfill our destiny," he said. "What I'm saying is that we feel that we are being joined to the MSI family in order to reach the world more effectively."

## STRATEGIC PARTNERSHIPS

The world is becoming a much smaller place, not only in terms of communications and commerce, but also in the exchange of ideas. Consequently, there has never been a greater opportunity to spread the Gospel and extend the kingdom of God. In order to take advantage of this unprecedented opportunity, however, local churches need to be a part of coordinated missions efforts.

Nothing sharpens your skills like competition, especially when the prize is your economic survival. Non-profit organizations, particularly churches, can learn a lot from secular companies whose success is regularly scrutinized by the stock market and analyzed in detail by those who read each quarterly earnings report. Jesus noted that, "the sons of this age are more shrewd in relation to their own kind than the sons of light."[16] His point was that, though the leaders in this world are wicked, they are nonetheless very wise when it comes to dealing with their own kind. Don't be like them in your motivation, He was saying, but learn from some of the smart things that they do.

Focusing on missions draws together others with a similar focus. Smart businesses recognize that they no longer operate in some discrete geographical box. Now their most formidable competitor in any market could be a business located on the other side of the world. As commerce and communications become more and more globalized, companies have been either merging or creating limited partnerships in order to more effectively do business on a worldwide scale. While airlines, financial institutions, technology companies and every other type of business imaginable are joining together in order to remain competitive, the Church has persisted in its tendency to fragment into little autonomous organizations, local congregations, that are not connected in a practical and meaningful way to any missions endeavor much bigger than themselves. (And that is assuming they even have a missions program. Many do not.) Consequently, their vision has become more and more localized, and their impact in this era of globalization is marginal at best. The Church needs to realize what secular corporations figured out a decade or two ago: if you don't compete well globally, then you are destined to lose both globally and at home.

## HIS PEOPLE MINISTRIES

Though the Church may be among the last to "get it," those who have been willing to expand their vision and join together with others are having a broad impact on the world. Those who do, end up having to overcome the many obstacles that invariably stand in the way of fulfilling the Apostolic Mandate. This is why Jesus encouraged His disciples with the promise that He would "be with them always, even to the end of the age."[17] He knew there would be tribulation—that the enemy wouldn't just roll over and play dead. As the apostle Paul advised the church at Rome, "We wanted to come to you…but Satan hindered us."[18] Any significant relationship will be challenged and consequently must be fought for.

This struggle was clearly seen in the joining of His People Ministries in South Africa with Morning Star International. As we saw earlier, Paul Daniel is the senior pastor of the fifteen-thousand-member His People Christian Church in Cape Town, South Africa. Together with Bill and Connie Bennot of Johannesburg, they formed an apostolic team to plant and cover churches that then spread throughout Africa and parts of Europe. Paul approached me in 1997 with a proposal: "We have the same calling. We're both reaching campuses, and we've embraced the same vision and values. There is only so much each of us can accomplish in our own lifetimes. But we could accomplish so much more together." It all sounded pretty simple and straightforward. Paul and his wife, Jenny, quickly became close friends of ours, and the process of joining our ministries together began. We soon found out that just being committed Christians and good friends wasn't enough to take us through the tough times ahead.

It took more than three years for this merger to become a reality. Working through the vision, values and mission of our two groups was a major factor in making this joining possible. Much prayer and fasting, as well as seeking the advice of fellow leaders was also involved. But the final confirmation of the urgency of the need for this relationship came to Paul in an unusual way. One day he was sitting in a theater watching the movie *Gladiator* with some friends. At one point, the movie depicts a reenactment of the battle of Carthage in the gladiatorial arena. The hero of the film, a former Roman general who is now a gladiator, shouts to the others who were facing certain doom in the arena, "If we stay together, we will survive." At that very moment, I just happened to call him on his cell phone from America to talk about the direction of our relationship. Listening to me while watching the hero escape certain death on the screen, the Holy Spirit spoke to him and said, "If you will stay with this team I'm bringing around you, you will make it as well." It was a defining moment for us. This key relationship has since born tremendous fruit and touched the nations. As Paul predicted, we have been able to work together and draw on the strengths of each other to reach further together than we ever could separately.

## THE AUTHORITY TO SEND

When I look back over the great things God has done, I realize how many of the significant events in Morning Star have hinged on people who were willing to be sent. This was certainly true of me as a young man. By the time I was ready to graduate from college, I had concluded that God was calling me to the ministry. "Wherever you need me," I eagerly told my pastors, "wherever you want to send me; I'm ready to go!" I can't claim any credit for this willingness. It came from the Lord. And it's a gift we'll have to walk in to win the world today.

In Chapter 2, I recounted how the Holy Spirit spoke to me in a dramatic way, calling me to get on the plane with my family and go to the Philippines. God began a church there that has grown into an extraordinarily effective apostolic missions center. It is important to note, however, that the most significant human ingredient to the growth and development of that church has turned out to be Steve and Deborah Murrell. To this day, I have never witnessed a clearer call from God on a particular couple to go to a particular place. Yet, Steve and Deborah were content with being campus directors at Mississippi State University and didn't sense the call to stay in the Philippines until they had been there for two weeks. At the outset, they were simply willing to go and serve wherever there was a need.

As the apostle Paul wrote, "How then shall they call upon Him in whom they have not believed? And how shall they believe in Him whom they have not heard? And how shall they hear without a preacher? And how shall they preach unless *they are sent*?"[19] When the apostles in Jerusalem heard that multitudes of people in Samaria were becoming believers, "*they sent them* Peter and John."[20] The Lord spoke to the leaders of the church in Antioch, instructing them to set apart Paul and Barnabas for the work to which He had called them. "Then, when they had fasted and prayed and laid their hands on them, *they sent them* away."[21]

Church planting overseas can get pretty complicated. I've thought at times of General Eisenhower assembling the Allied expeditionary force in preparation for the D-Day invasion of Normandy in World War II. Using this analogy, before anything can happen, we have to discern God's direction, select a landing site, raise a lot of money, organize prayer support, make contacts behind enemy lines, assemble a team, find the leaders and work out a thousand other little details that will all change if things don't happen on schedule. To use another analogy, the ministry of an apostolic team is like putting together a complex puzzle. It's a task that would be almost impossible without people who are willing to be sent. Of course, I'm in no way suggesting that we send out people who do not also sense the Spirit's leading in the same direction. What I am saying is that everyone needs to live a life of surrender to God and His purposes. That includes the apostolic team, the pastors, elders, lay leaders, families, students and anyone else in the Church. Like the prophet Isaiah, we should all be saying, "Here I am, Lord. Send me!"[22] This also means that those on the front lines are not the only ones who are important. When David took his small army to attack the Amalekites at Ziklag, the troops that stayed back with the supplies received the same reward as those who were on the frontline of the battle.[23]

## UTILIZING STRATEGIC RESOURCES

Too often, missionary work has been done the hard way. Hiking out into the wilderness in order to find a lost tribe or an unreached people group may seem exciting, romantic and somehow spiritual, but it's rarely an efficient or effective way of fulfilling the Apostolic Mandate. Sending an American family into a foreign culture where they have to learn another language is expensive, sometimes dangerous and usually a slow process. In some instances, it is not the best investment of time, energy, talent and money. Western missionaries have sometimes gone into the field carrying with them some unnecessary "baggage"—a conscious or a subconscious attitude of superiority and a tendency to view the Gospel through the lens of a western worldview.

The most effective way of reaching, establishing and multiplying the Church in non-Christian nations is by winning and training indigenous missionaries; that is, by raising up leaders from among their own people. Those who have studied the big picture of missions for any length of time invariably come to the same conclusion.

For churches in the West, probably the most strategic means of leveraging our missionary efforts is by reaching internationals in our midst, particularly students. International students studying at western universities are among the brightest young people from their nations, often coming from the most influential families. Visiting MSI churches, I've met several international students who were on fire for Christ and later learned that they were members of their nation's royal family or children of government ministers. These students can be discipled and then return to their nations to take positions of strategic spiritual and cultural importance. This is why the MSI strategy for international church planting has been built largely around winning, training and sending international students God has sent into our midst.

When MSI went into China, a couple of Taiwanese international students, who had been saved and discipled in one of our churches in the U.S., went with the team as translators. These two young people, both with advanced degrees, felt the call of God to stay and become the pastors of the newly planted church. This scenario has been repeated over and over again.

Though this strategy is highly effective, it doesn't mean that churches and Christians from developed countries are unnecessary or excused from being personally involved in other nations. Evangelism, discipleship and church-planting efforts desperately need the help and involvement of Christians from the United States and other nations where the Church is more solidly established.

One example of how established churches can help is a training program established by Pastor Ron Lewis in 1995. On a church-planting trip to Hong Kong, God spoke to Ron and his team in a dramatic way, instructing them to visit mainland China. Six months later, Ron and his family were in China, along with K. C., a former international student from their Raleigh-Durham church. God used a businessman who had been transferred to China from Ron's church to bring a steady stream of people to their hotel room, people who had never seen a Bible and had never heard of Jesus Christ. They readily received Christ and were being baptized in Pastor Ron's hotel room bathtub. That was the beginning of a new church plant in a city in southern China. This church today has already reached and baptized hundreds of Chinese, and their influence is beginning to spread to other cities.

Once home, Pastor Ron Lewis began contemplating another trip to China. Several years earlier he had met with one of the influential leaders in the Chinese underground church. As he thought and prayed about the when, where and how of a return, a visitor arrived unannounced. He looked up, surprised to see that this same Chinese leader had miraculously walked into his office. Through this contact, Pastor Ron, upon his return to China, was introduced to several leaders of the underground church movement. There are about twenty such underground church movements there. The numbers and growth rate of these movements are so incredible that western Christians have no frame of reference with which to compare them. Such phenomenal growth, however, in a nation where there are few Bibles, very little Christian literature and virtually no Bible schools, is accompanied by the critical need for leadership training. Since that first visit, Ron Lewis and King's Park International Church have been able to set up and fund numerous training centers throughout the country, and thereby, establish an effective partnership with one of the most explosive underground revivals in history.

Through these efforts, the Strategic China Initiative was started in 1996. It includes eleven training centers, has trained over 12,000 Chinese leaders, has disseminated twenty-five tons of leadership training materials and resources, and has distributed hundreds of thousands of Bibles in China. For most of these Chinese leaders, the centers provide their only formal training experience. They call the intense month-long training the only "sabbatical" they will ever have.

Again, what I am describing is like seeing that assembly of nations parading around the convention hall at a conference. It's thrilling to see large delegations of believers representing a particular nation. Then you see that one international student marching around all by himself, carrying his nation's flag. In my mind, that one person represents places where there are only a handful of Christians standing alone, sometimes at great personal cost. They bear the burden alone of reaching their nation for Christ. Seeing that lone flag bearer makes me want to join him, so he won't have to march by himself. I think

God pays special attention to these precious believers. The question is, *"Do you?"*

Spiritual battles critical to the spread of Christianity are being fought and won on the far-flung frontiers of the kingdom where the Gospel has either been suppressed or never before been preached. These places represent the most fertile fields for harvest in the world. And in these places, those who experience the love and forgiveness of Christ for the first time respond with a single-minded dedication that surpasses what most Western Christians have ever witnessed.

Many of the western Christians who encounter these faithful servants later confess: *"We are the ones who need to be trained by them."* Yet, they also realize that they have something to give as well. The leaders of the Chinese church are often young Christians, and some do not even have their own Bibles. We have heard biblical and theological basics so often that we are tempted to be bored with their familiarity; but to these believers, learning of them is like receiving manna from heaven.

If you've grown tired of trying to share the Gospel with people who feel no need for it, or if topics such as God's love for the world, Christ dying for your sins, forgiveness by the blood, justification by faith alone, sanctification, prayer in the name of Jesus and the baptism of the Holy Spirit don't seem as fresh to you as they once did—get out there on the front edge of the expanding kingdom of God and see what happens. After witnessing the power of the Gospel in the harvest field, you may never come back.

## CONCLUSION: BY FAITH

The eleventh chapter of Hebrews offers the spiritual key so that those of us with little to offer in our own strength and resources can participate in such a grand adventure. In this one chapter, it's as if God is summarizing the entire Bible. "By faith Abel… by faith Enoch…by faith Noah, Abraham, Isaac, Moses…" and on and on. Everyone who was anyone in God's eyes seemed to have this one thing in common: faith in God!

I realized early on that, besides my love for God and His creation, nothing else really mattered if I was motivated by faith. I also understood that faith was a trigger for all the big things that God would do through my life. The first of those things was my family coming to Christ; then different students; next came seeing entire campuses shaken; then cities; and finally watching the leaders of nations bow their knee before Christ the King. It all started by simply putting God's Word first in my life and allowing the power of the promises to take me out of the loop of failure and into a pattern of victory. This can be the destiny that awaits you as well.

As we look to the future, we must look with the eyes of faith. We should be stirred to reach the billions of people who have not yet heard the Gospel. We must be willing to step out in faith in order to see nations transformed. Don't think that someone else will do the impossible. Don't expect the heroes of the future to necessarily be people from the developed world, people with advanced education or high status. First Corinthians 1:27 declares that "God has chosen the weak and foolish things of this world to bring to nothing the things that are." He will use anyone who will humble himself and desire that God's will be done in and through his life—anyone who is trained to be a world changer.

My heart always goes back to Manila and the church that began in 1984. Through the years as I have gone back, it has truly become my favorite church in the world. The young people aren't from wealthy homes, but they're sold out to Christ. Their worship is passionate, and their faith is strong. It is from settings like these that the champions of the future will emerge. It will be from unexpected places like the Philippines and unsuspecting people like the Filipinos. Right now they are quietly getting ready—studying their Bibles, faithfully praying and looking for their moment to step out in faith and make a difference with their lives.

# "I WILL ARISE"

I f I had to choose my favorite scene in the Bible, it would have to be the one where Jesus was walking on the sea in the middle of a storm. As He approached the boat filled with His disciples, one brave voice spoke out, "Lord, if it's you…tell me to come to you on the water."[1] Jesus had conditioned His followers to put into practice what they saw Him do. Whether feeding the multitudes, healing the sick or now walking on water, the rule of thumb was, "If He does it, we do it."

In calling us into the nations with the Gospel, Jesus again is calling us out of the boat and into the storms of our times. In the confusion and darkness of our age, He has called His people to shine like lights in the midst of a dark and perverse generation.[2] If we want to walk with Him, then we must walk with Him into the very heart of His purposes.

The willingness to walk with Him in this way is what made the men and women of history great. They have raised a standard, and we must rise to that same level of commitment and passion. May the principles and lessons of this book lead you to abandon yourself fully to God's purposes in your generation. May we go beyond the prayers of blessing and personal convenience to the prayers for action and boldness to advance His kingdom at all costs.

As the old hymn implores, "Rise up, O men of God, be done with lesser things. Give heart and mind and soul and strength to serve the King of kings."

## BE STRONG AND COURAGEOUS

More than three thousand years ago, faced with a similar challenge to rise up and enter the Promised Land, Joshua was commanded to "be strong and very courageous."[3] It was a command with a promise— that he would lead God's people to possess their inheritance. It will take this same kind of courage to recover the Apostolic Mandate. The prophet Daniel said that those who "know their God shall be strong and carry out great exploits."[4] Being strong is not an option—taking action is the lifestyle of those who know Him. The secret of Joshua's courage was his faith in God's word. This is why he was commanded to be strong and then was commanded not to let the word "depart from your mouth, but you shall meditate on it day and night."[5] This is the mystery of how faith is produced in the human heart, and how it can ultimately move mountains of any kind, in any nation.

In the past season, there has been a revival in the area of prayer and intercession directed at seeing the nations open to the Gospel. Revolutionary understanding about spiritual warfare and spiritual mapping have mobilized Christians to pray as never before. Let it be understood that without prayer no significant work will be accomplished for God. Programs and strategies such as "Praying through the Window" have Christians praying for the nations in the "10/40 window." Prayer revivals in Asia, Latin America and Africa have shown what kind of dramatic results can be obtained when the Church prays. These prayers have opened doors worldwide.

Yet, the ultimate answer to these prayers will be a Church that rises up to fulfill its destiny and its mission by going through these open doors. In doing so, it casts off chains of unbelief, apathy and deception and becomes the influence in society it was intended to be. Prayer has set the stage for this dramatic "tipping point" to take place in every nation of the world—all that's left is for God's people to act.

Our dream is that a new generation of men and women will arise that will catch the flame of those who burned bright for the Apostolic Mandate in generations past. May we all so surrender our lives that the prayer of Patrick of Ireland will be our anthem:

# THE PRAYER OF ST. PATRICK

I arise today
Through a mighty strength, the invocation of the Trinity,
Through the belief in the threeness,
Through confession of the oneness
Of the Creator of Creation.

I arise today
Through the strength of Christ's birth with His baptism,
Through the strength of His crucifixion with His burial,
Through the strength of His resurrection with His ascension,
Through the strength of His descent for the judgment of Doom.

I arise today
Through the strength of the love of Cherubim,
In obedience of angels,
In the service of archangels,
In hope of resurrection to meet with reward,
In prayers of patriarchs,
In predictions of prophets,
In preaching of apostles,
In faith of confessors,
In innocence of holy virgins,
In deeds of righteous men.

I arise today
Through the strength of heaven:
Light of sun,
Radiance of moon,
Splendor of fire,
Speed of lightning,
Swiftness of wind,
Depth of sea,
Stability of earth,
Firmness of rock.

I arise today
Through God's strength to pilot me:
God's might to uphold me,
God's wisdom to guide me,
God's eye to look before me,

God's ear to hear me,
God's word to speak for me,
God's hand to guard me,
God's way to lie before me,
God's shield to protect me,
God's host to save me
From snares of devils,
From temptations of vices,
From everyone who shall wish me ill,
Afar and anear,
Alone and in multitude.

I summon today all these powers between me and those evils,
Against every cruel merciless power that may oppose my body
    and soul,
Against incantations of false prophets,
Against evil laws of pagandom,
Against false laws of heretics,
Against craft of idolatry,
Against spells of witches and smiths and wizards,
Against every knowledge that corrupts man's body and soul.

Christ to shield me today
Against poison, against burning,
Against drowning, against wounding,
So that there may come to me abundance of reward.
Christ with me, Christ before me, Christ behind me,
Christ in me, Christ beneath me, Christ above me,
Christ on my right, Christ on my left,
Christ when I lie down, Christ when I sit down,
    Christ when I arise,
Christ in the heart of every man who thinks of me,
Christ in the mouth of everyone who speaks of me,
Christ in every eye that sees me,
Christ in every ear that hears me.

I arise today
Through a mighty strength, the invocation of the Trinity,
Through belief in the threeness,
Through confession of the oneness,
Of the Creator of Creation.[6]

# ENDNOTES

## INTRODUCTION
## "THE TIPPING POINT"

1. Malcolm Gladwell, *The Tipping Point* (New York: Little, Brown and Company, 2000), p. 11.
2. Matthew 13:33.
3. Acts 19:20, NKJV.
4. William Peterson and Randy Peterson, *100 Christian Books that Changed the Century* (Grand Rapids: Fleming H. Revell, 2000), p. 16.
5. Ibid.
6. Rationalism—particularly the biblical variety that gave rise to modern science and technology—is still very much alive and well; for the most part blessedly. Where it ran out of gas, or more accurately *hit a wall*, is with its messianic promise to create a humanistic utopia. The French Revolution was the first major blow to its head; Communism in this century all but dug its grave.
7. Using the same type of militaristic language, on another occasion MacArthur called for a "battleship full of missionaries."
8. The National AIDS Control Programme, 1998, HIV/Syphilis Seroprevalence in Antenatal Clinic Attenders, The National AIDS Control Programme, Lilongwa, Malawi, report.
9. Acts 17:6, NKJV.
10. Andrew Murray, *The Keys to the Missionary Problem* (Fort Washington: CLC Publications, 2001), p. 27.
11. Nancy Gibbs, "Apocalypse Now," *Time*, 1 July 2002, p. 42.
12. Ephesians 3:10.
13. Isaiah 60:2–3; Ephesians 5:27; Luke 19:13, KJV.
14. Greek—*apostolos*; a delegate; specifically an ambassador of the Gospel; officially a commissioner of Christ, messenger; one that is sent. To help further demystify the term "apostle," keep in mind that the Latin word for "missionary" shares the same Greek root. Any missionary who works to plant churches is fulfilling the "Apostolic Mandate."
15. We go in the knowledge that "All authority in heaven and on earth has been given to [Jesus]" and that, furthermore, He "…will be with [us] always, even to the end of the age" (Matt. 28:18, 20).
16. John 14:6.
17. Jeffrey Sheler, *U. S. News & World Report*, 6 May 2002, p. 42.
18. See Hebrews 9:22.
19. See Matthew 16:21.
20. 1 Corinthians 2:2.
21. Revelation 1:5; 17:14; 19:16.
22. James Engel and William Dyrness, *Changing the Mind of Missions*

(Downers Grove: InterVarsity Press, 2000), p. 22.

23. Ephesians 4:12.
24. Philippians 1:12.

CHAPTER ONE
EVERY NATION IN OUR GENERATION

1. Some scholars would even go so far as to say that the Judeo-Christian worldview, more than mere geography, really defines the essence of what we mean by "the Western world."
2. George Barna, *The State of the Church 2002* (Ventura: Issachar Resources, 2002), p. 129.
3. Philip Jenkins, *New Christendom: The Coming of Global Christianity* (New York: Oxford University Press, 2002), p. 35.
4. Ibid., p. 89.
5. Gerald Zelizer in *USA Today*, 4 Sept. 2002. The previous low had been 52 percent during the televangelist scandals of the 1980s.
6. Matthew 7:16, NKJV.
7. Matthew 16:18, NKJV.
8. See 1 Samuel 17:45. One of the most common names for God in the Bible—used more than 270 times in the Old Testament—is the Lord (Jehovah) of hosts (a mass of persons, especially when organized for war; an army). Make no mistake about it, both the war and the ultimate victory belong to Jesus. (See 1 Samuel 17:47.) But more often than not, He uses His army, the Church, to accomplish the victory.
9. 1 John 5:4.
10. 2 Corinthians 4:8–9.
11. Luke 10:17.
12. Mark 6:41; John 21:9.
13. Mark 1:28, NKJV.
14. Mark 1:38.
15. John 12:31–32 (emphasis mine).
16. Matthew 28:18–19.
17. Romans 1:8; 15:19–20; 16:25–27; Colossians 1:23.
18. Reggie McNeal, *Revolution in Leadership: Training Apostles for Tomorrow's Church* (Nashville: Abingdon Press, 1998), p. 19.
19. Ibid., p. 20.
20. Acts 6:1.
21. Philip was the first of the initial disciples to start to "get it." After the encounter with the Ethiopian eunuch he hit the road, moving first west and then north until he ended up in Caesarea. But it is worth noting that this first missionary trip began when the Holy Spirit literally grabbed him and transported him to a city over forty kilometers to the west. Nothing like a good shove to start someone moving!

22. Philippians 3:4–5.
23. Acts 9:15.
24. Acts 1:8.
25. Philippians 1:6.
26. Acts 10:10ff.
27. Revelation 7:1; Isaiah 11:12.
28. Colossians 1:6. "All the world," of course, is an idiomatic expression that refers to the known world of the time.
29. Eric Pooley, "Person of the Year 2001," *Time*, 31 December 2001.
30. Thomas Cahill, *How the Irish Saved Civilization: The Untold Story of Ireland's Heroic Role from the Fall of Rome to the Rise of Medieval Europe* (New York: Doubleday, 1995), p. 102.
31. Ibid, p. 105.
32. Even more tragic—and prophetically symbolic—than the temporary triumph of humanism is the fact that the Druid religion has even experienced a revival of sorts.
33. Fred Barlow, *Profiles in Evangelism* (Murfreesboro: Sword of the Lord Publishers, 1976), p. 52.
34. Ibid.
35. John Clark Marshman, *The Story of Carey, Marshman and Ward: The Serampore Missionaries* (London: Alexander Strahan & Co., 1864), p. 8.
36. Taken from William Carey's sermon, "An Enquiry into the Obligations of Christians to use Means for the Conversion of the Heathens," 1792.
37. Ibid.
38. William A Beckham, *The Second Reformation: Reshaping the Church for the 21$^{st}$ Century* (Houston: Touch Publications, 1995), p. 227.
39. Hebrews 11:32–34.
40. As quoted by Dr. Dan Pierce, Princeton University Bible Fellowship, City on a Hill Symposium, from a manuscript entitled, "Robert Wilder and the SVM," Nov. 19, 1995, p. 8.
41. J. Herbert Kane, *A Concise History of the Christian World Mission* (Grand Rapids: Baker Book House, 1978), p. 105.
42. James Engel and William Dyrness, *Changing the Mind of Missions: Where Have We Gone Wrong?* (Downers Grove: InterVarsity Press, 2000).
43. Habakkuk 2:2, NKJV.
44. 1 Timothy 3:15.
45. Matthew 14:19; 13:33.
46. The original plan was every three years, but there has been a strong sense that we should pick up the pace.
47. Ephesians 3:20, NKJV.
48. Zechariah 4:6. The capstone that came down upon the holy mountain with shouts of "Grace, grace!" prophetically looks to the completion of the New Jerusalem.

49. See John 3:16.
50. 1 Peter 2:21; John 15:13.
51. 2 Corinthians 5:11, NKJV.
52. Curtis Chang, *Engaging Unbelief: A Captivating Strategy from Augustine & Aquinas* (Downers Grove: InterVarsity Press, 2000), p. 171.
53. Ibid.
54. 2 Peter 3:10.
55. Luke 19:12ff, NKJV.
56. Proverbs 24:16.

## Chapter Two
## The Miracle in Manila

1. See Acts 16:6–10.
2. Taken from John Wesley's Journal, 24 May 1738 (13). *The Works of John Wesley Bicentennial Edition, Vol. 18,* Journals & Diaries, I:249–250, copyright 1988.
3. Acts 1:8, NKJV.
4. Proverbs 18:12.
5. 1 Chronicles 4:9.
6. Luke 22:32.
7. Hebrews 3:14, NASB.
8. Psalm 78:72.
9. Hebrews 12:1–2.
10. 1 Timothy 1:18–19.
11. The name "Morning Star" is the title given to our Lord Jesus Christ taken from Revelation 22:16: "I, Jesus, have sent My angel to testify to you these things in the churches. I am the Root and the Offspring of David, the Bright and Morning Star." There is another ministry called Morningstar Ministries, led by Rick Joyner. The two organizations are totally unrelated. It's an interesting side note that choosing a name for a ministry that hasn't been used before can be challenging. There are a vast number of ministries that use the name "Victory," as well.
12. Esther 4:14.
13. Ecclesiastes 4:12.
14. See "God in the NFL," *Charisma*, November 2002.
15. VLI is accessible on the web at: www.vlionline.com
16. When Paul was bitten by a viper, Acts 28:5 says he "shook the creature off into the fire and suffered no harm" NASB.

## Chapter Three
## The Lordship of Christ

1. Michael Hart, *The 100: A Ranking of the Most Influential Persons in History* (New York: Carol Publishing Group, 1978), pp. 50–51.

2. Matthew 7:21.
3. 2 Corinthians 6:14–15, NASB.
4. Philippians 2:15, NASB.
5. Barna, *State of the Church*, pp. 125–127.
6. Ibid., p.127.
7. Matthew 10:32, NASB; Joshua 4:7b.
8. *Biblical Foundations*—twelve short Bible studies on the foundations of the faith. It is available through the MSI Store on our web site at: www.everynation.org.
9. Matthew 13:19.
10. Barna, *State of the Church*, p. 54.
11. John 8:46, NKJV.
12. John 14:30, NKJV.
13. Galatians 1:8.
14. Romans 3:30; 5:13, 20; 7:7–9; 1 Corinthians 15:56; Galatians 3:24.
15. Hebrews 2:3.
16. Romans 7:13b; 1:18–20; 2:14–16.
17. Matthew 10:16, NKJV.
18. "And the common people heard Him [Jesus] gladly" (Mark 12:37, NKJV).
19. Philippians 2:5–10.
20. And those words are not just the ones in red in your red-letter edition of the Bible. When Jesus told the Pharisees, "Before Abraham was, I AM" (John 8:58, NKJV), they sought to stone Him because they understood what He was saying: *I am Jehovah (Yahweh), the God who revealed Himself to your fathers in the Old Testament.* The entire Bible is God-breathed; all of it should be in red.
21. Matthew 24:35.
22. Luke 6:46.
23. John Stott, *The Incomparable Christ* (Downers Grove: InterVarsity Press, 2001), p. 30.
24. Ibid.
25. Dietrich Bonhoeffer, *The Cost of Discipleship* (New York: Simon & Shuster, 1959), p. 89.
26. Mark 4:17.
27. A book title used by by Francis Shaeffer.
28. Luke 6:49.
29. Hebrews 6:1, NASB (emphasis mine).
30. Acts 26:18 (emphasis mine).
31. Acts 2:36–38.
32. Acts 20:20–21.
33. 2 Peter 3:9.
34. Ephesians 2:8–9.
35. Romans 5:6, NASB.

36. Ephesians 2:8.
37. Romans 5:1–2.
38. Romans 5:17, NKJV.
39. Jude 4.
40. John 1:14.
41. Romans 6:14.
42. 2 Timothy 2:1.
43. 2 Timothy 2:2, NKJV.
44. 2 Timothy 2:22–23, NASB.
45. "The kings of the earth set themselves, and the rulers take counsel together, Against the LORD and against His Anointed, *saying*, 'Let us break Their bonds in pieces And cast away Their cords from us'" (Psalm 2:2–3, NKJV).
46. And at the end of the day, loving God's law and meditating on it day and night (see Psalm 119:97—something that's even more vital for us in A.D. times, because we have to bring the light of the New Testament into the Old and discern the law's new-covenant application) means a lot more than just being able to count the commandments off on our ten fingers. There is an entire worldview waiting to be drawn out of the Bible and much of it is found in the Pentateuch (the five books of Moses; the first five books of the Bible).
47. Matthew 5:13, NKJV.
48. Dr. Baehr tells how one big-name producer reportedly warned, "If the salt leaves, the meat will rot."
49. Emil Brunner, *Christianity and Civilization* (London: Nisbet, 1948), p. 62.
50. Henry Van Til, *The Calvinistic Concept of Culture*, (Grand Rapids, MI: Baker Academic), 1959, p. 44.
51. Cornelius Van Til, "The Impact of Calvinism on Culture," *Christian Statesman*, Vol. 14, #6, p. 3.
52. Herbert Schlossberg, *Idols for Destruction* (Nashville: Thomas Nelson Publishers, 1983), p. 324.
53. Matthew 5:13–14.

CHAPTER FOUR<br>REACHING THE "NEW" LOST WORLD

1. As quoted in "MTV Is Rock Around the Clock," *Philadelphia Inquirer*, 3 November 1982.
2. Luke 16:8, NKJV.
3. Deuteronomy 28:13, NKJV.
4. Ephesians 1:19, NKJV; 1 John 5:4.
5. Matthew 11:19, NKJV.
6. 1 Peter 2:9, KJV.
7. Isaiah 55:11.
8. Matthew 14:14, NKJV.

9. Matthew 9:13, NKJV.

10. Philippians 3:10, NKJV.

11. Luke 22:42.

12. Philippians 2:3; John 15:13, NKJV.

13. Matthew 9:36, NKJV.

14. Exodus 4:2.

15. 1 Corinthians 1:27.

16. Luke 7:34.

17. George Grant, *The Micah Mandate* (Nashville: Cumberland House, 1999), p. 15.

18. Romans 12:2.

19. Daniel 1:1–20.

20. Epimenides (Titus 1:12); Aratus (Acts 17:28); Cleanthes (Acts 17:28) and Meander (1 Cor. 15:33).

21. See, for example, his sermon atop Mars Hill in Acts 17:22–34. "Eternity in the heart" (Eccles. 3:11) refers to the truth that God has sown into every human soul and that is further reinforced by the created order. (See Romans 1:19–21.) Because that truth is there and is constantly bubbling to the surface, all religions and philosophies retain elements of it. Our job is to find those synchronicities—or points of contact—and use them as a springboard for presenting *the* Truth.

22. Terry M. Crist, *Learning the Language of Babylon: Changing the World by Engaging the Culture* (Grand Rapids: Chosen Books, 2001).

23. As quoted in *Time*, 19 August 2002.

24. For more information, please visit www.up2speed.us.

25. Daniel 1:17, NKJV.

26. 1 Corinthians 9:22.

27. Romans 9:3.

28. Matthew 11:19, NASB.

29. Romans 3:12.

30. Luke 19:10, NASB.

31. John 4:18.

32. Romans 1:16.

33. Proverbs 11:30.

34. Matthew 21:2.

35. James 1:20, NASB.

36. Isaiah 42:2–3.

37. 1 Corinthians 9:22.

38. 1 Corinthians 5:19–20, NASB.

39. Romans 9:3, NASB.

40. Ed Silvoso, *That None Should Perish: How to Reach Entire Cities for Christ Through Prayer Evangelism* (Ventura: Regal Books, 1994), p. 91.

41. Galatians 2:11–13.

42. Mark 16:15.
43. Acts 11:18, NASB.
44. See Acts 15.
45. Ephesians 3:4, 6, NASB.
46. Matthew 5:21–22.
47. 1 John 3:14, NKJV.
48. 1 Timothy 3:15, NASB.
49. Isaiah 59:19, NKJV.
50. 1 Corinthians 13:8.

CHAPTER FIVE
THE HEART OF THE MANDATE

1. Romans 4:25; Luke 24:49; Hebrews 11:13.
2. Matthew 16:24.
3. John 14:12, NKJV.
4. Matthew 16:24; Mark 8:34; 10:21, NKJV; Luke 9:23.
5. Bill Hull, *The Disciple-Making Church* (Grand Rapids: Fleming H. Revell, 1990), p. 11.
6. James H. Montgomery, *Dawn 2000: 7 Million Churches To Go* (Pasadena: William Carey Library, 1989), viii–ix.
7. Hull, The *Disciple-Making Church*, p. 11.
8. Robert Coleman, *The Master Plan of Evangelism* (Grand Rapids: Fleming H. Revell, 1993), p. 26.
9. Galatians 4:19, NKJV (emphasis mine).
10. There are several verses in Proverbs that touch on this truth, most specifically 22:6—"Train a child in the way he should go, and when he is old, he will not depart from it."
11. 1 Samuel 2:12 (see footnotes in the NKJV).
12. 2 Corinthians 2:14, NASB.
13. Hebrews 12:11, NKJV.
14. Proverbs 29:18.
15. Matthew 18:15–17; 1 Corinthians 5:5; 2 Thessalonians 3:6.
16. As quoted in *USA Today*, 18 September 2002.
17. Matthew 4:18–19.
18. Matthew 13:47.
19. The concept of "connectors" was actually developed by Malcolm Gladwell in his book *The Tipping Point* (see Chapter One, note 1). These are people who know a lot of other people and are uniquely gifted at linking them together.
20. See 2 Kings 5:1–15.
21. The *Biblical Foundations* book is purple; its color has become shorthand for the book itself.
22. See Luke 16:10.

23. Matthew 4:19; John 1:51; Matthew 19:28.
24. Romans 8:1–2, NKJV.
25. Ephesians 6:13, NKJV.
26. See John 14:30.
27. 1 Thessalonians 4:8, NASB.
28. Acts 14:3, NKJV.
29. 2 Timothy 2:2.
30. 1 Corinthians 3:4, NKJV.
31. Ephesians 4:15–16.
32. 1 Corinthians 4:15, NKJV.
33. Philippians 2:13.
34. Quoted by Reggie McNeal in *Revolution in Leadership* (p.15), as excerpted from the *Harvard Business Review*, January/February 1996, p. 154.
35. See Proverbs 20:21.
36. Acts 2:17.
37. As quoted in "The Third Coming of George Barna," *Christianity Today*, 5 August 2002.
38. James C. Collins and Jerry I. Porras, *Good to Great* (New York: Harper Business, 2001), pp. 37–38.
39. "Do not lay hands on anyone hastily, nor share in other people's sins" (1 Timothy 5:22, NKJV). To participate in the ordination of a leader who is unqualified is to risk sharing in the guilt for the mistakes (sins) they will likely commit. (See also 1 Timothy 3:6.)

## CHAPTER SIX
### THE GREATEST HARVEST FIELD

1. Michael S. Hamilton, "Generation X and the Waynesburg Experiment" (address given to the faculty of Waynesburg College, 18 August 1999).
2. Douglas Coupland, *Life After God* (New York: Pocket Books, 1995), p. 359.
3. James 3:15, NKJV.
4. Exodus 1:15, ff.
5. Matthew 2:7–18.
6. Acts 2:17.
7. Isaiah 53:2.
8. Though forty years old at the time, Caleb defined the expression "young at heart." Forty-five years later he was still a fighter and related how God had supernaturally given him the vitality of a man less half his age (see Joshua 14:6–11). Caleb gives hope to all of us on the other side of middle age. May God make Calebs of us all.
9. Numbers 14:26–30.
10. Jeremiah 1:7, NKJV.
11. 1 Timothy 4:12.

12. Titus 2:15.
13. Mark 16:5.
14. 1 John 2:14.
15. See Proverbs 20:29.
16. As quoted in "Still Dragging Kids Down After 20 Years," *Plugged In,* March 2001.
17. Proverbs 22:6.
18. Taken from the song, "A Rush of Blood to the Head" by Coldplay.
19. See Mark 10:15.
20. See Matthew 18:4–6.
21. Luke 1:38, NASB.
22. Luke 1:18.
23. See John 8:1–11, NKJV.
24. A. C. remained a virgin until his marriage in 2002. He retired after eighteen seasons holding the NBA record for the most consecutive games played (1,192). Rick Reilly of *Sports Illustrated,* in his 13 December 1999 editorial on A. C. entitled, "The NBA Player Who Has Never Scored," said that more remarkable than A. C.'s streak of consecutive games played, was his moral streak of maintaining his virginity.
25. John 7:17.
26. Romans 1:18, NKJV.
27. Joel 3:14.
28. Esther 4:14.
29. See Acts 13:36.
30. Martin Luther, "To the Christian Nobility of the German Nation Concerning the Reform of the Christian Estate, 1520," trans. Charles M. Jacobs, rev. James Atkinson, The Christian in Society, I (*Luther's Works,* ed. James Atkinson, vol. 44), p. 207 (1966).
31. Mark Beliles, The Providence Foundation.
32. Peter Singer, *Pediatrics,* 72 (July 1983):129.
33. Allan Bloom, *The Closing of the American Mind* (New York: Simon & Schuster, 1988), p. 25.
34. G. Richard Bozarth, "The Meaning of Evolution," *American Atheist,* 20 September 1979, p. 30.
35. Luke 19:12–13.

CHAPTER SEVEN<br>DISCOVERING SPIRITUAL FAMILY

1. Senge, Peter. *The Fifth Discipline* (New York: Currency Doubleday, 1990), p. 4.
2. Stormie Omartian, *The Power of a Praying Parent* (Eugene: Harvest House), 1995, pp. 142–143.
3. 1 Corinthians 4:15, NASB.

4.  1 Timothy 1:2, NASB.
5.  3 John 1:4.
6.  1 Timothy 5:1–2.
7.  For more on this subject, refer to Ray McCollum's tape series "Scandalon" which is available through the MSI Store at: www.everynation.org.
8.  1 Timothy 3:15, NASB.
9.  Matthew 12:25, NASB.
10. Donald MacLeod, *Shared Life: The Trinity and the Fellowship of God's People* (Greenville: Reformed Academic Press, 1994), p. 46.
11. Genesis 18:19.
12. 1 Corinthians 12:13, NKJV.
13. 1 Corinthians 12:18, NKJV.
14. 1 Corinthians 4:15.
15. 1 Timothy 1:2, NKJV.
16. See Genesis 11:6.
17. Senge, *Fifth Discipline*, p. 230.
18. Ibid.
19. Ibid., pp. 310–311.
20. Ibid., p. 210.
21. Proverbs 13:22.
22. Matthew 13:44, NKJV.
23. Senge, *Fifth Discipline*, p. 214.
24. Genesis 11:6.
25. Revelation 12:10, NKJV.
26. James 3:5–6.
27. Deuteronomy 8:13–14.
28. 1 Samuel 14:6, NASB.
29. 1 Samuel 17:45, NASB.
30. 1 Samuel 18:1, 3–4, NASB.
31. Ruth 1:16.
32. Ephesians 4:3, NASB.
33. Matthew 18:19–20, NKJV.
34. 1 Peter 3:7.
35. Excerpted from Omartian, *The Power of Praying Together.*
36. See Luke 11:1.
37. Matthew 6:10.
38. 2 Chronicles 7:14.
39. Hebrews 11:6.
40. Romans 10:17.
41. Isaiah 53:1, NKJV.
42. John 14:12, NKJV.
43. 1 Timothy 2:1–2, NKJV.

44. Romans 5:20.
45. George Otis, *Informed Intercession* (Ventura: Regal Books, 1999), pp. 39–40.
46. Psalm 68:5.

CHAPTER EIGHT
RECOVERING APOSTOLIC MINISTRY

1. Taken from the sermon "Gospel Missions" given by C. H. Spurgeon on April 27, 1856. Retrieved from Internet at Spurgeon.org/sermons/0076.htm.
2. C. Peter Wagner, *The New Apostolic Churches* (Ventura: Regal Books, 1998), p. 18.
3. McNeal, *Revolution in Leadership*, p.32. What is refreshing is that McNeal seems to write from an objective standpoint without the dispensational grid that causes many to avoid such "controversial" terms.
4. Larry Caldwell, *Sent Out! Reclaiming the Spiritual Gift of Apostleship for Missionaries and Churches Today* (Pasadena: William Carey Library, 1992), p. 133.
5. John 3:16, NASB.
6. 1 John 4:10, NASB.
7. Caldwell, *Sent Out*, p.11.
8. See Matthew 13:31–33.
9. Mark 3:13–14, NASB.
10. Luke 24:48, NASB; see also Acts 2:32, 3:15, 4:33, 5:32, 10:39, 13:31, 26:16.
11. Revelation 21:14, NASB.
12. Romans 16:7.
13. Colossians 4:14, NASB.
14. "…[They] searched the Scriptures daily to find out whether these things were so" (NKJV).
15. Romans 15:20.
16. Caldwell, *Sent Out*, p. 67.
17. Genesis 1:12b. It is an immutable law of nature as ordained by nature's God: Everything produces after its own kind. The true sign of the apostle is that he produces not just new life—the evangelist does that—but that the new life also begets new leaders.
18. Ecclesiastes 4:8, NASB.
19. Collins and Porras, *Good to Great*, pp. 37–38.
20. 2 Timothy 2:2, NASB.
21. Taken from "The Augsburg Confession," as submitted to His Imperial Majesty Charles V at the Diet of Augsburg in the year 1530 by certain princes and cities, p. 4.
22. Jim Laffoon, *A Divine Alliance: How to Build Effective Relationships Between Apostles and Prophets* (Colorado Springs: Wagner Publications, 2000), p. 13.

23. See Ecclesiastes 4:12.

24. No secret here—godly, anointed, apostolic men from Whitefield to Wesley have had their own way of doing things because of their traditions and theology. As much as we would all like to say that our way is the Lord's way, we all still look "through a glass darkly" (1 Cor. 13:12, KJV). In trying to sincerely serve the Lord and be faithful to His Word, we have developed a certain style and way of doing things that will likely be different in some respects from other apostolic movements. And, of course, we are always open to learning and changing to get ever closer to the mark. (*Ecclesia reformata, semper reformenda*—"The Reformed Church is always reforming.") But if we're going to move ahead in faith, well, there's no secret here either—we must move ahead. That means walking in what you know and always preserving unity.

25. Caldwell, *Sent Out*, p. 67.

26. Matthew 5:15, NKJV.

27. Acts 17:16–34.

28. Luke 11:21–22.

29. C. Peter Wagner, *Churches That Pray* (Ventura: Regal Books, 1993), p. 139.

30. 1 Corinthians 3:4.

31. Psalm 68:6.

32. Ephesians 4:16b.

33. Genesis 50:20.

34. Deuteronomy 24:7.

35. See Luke 4:18.

36. 1 Thessalonians 1:5, NKJV.

37. Hebrews 13:8, NKJV.

38. Charles H. Kraft, *Christianity with Power* (Ann Arbor: Servant Publications, 1989), p. 6.

39. Luke 9:1ff; John 14:12.

40. Matthew 28:20.

41. Wagner, *New Apostolic Churches*, p. 14.

42. Joel 2:28; Acts 2:17.

43. Psalm 110:3.

44. Matthew 16:4, author paraphrase.

45. Luke 16:19–31.

46. Acts 17:19–21.

47. Proverbs 11:14, NKJV.

48. Senge, *Sent Out*, p. 11.

49. Ephesians 4:14, NKJV.

50. 2 Corinthians 11:9,19–21.

51. 2 Corinthians 12:14.

52. 2 Corinthians 10:18.

CHAPTER NINE
THE MOST EFFECTIVE FORM OF EVANGELISM

1. Daniel Eisenberg, "Can McDonald's Shape Up?" *Time*, 30 September 2002, p. 52.
2. Caldwell, *Sent Out*, p. 154.
3. Bakke, Ray. *A Theology as Big as the City* (Downers Grove: InterVarsity Press, 1997), p. 12.
4. *People and the Planet*, 18 September 2002.
5. Silvoso, *That None Should Perish*, p. 21.
6. Jeremiah 6:14.
7. Matthew 25:21.
8. See Deuteronomy 28:1–2.
9. Isaiah 45:3, NKJV.
10. Bakke, *Theology as Big as the City*, p. 117.
11. Matthew 13:31–32.
12. Acts 8:39, NASB.
13. Irenaeus, one of the leaders in the early Church, wrote about him in *Against Heresies* (iii.12.8).
14. Acts 17:34ff, NASB.
15. *Ecclesiastical History*, iii. 4.11; iv. 23, 3.
16. Proverbs 12:24.
17. Mark 11:17.
18. Luke 14:31–32.
19. All told, nearly 500 internationals from ninety-one countries lost their lives in the September 11 attack.
20. www.unitingthenations.com.
21. 1 Peter 5:2–4; Hebrews 13:17.
22. 1 Timothy 5:17.
23. James 3:1, NKJV.
24. 1 Timothy 3; Titus 1:15–16.
25. Revelation 12:10, KJV.
26. Senge, *Sent Out*, p. 288.
27. See 2 Timothy 1:13–14.
28. Ephesians 4:12, NKJV.
29. Jeremiah 31:34.

CHAPTER TEN
A LIGHT TO THE NATIONS

1. Acts 6:15, NASB.
2. Murray, *Keys to the Missionary Problem*, p. 24.
3. Matthew 22:3; see vv. 1–14.
4. John 3:16; Revelation 5:9, NASB.

5. Matthew 13:31.
6. Acts 17:6, NKJV.
7. This is a broad designation for churches that accept the gifts of the Spirit as a present reality.
8. Jenkins, *New Christendom,* p. 8.
9. Patrick Johnstone, *The Church Is Bigger Than You Think* (Christian Focus Publications, 1998), p. 94.
10. Acts 19:20, NASB.
11. Matthew 6:33, NKJV.
12. Matthew 28:18–19, NASB.
13. Acts 1:8, NASB.
14. Johnstone, *The Church Is Bigger Than You Think,* pp. 181–192.
15. Ted Haggard, *The Life Giving Church* (Colorado Springs: Regal Books, 2001), p. 146.
16. Luke 16:8, NASB.
17. Matthew 28:20, NASB.
18. 1 Thessalonians 2:18, NKJV.
19. Romans 10:14–15, NKJV (emphasis mine).
20. Acts 8:14, NASB (emphasis mine).
21. Acts 13:3, NASB (emphasis mine).
22. See Isaiah 6:8.
23. 1 Samuel 30.

## CONCLUSION
## "I WILL ARISE"

1. Matthew 14:28.
2. See Philippians 2:15.
3. Joshua 1:7.
4. Daniel 11:32, NKJV.
5. Joshua 1:8, NASB.
6. Reprinted from Cahill, *How the Irish Saved Civilization,* pp. 116–117.

# UNITING THE NATIONS

Read abo
Church of the Natio
New York City
pages 203-20

CHURCH OF THE NATIONS
NEW YORK CITY

Sunday Nights • 7:30pm • The Lamb's Theater • 130 W. 44th Street, New York, N
www.unitingthenations.com

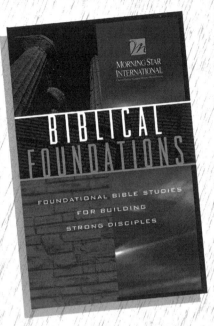

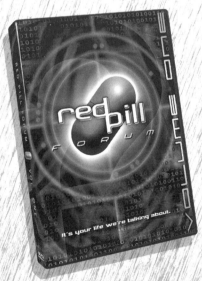

# ABOUT THE AUTHOR

Rice Broocks is the president of Morning Star International (MSI), a family of churches and ministries currently operating in thirty-five nations. He is also the senior pastor of Bethel World Outreach Center in Nashville, Tennessee, where he lives with his wife and their five children.

Rice is a graduate of Mississippi State University, with a degree in business administration. He also holds a Masters Degree from Reformed Theological Seminary in Jackson, Mississippi. He serves as an adjunct instructor for Fuller Theological Seminary in Pasadena, California, and is the co-founder of Champions for Christ, a ministry to college and professional athletes. He is also the president of Victory Campus Ministries, reaching out to hundreds of university campuses around the world.

MSI's passion for uniting the "fire" of the Holy Spirit within the theological "fireplace" of the historic Christian faith has produced a three-year Bible School, Victory Leadership Institute, which is also available online. For more information, visit www.everynation.org.